LIFESTYLE SHOPPING

In shopping malls and markets the world over new modes of subjectivity, inter-personal relationships and models of social totality are being 'tried on', 'taken off' and 'displayed' in much the same way that one might shop for clothes. These are not the modernist spaces of goal-directed individuals and utopian projects. Rather, contemporary consumption sites are spaces of carnivalesque inversions of the present order of things. The multiple masks of the postmodern person who 'wears many hats' in different groups and surroundings form a veritable *dramatis personae*. In such masks of the individual and the social world may be found a new spatialization and new intuitive perceptions of time and space.

This representation of contemporary social life grows out of the work of Henri Lefebvre, Michel Maffesoli, Walter Benjamin and Mikhail Bakhtin. It is an attempt to take seriously the idea that we live in a postmodern consumer culture and to follow through the implications and possibilities of this idea. Cases are drawn from Britain, the United States, Canada, Australia, Japan and Singapore to illustrate the new intersections between people, mass culture and consumption. It will quickly become required reading on courses in the sociology of culture and cultural studies.

Rob Shields is Assistant Professor in the Department of Sociology and Anthropology at Carleton University, Ottawa, Canada.

INTERNATIONAL LIBRARY OF SOCIOLOGY
Founded by Karl Mannheim

Editor: John Urry
University of Lancaster

LIFESTYLE SHOPPING

The Subject of Consumption

Edited by
Rob Shields

London and New York

First published in 1992
by Routledge
11 New Fetter Lane, London EC4P 4EE

Simultaneously published in the USA and Canada
by Routledge
a division of Routledge, Chapman and Hall Inc.
29 West 35th Street, New York, NY 10001

Phototypeset by Intype, London
Printed and bound in Great Britain by
Biddles Ltd, Guildford and King's Lynn

British Library Cataloguing in Publication Data
A catalogue record for this book is available from the British Library.

Library of Congress Cataloging in Publication Data
Lifestyle shopping: the subject of consumption / edited by Robert
Shields.
p.cm.–(The International Library of Sociology)
Includes bibliographical references and index.
1. Lifestyle–Case studies. 2. Consumers–Psychology–Case
studies. 3. Shopping malls–Social aspects–Case studies.
4. Postmodernism–Social aspects–Case studies. I. Shields, Rob,
1961– . II. Series.
HQ2042.L54 1992
306.4–dc20   91-43287
                                                                CIP

ISBN 0–415–06059–1 (hbk)
ISBN 0–415–06060–5 (pbk)

CONTENTS

v

CONTENTS

ILLUSTRATIONS

CONTRIBUTORS

Beng Huat Chua is Senior Lecturer in the Department of Sociology at the National University of Singapore.

John Clammer is Professor of Anthropology and Sociology in the Department of Comparative Culture, Sophia University, Tokyo, Japan. His research interests focus on the sociology of consumption, urban life patterns, the sociology of knowledge and belief and social change, all in the context of contemporary East and Southeast Asia.

Jill Delaney is in the doctoral programme in the Program in Art and Architectural History, Department of Fine Arts, State University of New York, Binghamton. She is a Social Sciences and Humanities Research Council of Canada Doctoral Fellow. Recent publications include 'Superblock as Garden City-Infill. The Design of Community in the Public Housing of Alexandra Park, Toronto', *a/r/c* 3 (winter/spring, 1992).

Harvie Ferguson is in the Department of Sociology at the University of Glasgow, Scotland.

Kevin Hetherington is a doctoral student in the Department of Sociology at the University of Lancaster, Lancaster, UK.

Lauren Langman received his degree in Human Development from the University of Chicago in 1969. His interest was cross-cultural study of social structure and personality. His current project is a historical study of the relation of subjectivity and politics, from subjects of the crown, to citizens of the nation and now audiences of the simulations of politics.

Sean Nixon is Lecturer in Cultural Studies in the Department of

Media and Cultural Studies at Liverpool Polytechnic, UK. His chapter comes from a more extensive work to be found in 'Hard Looks: Masculinities, the Visual and Consumption in the 1980s' (PhD thesis, The Open University).

Gail Reekie is a historian and lecturer in Australian Studies at Griffith University, Brisbane, Australia. She has published mainly in the areas of Women's History and Gender Studies, and has just completed a book on the sexualization of selling in Sydney's department stores since 1880.

Rob Shields is Assistant Professor in the Department of Sociology and Anthropology at Carleton University, Ottawa, Canada. Previously he was a Postdoctoral Fellow at the University of Lancaster and later at the Centre d'Etudes sur L'Actuel et le Quotidien, Université de Paris V (Sorbonne) and held a Commonwealth Scholarship at the University of Sussex. He is author of *Places on the Margin, Alternative Geographies of Modernity* (Routledge, 1991).

Janice Williamson writes and teaches English and Women's Studies at the University of Alberta. She has published essays on feminist cultural studies and Canadian women writers. She co-edited (with Deborah Gorham) *Up and Doing: Canadian Women and Peace* (1989), and co-curated and co-wrote (with Bridgett Elliot) *Dangerous Goods: Feminist Visual Art Practices* (1990). Her innovative fictions are collected in *Tell Tale Signs* (1991). She is the author of *Sounding Differences: Conversations with Seventeen Canadian Women Writers* (1992).

1

SPACES FOR THE SUBJECT OF CONSUMPTION[1]

Rob Shields

LIFESTYLE SHOPPING

This is a many-voiced text which attempts to look beyond sites and the physical architecture of shopping malls and city-centre redevelopments. Our interest is the interface between media images, 'consumption sites' where such images can be purchased as ready-to-wear 'masks', and the personalities and tribes that form a social 'architecture' of lifestyles and 'consumption cultures'. Following in the tracks of Walter Benjamin's study of the shopping arcades of nineteenth-century Paris (1989), in these contemporary sites we find the implicated shadows of self, desire and consumption in amongst the goods on display and the crowds of people. *Lifestyle Shopping* is thus not intended as another celebration of the triumph of an ideology of lifestyles and marketing (Gardner and Sheppard, 1989) but a critical marking of the interdependence of the private spaces of subjectivity, media and commodity consumption, and the changing spatial contexts of everyday public life. This includes shopping malls which have developed as privately owned 'public' spaces for retailing, traditional public spaces such as markets, public buildings and monuments such as museums or heritage sites like Stonehenge, as well as the ephemeral 'public' space of the mass media.

Already broached under the rubric of 'postmodernism', changes in contemporary urban cultures have raised important issues which the authors in this volume do not intend to resolve. Rather we intend to set the agenda for debates in which closure cannot be evoked at this time. The following contributions are thus prelimi-nary but are part of the larger postmodern project of remapping and rewriting the classical schemas of the human sciences, which

1

located the subject in an abstract space of the bourgeois individual, de-spatialized and unrelated to place and context, and canonized in the positivism of social science.

The 'postmodernism' controversy lies at the intersection of contemporary cultural change and the political economy of commodity exchange. This debate concerns the changing role of consumption sites, such as shopping centres, market places, malls, museums and redeveloped downtown commercial areas with their pedestrian streets and interior arcades. The regional shopping centres and malls such as the MetroCentre, the West Edmonton Mall, Le Toison d'Or in Dijon or, indeed, local shopping centres, well established markets and the noon-hour shopping arcades being built in the London Docklands are significant as the ideal topoi in which the implications of new cultures, changing spatial practices and representations, may be seen.[2]

In general, the modernist separation of economy and culture has left little room for serious engagement with consumption practices. Critiques have been often motivated by the anomalous character of consumption which does not fit easily into the frameworks of productivist economics nor the *Arbeitsgemeinschaft* sociology of work cultures. Tomlinson, in his introduction to consumer cultures, has called the critiques 'sad, dislocated, elitist, perhaps menopausal' (Tomlinson, 1990: 17). A serious engagement with consumption must be open to discovering that lifestyles and consumption cultures are not '*confusions* over class, regional, generational and gender identities' (Tomlinson, 1990: 18) but the emergence of new 'identifications'. There is a need, therefore, to treat consumption as an active, committed production of self and of society which, rather than assimilating individuals to styles, appropriates codes and fashions, which are made into one's own (de Certeau, 1984: 166). In the process, hegemonic systems find themselves undermined,

> confronted by an entirely different kind of production, called 'consumption' . . . characterized by its ruses, its fragmentation . . . , its poaching, its clandestine nature, its tireless but quiet activity, in short by its quasi-invisibility, since it shows itself not in its own products, but in an *art of using* those imposed on it.
>
> (de Certeau, 1984: 31, italics added)

2

MALLS AND MARKET-PLACES

Every epoch has its cathedrals, monuments to the era, that come to signify or embody the cultural *Weltanschauung*. Buildings such as train stations or palaces, urban projects such as defensive city walls or pedestrian boulevards have direct impacts on behaviour and, indirectly have a discursive impact on thought and cultural practices. Architecture has a legitimating function as it attempts to express the essence of social needs resolved in a project and in so far as it influences norms of conduct. Like the castle or factory, the shopping centre and mall invite interpretation, being both structures and discursive statements. They can be studied for the cultural presuppositions and power relations which they impose by presupposition.

Culture has its contexts. It may vary over the course of a few city blocks, from site to site or from urban space to space. And, as culture varies, so this book sets out to argue that individual subjectivity may also be more fickle, more contextual than is readily acknowledged by modernists. In the essays that follow, Langman, for example, notes that

> the relationships of social spaces and individual subjectivity remain little explored, especially in so far as elite power and privilege are secured by the everyday behaviours and habitual understandings that transpire in such spaces. Most critiques of subjectivity fail to contextualise its emergence in specific times and spaces.[3]
>
> (Langman, 1992: n.p.)

The genealogy of the mall has two roots, the luxurious arcades built for the European bourgeoisie in the nineteenth century (see Benjamin, 1989; Geist, 1983) and the emporia or department stores in which mass produced household commodities and clothing became available in settings designed as palaces of consumption (see Chaney, 1991). Cast-iron engineering allowed new architectural effects such as multi-storey atria which amplified the effect of a spectacular, simultaneous display of a vast quantity of goods on offer. For a moment, shoppers, mostly women, were treated as royalty and could shop for bits of luxury (see Reekie, Ch. 9; Bowlby, 1985). To this background one might add a darker touch of the Foucauldian panopticon prison where visibility and surveillance reigned supreme.

3

While market-places are familiar to all, the shopping mall, especially as it is known in North America and more recently in Europe, is typically based on a galleria or arcade of boutiques and shops on one or more levels between two major stores which 'anchor' the dumb-bell-shaped plan by providing the functional poles of attraction for shoppers. A large food store at one end attracts shoppers from a large department store at the other end, or vice versa. The process ensures a steady flow of shoppers or even strollers, window shoppers and 'hangers-out', elderly people savouring the lively crowd, or adolescent 'mall-rats' and 'mall-bunnies' as one journalist called them (Kowinski, 1985). 'Malls' are typically more grandiose than shopping centres which, in their smaller 'community' versions, may be simple strips of small stores fronted by parking. In the malls, the plan becomes more complex (triangular, figure of eight), everything is larger, the architecture more monumental (expensive finishes such as marble, skylit arcades, soaring ceiling heights, dizzying mezzanines, sculpture, indoor tropical gardens), the major 'anchor stores' multiply and the functions increase with the addition of cinemas, hotels, zoos, recreation complexes featuring pools, ice-rinks, stadia, fairground rides and so on, office towers, conference centres, libraries, churches – in short almost any urban activity one can imagine. Malls now form the architectural typology for office buildings whose elevator lobbies grew first into atria then into malls (Shields, 1989), and international airport terminals where duty-free shopping is a major activity (Terminal 3, Toronto (*Globe and Mail*, 21 April 1991: C1–8); Schiphol, Amsterdam). More insidiously, their 'social logic' of retail capital mixed with the social ferment of crowds of people from different backgrounds and all strata forms the model for conceptions of community and the public sphere which later emerge, concretized, in public projects such as museums, as Jill Delaney notes in Chapter 7.

The building itself is completed by the provision of parking for several tens of thousands of cars. In suburban locations, or areas where land was available when the mall was built, parking forms a great asphalt girdle completely encircling it. Such malls often lie at the intersection of major 'feeder' roads. The mall and inter-section are typically ringed by apartment towers and schools sited near by according to modernist theories of urban zoning. In this configuration (a new and little-remarked upon urban morphology), the mall forms the centre of an urban constellation and a social community is born which appropriates the mall as a surrogate town square. As major users of such malls, the elderly walk from the nearby apartments and the adolescent 'mall jammers' migrate from schools in the vicinity to match wits with security personnel, in search of less controlled areas than the schoolyard. Others arrive by car or on buses which, symbiotically exploiting the conjunction of parking space and enclosed waiting areas patrolled by the mall owners' security guards, serve the malls as nodes in the public transport system.

Ease of access, controlled climate, and reduced price based on a higher market volume are the functional attractions of the mall. But the articles in this book show that for all consumption sites, these benefits are quickly outstripped by the symbolic and social value of the mall as a site of communication and interaction. The broadening of access to credit through bank and store credit cards allows a wide cross-section of society to participate, with new marginals being created from those denied access, based on the flimsiest of judgements and reasoning, by security guards (private armies who ensure retailers conform and shoppers 'behave'). As will be further argued, purchases often represent very minor expenditures (for example, a cup of coffee) and the spending of money is not required in any case. The mall's benefits which derive from its internal environment and milieu are, like the market, a public good, 'free' to the individual user. It is here that groups meet, that face-to-face communication if not community is a practice for a huge number of people in the televisual age. This typology applies to a range of sites from shopping malls to outdoor markets and from Disneyland to 'alternative' festivals such as Glastonbury which Kevin Hetherington chronicles below. Langman (see Chapter 3) has remarked that,

> Whatever one's status or job in the world of work or even without job, there is an equality of just being there and looking at the shows of decor, goods and other people. Malls appear democratic and open to all, rich or poor, young or old. Age is often the only visible marker of difference given androgynous fashions, embourgeoisement of the masses and affluent slumming. This is the realm where the goods of the good life promised in the magazine ads and television commercials can be found.
>
> (Langman, 1991: 2)

CONSUMPTION SPACES AS TOPOI: SITES OF CULTURAL CHANGE

The significance of consumption for the economy and for the culture of people's everyday lives is in change. *Lifestyle Shopping* focuses on cultures of consumption, and their impact on individuals and societies, in the great urban societies of the late twentieth century. The significance of these new consumption sites is not that their content of characteristic social activities and spatial practices is new. It is the *combination* of practices and behaviours kept apart according to classic portraits of modernity. In their totality, postmodern consumption sites are characterized by a new spatial form which is a synthesis of leisure and consumption activities previously held apart by being located in different sites, performed at different times or accomplished by different people. Modernism in this and many other ways is marked by what Max Weber described as the segmentation of culture and the separation of life into separate value spheres: culture differentiated from economy; both separated from religion. Most notably in the shopping mall, a new spatial and cultural form (Chaney, 1991; Simmel, 1950) results from a combination of two sets of spatial practices and understandings; practices which characterize the spatial performance typical of leisure spaces and spatial practices which characterize the performance of commercial sites.

Typical of such sites and areas are refurbished, 'preserved' and converted buildings, often factories or warehouses, those 'back stages' of earlier commercial activities.[4] Often, buildings built for production activities have been converted to host consumption. For example, processing facilities such as a wholesale fish market may be converted into market buildings which combine eateries and leisure browsing in fashionable boutiques with traditional, more functional food-shopping activities (South Street Seaport in Manhattan).

In these sites, the new combination of those consumption activities long thought to be 'ordinary' with leisure activities marks a new phase in the recent history of urban centres and consumerism. Everyday shopping activities are foregrounded as if on a theatre stage, to be observed by passers-by who may vicariously participate in the bustle and lively activity of consumption without necessarily spending money. Attention wavers from rational economic activities: the site hosts a scene in which at least some of the people may take the opportunity to elaborate more complex social behaviours, to engage in more roles, even to contest the economic rationale and rationalized norms of the site. Hence the genesis of a site of cultural change, of social experimentation, a theatre of everyday life.

Again consumption, which might have once been regarded as merely part of the reproduction of labour, comes to share its spaces with leisure activities. Questions of inequality and power become complex. Discrepancies arising from economic class differences are met with compensating cultural inventions, lack of political power is displaced by superior 'performance' in a site which endorses a certain theatricality in which all participate at the same time as forming an audience. A *spectacle*, then, which is marked by the exchange of looks and gazes, complements the theatrical display of goods and commodities (Debord, 1970; see Nixon, Ch. 8).

In short, at the level of individual behaviour and group sociation (Simmel, 1950), changes in the built environment are accompanied by a stress on various forms of *flânerie* (loitering, aimless strolling) and leisure, a marked shift from the purposive behaviour which provided the *raison d'être* of the old consumption sites and the first malls. It is not a question of the built environment encouraging a new form of behaviour in a deterministic way, but the buildings are renovated to accommodate and host the new combination of leisure and consumption activities. Whether or not the foreseen and planned-for behaviour actually occurs is then a question of users' appropriation of the site and buildings as a place for particular activities, a particular set of spatial practices. The sum of these contradictory and multiple practices are a postmodern spatial performance, for example, a 'crowd practice' which specifies the 'form' the various collective behaviours may take but is less specific as to its content.

Leisure spaces

The performances of leisure sites include spatial practices of displacement and travel to liminal zones, thresholds of controlled and legitimated breaks from the routines of everyday, proper behaviour (Zukin, 1991). Examples of this include the classic case of pilgrimages (Turner, 1979), eighteenth-century and nineteenth-century trips for a spa cure (Shields, 1991), and some aspects of contemporary tourism (Cohen and Ben-Yehuda, 1987; Urry, 1990). Liminal zones were once completely outside of the civilized realm of every-day community life. Deserts, wilderness, forests and the sea became zones of quests and searches for alternative social arrangements and new social statuses for individuals. These were also the zones of the excluded, shunned and leprous, zones of death. Initiatory rituals and rites of passage mobilize the symbolism and spatial practice of liminality to mark the symbolic death of one type of person and their social rebirth as a 'new' person of another rank and type. While in the liminal zone, even if it is simply a hut set aside for the purpose and symbolically consecrated as liminal, initiates are 'betwixt and between' social ranks and statuses, they loose their social identity (with major repercussions for their psychological self-identity which is entwined with social status, gender, class and so on) to be *endowed* with another one (Turner, 1979). Leisure spaces are controlled *limen*: like the classic cases, they are truly a threshold, but leisure spaces are an adjunct to everyday life – not fully differentiated, not fully liminal as the more uncompromising spaces just discussed. In this tension, leisure spaces are open to the liminal chaos which places social arrangements in abeyance and suggests their arbitrary, cultural nature (Shields, 1991).

Leisure and legitimation share the same Latin root, *lex*, law. As such, leisure spaces are zones of permitted, *legitimated* pleasure (Rojek, 1985), still very much within the grid of social control and repression (misunderstood by Lefebvre, the Situationists and the motivators of the May 1968 'festival' in France). Rather than the complete suspension of morality one finds the lifting of the curtain of morals followed by embarrassed or guilty returns to moral codes.

None the less, it is important not to overstress social control in leisure spaces. A second factor operating in such sites is what Bakhtin calls the carnivalesque, the inversion of social norms and codes within the spaces of everyday life (Bakhtin, 1984; Stallybrass and White, 1986). While this may simply take the form of ironic remarks or parodic actions which only momentarily destabilize the authority of the social order at the micro-scale, in some cases the carnivalesque is marked by full-scale revolts, eruptions of violence and major transgressions of social norms. Leisure in this case overflows into serious carnival, loosing its relaxed, uncommitted mood in favour of more wholehearted and engaged festivity.

Yet these are *not* simple sites of the carnivalesque, a characterization that would be more appropriate to fairs with roots in medieval feasts and market days. Bakhtin describes these as festivals of apparent anarchy, the inversion of social codes, the transgression of hierarchy and place, and the breaking down of individual propriety, difference and rank in the name of distinguishing a deeply bonded *Gemeinschaft* community against all outsiders and newcomers. Neglected, however, are the commercial relations which penetrated these feasts and even served as their *raison d'être* in the case of market days. Even in its most carnivalesque forms, social exchange is marked by economic exchange.

Economic spaces

Similarly if these are obviously economic spaces, the commercial exists in a tense dialectic with the festive and carnivalesque aspects of leisure. There is no permanent equilibrium by which commercial interests succeed in mastering, directing the carnival. Rather an ongoing and daily struggle is waged between what are opposed interests and purposes. Consumption spaces may therefore include discouragements to carnival. Most obviously, security guards, wardens, guides and 'hostesses' monitor the action in the site, and may reprimand or eject boisterous groups.

Additionally, however, control may be exercised through ticket booths permitting only certain people to enter or excluding certain ethnic, racial or economic groups. Music designed to influence the tempo of activities may be played over loudspeakers at certain times, or this 'muzak' may be played loudly to discourage standing about and talking so that even chance meetings of acquaintances are dampened. Similarly, benches, tables, or other common facilities which permit loitering or any unapproved (read unprofitable) activity by mall users and habitués may be removed (as discovered by Ploegaerts and Momer, 1989).

The scale of investment, the commitment of urban transportation resources, and the number of patrons suggest that shopping malls and other postmodern consumption sites are highly integrated into the distribution of urban goods and services. The economic contribution of consumption sites is such that they form central crucibles of the service economy. Numerous personal services – barbers, shoemakers and so on – as well as banks, travel agencies, doctors and government offices may now be found in malls. Many markets have diverged from functional provisions and cut-rate goods to embrace craft stalls and boutiques in surrounding

9

stores whose specialty wares can only be supported by the presence of large crowds. Restaurants and cafés offer vantage points and settings which exploit the colourful atmosphere of the 'market' thus created.

Consumption spaces which include retail, service, restaurant and even marginal occupations are thus the locus of employment for many people (Dawson and Lord, 1983). Major consumption spaces attract shoppers from quite distant areas (Shields, 1989; Lorch and Smith, 1988). In connection with tourist shopping, such service economies far outstrip all other economic sectors (Lorch and Smith, 1988). The importance of credit and consumer spending is manifest. Even in Canada, a country with an economy often pictured as dominated by resource industries and their servicing, consumer spending buys 60 per cent of all goods and services (Conference Board of Canada, cited in *Vancouver Sun*, 20 May 1982: A12).

It is also difficult to present statistics showing the exact numbers of people who patronize the more controlled environments of malls. Mall owners and developers who have such studies generally refuse to divulge their contents, nor do they grant permission for impartial surveys on their property. The question remains of how many people revealed by surveys of parking lots or exit counts actually make purchases. In France, one study found that one-third of people exiting from suburban Parisian shopping malls had made no purchase and between 8.8 and 10.75 per cent were only either strolling in the mall or passing through (Moise, 1983; see Anand, 1987 concerning the use of malls as pedestrian short-cuts). Most of those people would make a purchase at another time, thus guaranteeing the commercial viability of the mall. However, suffice to say that a simple extrapolation of the number of non-purchasers and people who make only small, legitimating purchases in any one mall accumulates to a significant number at the national scale – enough to question the simplistic assumption that all mall users are always and only there for simply functional reasons; arrive, choose goods to maximize their advantage and monetary and time resources, purchase and leave.

Beyond purposive exchange and 'responsible consumerism', some have argued that consumption regains the quality of a primitive ritual of symbolic exchange (Kroker and Cook, 1988). Consumption expands beyond need in a kind of neo-potlatch based on the easy availability of credit (Finkelstein, 1991: 117–18), of cheap mass-produced copies of even the most exclusive and expensive merchandise and marques. Shopping, as a leisure activity, embraces not only the literal forms of consumption which involve purchase and economic exchange. In addition, it is elaborated by practices of browsing, looking, consuming the environment of various purpose-built 'consumption spaces' including out-door markets, department stores, boutiques decorated in the most avant-garde minimalist manner, glitzy shopping malls, the air-conditioned tropical forests of office tower atria, and the eclectic atmosphere of run-down market halls.

FASHIONED SELVES IN THE LAND OF CONSUMPTION

Gail Reekie traces the broadening, leisure character of malls and other consumption sites which is reflected in fundamental shifts in retailing consumption, shopping patterns and lifestyles over the last decades. Recent redevelopment of the old McWhirters department store in Brisbane as a 'festive shopping galleria' on four floors marks a change from older gendered traditions of shopping as a distinctly feminine activity and the loss of a distinctive women's space (see Dowling, 1991). Changes in the interior of the building and the spatial arrangement of retail goods within it reflect a 'masculinization' of shopping where sexual difference constitutes a primary organizing principle of the spatial layout of the department store. Changes in the physical infrastructure of this 'Adamless Eden' cannot be fully understood without reference to the changing social and spatial context of gendered inequalities in which developments are embedded (Chapter 9).

The specifics of the experience of leisure shopping are elaborated in Harvie Ferguson's study of Princes Square, Glasgow where retail space is given a gloss of the sensation of being in a museum or theatre. Without giving away too much of the story, it is germane to mention the unexpected appearance of a replica of Foucault's Pendulum, suggesting a distinction between a 'cosmic' motion of commodities and the 'local', resisted motion of consumers. Applied to the 'psyche', Ferguson builds a metaphor of the difference between the internal 'movements' of desiring and wishing. Prince's Square teaches a lesson in the wishfulness concealed within the 'normal' relations of desire. It is a kind of Foucault's Pendulum of the modern psyche, founded upon a myth-

11

ology of the isolated ego moving in the 'ideal space' of society. The person is a privileged 'object' within a world of objects merely by possession of the consciousness of its own activating mechanism; it 'feels' the local motion we call desire (see Chapter 2).

Indeed, these desperate and interlinked activities which are taken for granted as 'shopping', expose new geographies of the self, giving the lie to nineteenth-century social constructions of the subject as masterful, monadic, rational and independent. Instead, Langman extends a Kleinian psychology to argue that the subject in the mall is apt to be a casualty of not only desire but anxiety and envy (see Chapter 3). The refrain of 'Lost in the Supermarket', by the British group, the Clash, (*London Calling* album, 1979), goes something like:

> Lost in the Supermarket
> can no longer shop happily,
> I came in here for a special offer
> 'Guaranteed Personality'.

The lyric encapsulates some of the contradictions experienced today by the 'subject of consumption'. New linkages between desire, lack and consumption suggest a more contingent and ethereal construction of a postmodern subjectivity. While gendered, and reflecting ethnic and class origins, the common construction of this subjectivity out of the resources of the social and environmental milieu gives it a certain cross-class and trans-gender consistency. It thus becomes essential to separate the common elements of the subjectivity of what we below call the mass-consumption 'persona' from the varying degrees of personal privilege which differentiate people's lives. The lack of opportunity for less privileged socio-economic and cultural strata, together with the constraints of patriarchy, amplify the pressures of inequality and disadvantage, poverty and exploitation. The divisions of gender–ethnic–class privilege and power give a weighty, earthbound cast to the 'lightness of being' of shoppers in the mall.

Yet the conundrum of consumption spaces, be they markets (as is their tradition – see Stallybrass and White, 1986) or malls, is their appropriation as sites of deflected and displaced resistance. Even the most disadvantaged have demonstrated an ability to steal the opportunity for pleasure in the 'clever art' of appropriation; an invasive 'poaching' (de Certeau, 1984: 174) of luxurious and 'climatized' environments (air-conditioned and heated, humidified and dehumidified until just right) through vicarious observation, gratuitous *flânerie* and window shopping, or cheap luxury. All ranks and stripes are here, 'acting out' (Langman, Ch. 3; Shields, Ch. 5), 'hanging out', engaging in forms of neo-*flânerie* (Wolff, 1985), skirting the security patrols – even occasionally taking over washrooms as temporary, informal brothels in the hopes of intercepting the odd affluent male – and above all masking themselves in the symbolic guise and 'persona' of middle-mass purchasers by carrying shopping bags (Shields, 1989).

Langman notes, 'selfhood has become a plurality of intermittent disconnected recognition-seeking presentations.' The challenge is to theorize the emergence of new forms of subjectivity and thence new social practices in the context of times (*fin de millénium*, the recurrent crisis of western economies) and spaces (the urban consumption spaces of divergent industrial societies and cultures). This gendered persona is addressed through carefully crafted strategies of retail display, advertising and shop layout. Sean Nixon considers the way men are addressed and positioned within contemporary 'shopping spectacles' and what's at stake in these new visual addresses within the practices of shopping (see Chapter 8). The design and layout of stores informs and incites acts of looking, offering visual pleasures which supplement the goods arranged for display and purchase. On one side, specific, segmented addresses to men as consumers are attempted, but less theorized is the other side of this equation. How are we to think of the shopper's gaze, the incitement and exchange of looks – what is proposed as a language of looks – that make up a large and often neglected part of the experience of shopping?

If consumers are agents who engage in an ironic self-implication in capitalist structures of fashion and retail in the elaboration of a 'personal' practice of the self through narcissism and the appropriation of symbolic commodities, this is not everywhere the same. Rather than reading across magazines and store environments as does Nixon, or using a historical approach to degage the 'secret histories' of everyday life, Beng Huat Chua illustrates the possibilities of observational method in the milieu of women's fashion boutiques in Singapore. Shopping remains for many a backstage activity of preparation and 'programming' and the presentation of self for an audience. However, again one finds the development of social ties around favourite boutiques in the construction of an elaborate community of formal relationships between patrons and clerks (Chapter 6).

THE TRIBALISM OF CONSUMPTION

The disaggregated market of 'life styles' and 'consumption classes' (Saunders, 1978) reflects both the cross-hatching of socioeconomic stratification with cultural groupings and the absence of any truly 'mass' culture. To recover some critical sense for the term, 'life-styles' will be treated less as the macro-social phenomena of marketing lore and more as the expression of continuous social change and the development of unreified, affective groupings (Weber, 1978, 1: 6–7, 40–5; 2: 1376–7), or what Simmel once called 'socia-tions' (1950), which emerge through the medium of shared symbolic codes of stylized behaviour, adornment, taste and *habitus* (Bourdieu, 1971). Such lifestyles are generally regarded as irrelevant in politico-economic studies of class and power. Yet in so far as these life style 'tribes' (Maffesoli, 1988) cross genders and ethnic groups, as is argued below in 'The individual, consumption cultures and the fate of community', they represent an often observed but under-theorized factor in social differentiation, conflict and stratification (see Chapter 5).

Considering festival consumption spaces, Kevin Hetherington argues that the swarming fragmentation of the mass originates in the 'culture of displacement' of the disaffected and disempowered young middle class whose cultural identity is neither bourgeois nor proletarian but centreless (Chapter 4). Social, educational and spatial mobility, and gender and occupational displacement undermines a shared social existence. 'Tribes' are intense but unstable sociations, unfixed by institutional parameters. Although foregrounded at Stonehenge and Glastonbury, they are also common amongst young mall-jammers at mundane city malls and shade off through all the affective groups found in consumption sites (Anand, 1987; Fowler, 1988). The knots of friends, groups who appear to be clones of one fashion-style or another, interest groups and clubs were labelled *Bündes* or 'communions' by Schma-lenbach (1977). Rather than representing a true *Gemeinschaft* community, they are achieved rather than ascribed and maintained through the active monitoring of group solidarity. The perpetuation of the group itself thus becomes the primary goal. Hethering-ton suggests this social form of tribalism as a 'site of synergy' of aesthetic, ethical and expressive styles welded into passionate group identifications centred around charisma (Weber, 1978, 1: 242–3): magnetic leaders, compelling, charismatic aesthetics and fervent belief.

Similarities to the more familiar, anthropological use of 'tribes', continue with the elevation of symbolic practices of the moment (as against the future-oriented projects of social movements), rituals of initiation and renewal (as compared to the rational procedures of other groups), and a conservative closure against outsiders (as opposed to the universal, accepting humanism of society as a whole). 'Heavy metals' and 'punks' glare at each other across the street. In 'Neon cages', Lauren Langman isolates yet more possible 'identifications' (Maffesoli, 1985; 1988) that may be taken on (see Chapter 3). But in contrast to more widespread understandings of 'primitive tribes', *Bündes* are short-lived flashes of sociality (Shields, Ch. 5) whose only sanction against their members is exclusion if and when their interests change from those of the group. Membership is thus short-term and even multiple. For example, there might be a simultaneous and exhausting set of personal 'identifications' with the 'gang' at the bar, the group of daycare volunteers, the pals of the sports club (a type of consumption site not examined in this volume), not to forget comrades in the neighbourhood 'people against — '.

Thus for the Japanese, shopping is not merely the acquisition of things: it is the buying of identity; an 'aesthetics of self' which establishes one's 'social being'. John Clammer argues that this is true even of the consumption of 'necessities' in any situation where choice reflects decisions about self, taste, images of the body and social distinctions (see Chapter 10). Japanese consumption is situated in a postmodern context, familiar yet disturbingly different. It is a society semiotically charged, but in unfamiliar ways, which express a sensibility in which aesthetic values and social order interact continuously. Consumption both solidifies the sense of personal self, and confirms it *as social* through common membership in a shopping fraternity.

In contemporary consumption sites it is hypothesized that new modes of subjectivity (at the level of the person), interpersonal relationships (at the level of the small group) and models of social totality are thus being experimented with, 'browsed through' and 'tried on' in much the same way that one might shop for clothes. In the context of these 'tribes', a re-valorized sense of self is a specific, reflexive configuration of the body and psyche. While it is a form of 'individualism', its emphasis on expression, body-centredness, and connection to a social and spatial milieu distinguishes it from the autonomous rational *individuum* which is the ideal type of classic forms of individualism. Maffesoli has argued that the multiple 'identifications' of a person in a series of site-specific tribes are the multiple masks of a postmodern 'persona' who 'wears many hats' in different groups and surroundings. A *logic of identity* is replaced by a more superficial, tactile *logic of identification*; individuals become more mask-like *personae* (Maffesoli, 1988) with mutable selves (Zurcher, 1977; Carrithers, Collins and Lukes, 1985). Their multiple identifications form a private *dramatis personae* – a self which can no longer be simplistically theorized as unified, or based solely on an individual's job or productive function. The multi-faceted subjectivity of the persona is supported by easy, generalized public access to a multiplicity of sites which are appropriated and become socially important not only for their empirical facilities but for their qualities as what William Whyte once called 'schmoozing' spaces which support personal and group identifications (1980).

In such representations of the subject and of the social world may be found a new spatialization – new intuitive perceptions of time and space which structure everyday practices and representations of the world alike. The individual is re-spatialized into a form more dependent on social and spatial context. Consumption for adornment, expression and group solidarity become not merely the means to a lifestyle, but the enactment of lifestyle. These *personae* are more like spiders at the centre of social and stylistic webs of their own making which extend the body in space, rather than the autonomous, disconnected and monadic ego-centred identities of bourgeois individuals. It is thus that one may properly argue that the reliance on group-imposed and endowed personal identifications represents a breakdown on individualism even in the midst of the motion toward identification. This breakdown challenges, even if only momentarily, social identities based in class and regional cultures and possibly traditional gender roles.

Both major and minor consumption sites, such as any one of the multitude of sub-regional shopping centres everywhere in the developed world, have emerged as key centres of cultural change. Consumption spaces are host to unique cultural forms by combining economic and leisure forms which demand new practices such as tribalism, and the elaboration of *personae*. Correspondingly new representations and understandings are attempted below. These are not the modernist spaces of rational, goal-directed individuals and utopian projects. The civic culture of consumption sites and spaces is a culture of the present, of carnivalesque inversions and alternatives to rational social order. Alone this introduces a slippage in the purchase and explanatory power of narratives built around the presupposition of goals in social action. Leisure forms such as browsing and sampling, and non-rational, spontaneous purchases from which retail capital benefits and increases its socioeconomic importance, provide a measure of circumstantial evidence for this culture of consumption which transcends its many, transient lifestyles.

NOTES

1 Parts of this introduction were directly inspired by the work of the authors in this volume, to whose faith and enthusiasm in this project I owe a great debt.

2 The MetroCentre is in cleared industrial land on South Tyneside, in Yorkshire, UK and the West Edmonton Mall is in suburban Edmonton, Alberta, Canada. Both projects combine leisure in the form of fairground ride-filled 'Fantasylands' with the more typical retail stores and services. The London Docklands project to construct a new city in the old Albert and Victoria docks in the East End of London was carried out partly by the Canadian developers Olympia and York at Canary Wharf.

3 Despite the borrowing of geographic metaphors (e.g. *Gestalt* 'field') by psychology, this is a recent area of research. See Harvey's work on the urbanization of consciousness (1988). I have also given over space to this question in an earlier work (1991).

4 Traces of the organic history of sites are framed in new ways so that one now sees only those past realities of warehouses and work-a-day markets which have been *selected* for preservation as 'heritage'. Often the grot, the sweat and competitive toil is erased. What remains after the transformation is but a moment of the old built artifact, for example, the architectural 'original' without the makeshift modifications generations of inhabitants have made to buildings to make them more suitable to their use. It was the unpredictability of everyday life, the vitality not accounted for in the architectural design, which required the ongoing modifications – for example, the addition of tin and corrugated steel shacks to the sides of neoclassical markets. The 'original' speaks of a rarefied professional vision of social life without contradictions, change or daily vicissitudes. Often heritage architecture is preserved or adapted in such a way that no trace of the buildings' inhabitants

remains. What remains of the past is only a vision of historical social life without people.

The redevelopment of buildings is extended in the reconstruction of entire urban districts and also the reconfiguration of social activities in them. Even where areas are designated 'heritage' zones, only certain aspects are selected for preservation. For example, the buildings of the nineteenth century may be wiped out in favour of buildings of the eighteenth. Focusing on one historically defined epoch or historical activity allows areas to be advertised to tourists or city inhabitants who will be given a clear expectation of what will be found. New facilities for these 'urban tourist-consumers' replace the extraneous buildings which are, in a sense, 'edited out' of the urban text. The reduction of complexity is thus both at the level of function and history.

REFERENCES

Anand, R. (1987) *Task Force on the Law Concerning Trespass to Publicly-Used Property as it Affects Youth and Minorities*, Toronto: Ministry of the Attorney-General's Office.

Anon. (1982) 'Canadian consumers cautious about making major purchases', in *Vancouver Sun*, 20 May: A12.

Anon. (1991) 'Trillium terminal three', supplement to the *Toronto Globe and Mail*, 21 April: C1–8.

Bakhtin, M. M. (1984) *Rabelais and His World*, London: Midland.

Benjamin, W. (1989) *Paris, Capitale du XIXe Siècle. Le Livre des passages* (tr. J. Lacoste), Paris: Editions du CERF.

Bourdieu, P. (1971) 'The Berber house or the world reversed', in M. Douglas (ed.) *Rules and Meanings*, Harmondsworth: Penguin: 98–110.

Bowlby, R. (1985) *Just Looking: Consumer Culture in Dreiser, Gissing and Zola*, Andover: Methuen.

Carrithers, M., Collins, S., Lukes, S. (1985) *The Category of the Person*, Cambridge: Cambridge University Press.

Chambers, I. (1985) *Urban Rhythms. Pop Music and Popular Culture*, London: Macmillan.

Chaney, D. (1991) 'Subtopia in Gateshead: the MetroCentre as a cultural form; *Theory, Culture & Society* 7: 49–68.

Cohen, E., Ben-Yehuda, N. and Aviad, J. (1987) 'Recentering the world: the quest for "elective" centers in a secularized universe', *Sociological Review* 35(2): 320–46.

Dawson, J. and Lord, J. D. (1983) *Shopping Centre Development*, New York: Longman.

Debord, G. (1970) *Society of Spectacle*, Detroit: Black and Red.

de Certeau, M. (1984) *The Practice of Everyday Life*, Berkeley: University of California Press.

Dowling, R. (1991) 'Shopping for pleasure? The Woodward's department store and femininity in the 1950s', outline of an MA thesis presented at the Canadian Association of Geographers' annual conference, Kingston, Ontario, June: Dept. of Geography, University of British Columbia.

Finkelstein, J. (1991) *The Fashioned Self*, Cambridge: Polity.

Fowler, D. (1988) ' "Centerites", making public use of private property: the case of urban shopping centres', MA thesis, McGill University, Montreal.

Fox, K.J. (1987) 'Real punks and pretenders. The social organization of a counterculture', *Journal of Contemporary Ethnography* 16(3) (Oct.): 344–70.

Gardner, C. and Sheppard, J. (1989) *Consuming Passion*, London: Unwin Hyman.

Geist, J-F. (1983) *Arcades*, Cambridge, Mass.: MIT Press.

Harvey, D. (1988) *The Urbanization of Capital: Studies in the History and Theory of Capitalist Urbanization*, Baltimore: Johns Hopkins University Press.

Haug, W.F. (1986) *Critique of Commodity Aesthetics. Appearance, Sexuality and Advertising in Capitalist Society*, Minneapolis: University of Minnesota Press.

Kowinski, W.S. (1985) *The Malling of America*, New York: Morrow.

Kroker, A. and Cook, D. (1988) *The Postmodern Scene. Excremental Culture and Hyper-Aesthetics*, Toronto: New World Perspectives and Macmillan.

Lakoff, R. cited in Pred, A. (1990) 'In other wor(l)ds: fragmented and integrated observations on gendered languages, gendered spaces and local transformation', *Antipode* 22(1): 39–52.

Langman, L. (1991) 'Goffman meets Marx at the shopping mall', paper presented at the ASA Annual Conference.

Lorch, B.J. and Smith, M.J. (1988) 'Shopping centre sales promotions and consumer behaviour: a marketing geography case study', *Canadian Geography* 32(1): 56–62.

Maffesoli, M. (1985) *L'Ombre de Dionysos. Contribution à une sociologie de l'orgie*, Paris: Méridiens Klincksieck.

Maffesoli, M. (1988) *Le temps des tribus*, Paris: Méridiens Klincksieck.

Miller, D. (1987) *Material Culture and Mass Consumption*, Oxford: Basil Blackwell.

Moise, P. (1983) *Attractivité des centres commerciaux régionaux le samedi. Les Cas de Rosny II et de Créteil-Soleil*, Paris: Institut d'Aménagement et d'Urbanisme de la Région d'Ile-de-France.

Morris, M. (1988) 'Things to do with shopping centres', *Culture Studies*, WP 1 Centre for Twentieth Century Studies, University of Wisconsin-Milwaukee, 1: 2.

Nava, M. (1987) 'Consumerism and its contradictions', *Cultural Studies* 1 (2): 204–10.

Ploegaerts, L. and Momer, B. (1989) 'L'Appropriation des espaces commerciaux par les personnes agées', *Metropolis* 87: 31–42.

Rojek, C. (1985) *Capitalism and Leisure Theory*, London: Tavistock.

Saunders, P. (1978) 'Domestic property and social class', *International Journal of Urban and Regional Research* 2: 233–51.

Schmalenbach, H. (1977) *Herman Schmalenbach on Society and Experience*, (eds and tr. G. Lüschen and G.P. Stone), Chicago: University of Chicago Press.

Shields, R. (1984) 'A site and space of consumer jouissance and liminality:

the Toronto Eaton's Centre', *Frontenac Review*, Queen's University Dept. of French Studies.

Shields, R. (1989) 'Social spatialisation and the built environment: the case of the West Edmonton mall', *Environment and Planning D: Society and Space* 7 (2): 147–64.

Shields, R. (1991) *Places on the Margin. Alternate Geographies of Modernity*, London: Routledge.

Simmel, G. (1950) *The Sociology of George Simmel* (ed. K. Wolff), New York: Free Press.

Smith, D. (1990) *Texts, Facts, and Femininity: Exploring the Relations of Ruling*, London: Routledge.

Stallybrass, P. and White, A. (1986) *The Poetics and Politics of Transgression*, London: Methuen.

Tomlinson, A. (1990) 'Introduction: consumer culture and the aura of the commodity', in *Consumption, Identity and Style*, London: Routledge.

Turner, V. (1979) *Process, Performance and Pilgrimage*, New Delhi: Concept.

Urry, J. (1990) *The Tourist Gaze*, Beverly Hills: Sage.

Weber, M. (1978) *Economy and Society* (2 vols.) (tr. G. Roth and C. Wittich), Berkeley: University of California Press.

Whyte, W. (1980) *Social Life of Small Urban Spaces*, Washington: Conservation Foundation.

Wolff, J. (1985) 'The invisible *flâneuse*: women and the literature of modernity', in *Theory, Culture and Society* 2, 3: 37–47.

Zukin, S. (1991) *Landscapes of Power. From Detroit to Disney World*, Berkeley: University of California Press.

Zurcher, L. A. (1977) *Mutable Self: a Self-concept for Social Change*, Beverly Hills: Sage.

2

WATCHING THE WORLD GO ROUND

Atrium culture and the psychology of shopping

Harvie Ferguson

Consumption is a selective process aimed at isolating the really new and indestructible aspect of production.

(Tournier, 1981: 75)

GLASGOW'S LEISURE REVOLUTION

Glasgow was designated 'European City of Culture' for 1990. This unlikely palm was sought, and subsequently used to justify, a dramatic shift in the national and international image of the city. From being a historic centre of industrial production, ruined by structural shifts in the economy and political neglect, its domestic architecture all but destroyed by the construction of urban motorways and short-sighted housing policies, Glasgow was to be reborn as the leisure capital of the north; a modern city of consumption. Nineteen-ninety was, in fact, the culmination of at least fifteen years of promotional image-making on the part of the city authorities. Whatever justification this policy might have had, and whatever benefits it might have brought (or more likely not brought) to the majority of its residents, central Glasgow, during this period, has been radically altered. Victorian façades have been cleaned and lovingly restored as office accommodation or preserved as traditional housing. And, though there has been much unimpressive speculative construction, more self-confident modern building has also begun to appear. The Royal Academy of Music and Drama has been imaginatively relocated adjacent to the new Royal Concert Hall, which was the most ambitious building project to be completed during 1990. On the south side of the city, in the grounds of Pollok House which had been gifted to the city some years earlier, a modern and innovatively designed museum was erected as the permanent home of the Burrell Collection.

The reconstruction of Glasgow's cultural infrastructure, which was an essential prerequisite of the remaking of Glasgow's image as a cultural centre and tourist 'destination' ('resorts' are strictly for package-deal suntans) went hand in hand with the redevelopment of central Glasgow's shopping facilities. 'Culture' in the form of art treasures, live performances, and picturesquely presented architecture (though with the exception of Templeton's carpet factory, whose exotic Victorian brickwork has long been an 'attraction' to the more architecturally minded tourist, this was notably lacking in restored industrial buildings) might attract visitors, but to get the most out of such a resource depended on persuading them to spend freely while in the city. Hotel accommodation, restaurants, bars and shops were extensively redeveloped.

MODEL SHOPPING VENUES – SPORTS HALLS AND THEATRES

Two recent developments in Glasgow serve to highlight contrasting modern architectural traditions in the provision of shopping facilities, each apparently hinting at implicit and divergent psychologies of consumption.

St Enoch Centre is a large 'mall' construction containing two levels of general High Street stores (British Homes Stores, Boots, Mothercare, etc.). It is an extensive enclosure on a city-centre site which had been left undeveloped for many years after the closure and demolition of St Enoch railway station. The importance of the site has been recognized in a somewhat half-hearted concession to the spirit of architectural innovation. A flamboyant glass shell has been erected over a conventional ground-plan, creating the impression of a large glass circus tent.[1] Yet this is no Crystal Palace. The evocation of the great International Expositions which, during the second half of the nineteenth century, and particularly in Paris, advertised and instituted the age of mass consumption, is timid and muted.[2] And compared to the subtle use of glass in the Burrell Museum which allows light to filter through late medieval stained glass, or at points abolishes the boundary between the exhibition area and the 'natural' wooded environment beyond, its use in the St Enoch Centre, opaque but non-reflective from the outside, obscured by structural features on the inside, lacks the essential quality of translucence.

The modern association of shopping with leisure, and particularly healthy sporting activity, initially played a central part in the design for the St Enoch Centre with the proposed inclusion of an ice-rink. This plan was subsequently revised, the ice-rink considerably reduced in scale, repositioned and given a separate entrance. It is, in fact, rather difficult to find and constitutes a separate facility associated with, rather than an integral part of, the overall structure. Yet there remains, conveyed in its tented glass canopy and open interior finished in a garish high-tech style, the sensation of entering the sports complex of one of the more popular Mediterranean holiday resorts. One expects to find a swimming pool, squash courts, or even a running track rather than a shopping arena. But this is a temporary illusion, and, as it contains none of these things, the curious visitor has no reason, other than the strictly limited convenience of its range of shopping (all of which is more interestingly replicated in the adjacent streets), to return. It is, in fact, a somewhat austere and practical construction, a misplaced shopping mall which, though something of a spectacle from the train as it crosses the Clyde, remains a building to be entered only when strictly necessary, when the shopper requires something he or she knows to be housed within it.

Very different, and the most successful recent shopping development in Glasgow is Princes Square. This is a fashionable 'gallery' of small units constructed from existing city-centre buildings. A block facing on to the recently pedestrianized Buchanan Street has been 'turned inside out' by covering the central courtyard (originally the 'backcourts' used for storage and collection of rubbish)[3] with a Victorian-style glass roof. The resulting atrium becomes the central focus of a new theatrical interior with shops and restaurants on three levels served by ornamental balconies, escalators and lifts. The shops are small, and either highly specialized (The Pen Shop), fashionable boutiques (Monsoon, Katherine Hammett), or miniature extensions of famous names (Crabtree and Evelyn, Vidal Sassoon). A curved staircase, with art-deco wrought-iron balustrades, rises elegantly from the central well of the building in imitation of the eighty-year-old interior of the Galerie Lafayette in Paris.

The feeling of being in a museum or theatre (where something

Figure 2.1 Interior view of Princes Square, Glasgow, Scotland
Source: Photograph taken by the author, Harvie Ferguson

is just about to be exhibited or performed) is heightened not only by the provision of a central, and generally empty, 'performance space', but also by the unexpected appearance of Foucault's Pendulum, a replica of which describes a leisurely arc in the space

24

bounded by two sets of escalators. Foucault's wonderful demonstration of the earth's rotation, carried out in Paris, beneath the dome of the Panthéon in 1851, created a considerable public sensation at the time and has since become a rather popular scientific 'spectacle' now routinely included in the interior decoration of many large public buildings.

The fascination of Foucault's original demonstration lay in the elegance and economy with which it revealed the rotation of the earth. It allows the observer, literally, to 'watch the world go round'.[4]

The pendulum's plane of oscillation remains fixed in relation to the earth's rotational movement. This does not mean, as Eco's observer believes, that 'along the infinite extrapolation of its wire . . . up toward the most distant galaxies, lay the Only Fixed Point in the universe, eternally unmoving' (Eco, 1989: 5). Its independence from the earth's rotation does not 'prove' the existence of such an absolute frame of reference. But it does reveal, without leaving its surface, the fact of the earth's motion. We can stand and watch the earth turn beneath the pendulum's 'serene breathing'.

MOTION AND DEPTH

The appropriateness of this 'exhibit' to a modern shopping development is more than superficial. The pendulum reveals to us a type of movement which, by virtue of our inclusion within it, is normally concealed. We cannot directly 'feel' the rotation of the earth, even though it is more general and 'fundamental' than the various forms of 'local motion' of which we do become conscious. And unlike such 'local motion', which always requires a specific 'cause', this cosmic rotation is 'effortless' (Koyré, 1978).

The distinction between a normally unremarked, and effortless 'cosmic' motion, and a 'local' resisted motion, played an important part in the formation of modern physical theories. In general the primacy of 'cosmic' motion, as the fundamental model for dynamics, gradually replaced the 'common sense' immediacy of 'local' or 'forced' motion. Similar dualities emerged in the theoretical understanding of other aspects of nature, and, more significantly from the present perspective, in efforts to conceptualize human action. This is revealed not only in the emergence of psychoanalysis and other 'depth' psychologies, but much more generally in the continuous search, within academic psychologies since the scientific revolution, for an 'underlying' psychic mechanism deemed to be explanatory of the phenomenal world.

The psychic equivalent of the 'classical' scientific perspective of inertial cosmic motion through absolute space is found in the notion of 'desire' as an 'absolute' or groundless force propelling the individual to action. Everyday human activities are ultimately the outcome of such hidden forces. Only rarely, however, are these desires openly expressed. More generally they are 'deformed' in being expressed through the medium of everyday social conventions.

The classical psychology of the bourgeois era is concerned almost exclusively with desire, that is with the restless energy of the 'ego' seeking to express itself in the world of practical activities. The notion of desire is founded upon a mythology of the isolated ego moving in the 'ideal space' of society. The person is a privileged 'object' within a world of objects, constituted simply by possession of the consciousness of its own activating mechanism; it 'feels' its tendency towards self-actualization, and has privileged access to the stable realm of desire from which it manufactures the 'local motion' of 'rational' action. Thus, even for the most stringent utilitarian tradition, the person is held to be activated by an invisible inner force, which, dimly felt, was only partially revealed to others. Indeed, it is just because 'society' constitutes a world of shared experience that it can be characterized, in relation to such inner personal forces, as superficial, artificial and even unnatural. In society, 'we no longer dare seem what we really are', and consequently 'we never know with whom we have to deal'. The 'real' self is hidden 'beneath the uniform and perfidious veil of politeness' (Rousseau, 1973: 6).

WANTING AND WISHING

In its simplest form, then, a bourgeois psychology of shopping elevates the difference between the person and commodity into an ontological distinction. The shop is essentially a market, a convenient means of realizing the rational exchanges immanent within the division of social labour.

Even within the Enlightenment, such a rationalist model of consumption was subject to development and revision. In the psychology of the *philosophes* 'need' was progressively interpreted as a social, and thus conventional, phenomenon, rather than as a naturalistic category. These developments, therefore, all involve, though in different ways, attempts to explicate the notion of 'want'.

Initially, that is to say, the urge to procure goods was viewed simply as the outcome of an individual and rational market choice. The inner 'needs' or 'wants' of the isolated individual were held to be the sovereign and irreducible basis of consumption. However, just as in terms of sensory psychology the person was held to be unaware of 'colour' in general, or even of some particular colour, such as 'greenness', it was not desire or wants in general, but the desire for a specific object, which seemed to animate the individual. Whatever the 'deeper' origin of the passions, they could exist for us only as the 'secondary qualities' of particular wants. The urge to consume was, thus, a link between the unknown realm of the passions and the rational construction of the everyday world.

The variety of such wants appeared to be infinite, so that the sphere of consumption, approached in terms of any rational psychology seemed to lead immediately into a dizzying abyss. Attempts to make sense of such a sphere, to close the gap somewhat between the original simplicity of the passions, and the incomprehensible complexity of everyday 'wants' was a scientific challenge not dissimilar to that guiding the search for simple 'underlying' laws expressive of some primitive natural unity. Thus, in spite of the difference in language and philosophical tradition there was a close relation between the development of reductionist psychologies, which sought this unity in a physical 'mechanism', and the emergence of 'dialectical' psychologies of desire as the internal movement of 'self-expression'.

More particularly there was developed, as the unifying conception 'underlying' the variety of wants, a conception of selfhood as individuated personal identity. The self, as any other 'universal', could become conscious within us only through the medium of some particular content, some specific set of events or desires. The 'self' which exists potentially within us, it was held, becomes actual through the process of consumption.

All consumption became conceivable as the desire, *for*, as well as the desire *of*, the self. There lay in every want the aching need for self-expression. The unknown depths of desire announced their presence within us in the specificity of 'wants', that is as a sense of loss or absence which could be made good through the appropriation of some specific thing. But however varied such wants, they were connected in the urge to 'complete' the self.

The 'exteriority' of consumption was, therefore, an illusion. Rather than grasp the process as one of 'attraction', and attempt to describe and classify just those characteristics of external objects which made them attractive to us, the psychologist of desire sought to discover in the attractiveness of objects the reflected image of an inner self-movement. All attractiveness was the result, and not the cause, of desire. Desire spontaneously moves outward. An image of the self is projected into the world and renders some aspects of it attractive; 'all possess in themselves the original of that beauty which they look for externally' (Pascal, 1850, 2: 133). It endows the world of objects with their psychological tone or tension, it makes them desirable. We then seek, in consuming such objects, to incorporate an idealized self, to make the self more real, and to end the inner despair of not having a self. The psychology of passionate individualism, developing in parallel with the utilitarian, mechanistic and reductionist psychologies of the ego, stretches from Pascal through Kierkegaard to Proust (Ferguson, 1990: 199–218).

Taken together these traditions represent certain possibilities within the framework of bourgeois psychology. Consumption could be viewed variously as a simple want for things whose inherent attractiveness was a property of nature (utility), as a want for things whose attractiveness depended on the assumption that they were wanted, or already possessed, by others (envy), or as a want for things whose attractiveness was the reflex image of the self (desire).

Interestingly enough the great revolution in shopping which took place during the second half of the nineteenth century and which, in a variety of different ways, has continued to the present, is comprehensible only on the basis of quite different psychological assumptions. Boucicat, the founder of the Bon Marché in Paris, or Macy, or Wannamaker, understood the situation much more profoundly than did their academic contemporaries.

The creation of the department store might, at first sight, seem to confirm the centrality of envy in modern bourgeois culture. The unprecedented concentration and display of commodities might be seen, thus, as a mechanism for facilitating the social comparisons upon which 'wanting' was based. A brief examination of the nature of the early department stores, however, suggests there is something rather different in the style of consumption which they encouraged.

The department store opens itself to the passer-by. Its windows are larger, better lit, and fuller of merchandise than earlier, specialized, shops. Even a visitor from somewhere as cosmopolitan as Vienna could be astonished by the luxuriousness of Parisian stores of the 1880s. It was 'the infinite variety of attractively displayed goods' that caught Freud's attention during his first visit to Paris in 1885, to study under Charcot. To him Paris seemed to be a place whose populace had become 'given to psychical epidemics' (Freud, 1960: 199–200, Letter to Minna Bernays). He was little different, in fact, to the modern 'guest worker' who spends his first day in the city in mesmerized procession 'from shop window to shop window' (Tournier, 1988: 144). The window-displays flaunt the commodity; offering it to the casual passer-by in a tantalizingly incomplete manner. It forms 'an enclosed area, at the same time totally exposed to the gaze and inaccessible to the hands, impenetrable and yet without secrets, a world you may only touch with your eyes but which is nevertheless real, in no way illusory like the world of photography' (Tournier, 1988: 144). The shamelessness of the commodity, is literally 'arresting'; hinting at the proximity of an entire world of related items.

Its windows, therefore, though unprecedented in their size and in the elaborateness of their displays, are insignificant in relation to the totality of their structures, which, 'massive and impressive spectacles', rivals in scale, solidity, and classicism, the most splendid of public buildings' (Benson, 1986: 18). Only the most formidable mass could contain the entire world at which its windows hinted.

The fundamental character of the department store, therefore, is sheer size; it is overwhelmingly extensive. Not all occupied an entire city block, like Macy's New York store with its more than two million square feet of floor space (Hendrickson, 1979: 61), but each strove to represent itself as an entire *world*, self-sufficient and abundant. The consumer need go nowhere else, she (less frequently he) could wander aimlessly in an 'Adamless Eden', drawn from one part of the store to another by the spectacle of the commodity itself, by its endless variety and its infinite capacity to replenish itself.

But it was not simply larger and more magnificent than any shop, for the first time offering a multiplicity of merchandise at fixed price, it deliberately broke down the distance between the autonomous 'person' and the commodity which was to be purchased and consumed (Miller, 1981: 165). It brought the commodity closer, and made it seem more available. The department store was a public place, and encouraged casual visitors. Entering the building, as had been the case with earlier shops, did not place anyone under an obligation to purchase something. Not only merchandise, therefore, but a host of ancillary services were provided to attract the customer. Nurseries, writing-rooms, art galleries, meeting-places for women's clubs, were all provided, particularly in American stores (Benson, 1986: 84–5). There is more to this than capitalist trickery, or cynical manipulation. The psychological distance between the inner world of wants and the externality of the commodity became blurred, and the categorical distinction among commodities abolished. All could be housed in the same place because all were becoming fundamentally alike, and all became more alike in being located in the same place.

The department store is ideally a building which absorbs and swallows the shopper. There is nothing limited or precise about the stimulus required to enter its doors. And once within, there is no boundary beyond which the commodity is kept in seclusion and safety. The shopper mixes with the commodity, lives amidst its forms. The 'chaotic-exotic' interiors inspired particularly by the sumptuous orientalism of the Trocadero exhibit at the Paris Exposition of 1900 seized upon anything distant and unusual, recreating for the Parisian imagination at least, the 'decor of the harem' (Williams, 1982: 69). Merchandise is no longer just a collection of items for sale. Commodities are not arranged in a passive landscape upon which the discriminating searchlight of the ego might be turned to illuminate just those items best adapted to the 'wants' of each particular customer. They constitute, rather, an active mass which overwhelms the ego, absorbs and transforms the observer, arousing in her completely new sensations. Zola's *Au bonheur des dames* (1980, originally published in *Le Gils Blas*, 1882–3) quite accurately characterizes this assault on the senses. He sees in the department store the 'poetry of modern life', a new and irresistible sensuousness. The consumer cannot withstand the abundant luxury of huge open displays, she is 'seduced, driven crazy' (Bowlby, 1985: 74–5).

The mechanism of wanting or desiring depended on the maintenance of a psychological distance between 'ego' and 'object', and the creation of an inner tension which was felt as a 'want'. But in the department store, distance is abolished; there is an immediately sensuous world of things with which the shopper can effortlessly identify. And where the facilitation of desire was founded upon comparison, vanity, envy and the 'need' for self-approbation, nothing underlies the immediacy of the wish. The customer is swept away by the illusion of luxury. The purchase is casual, unexpected and spontaneous. It has the dream quality of both expressing and fulfilling a wish, and like all wishes, is insincere and childish.

The display of commodities within the department store is overwhelmingly diverse and abundant. Its centre, the very core of the building, is given over to a literal mountain of goods. The atrium construction favoured by the designers of the early department store (in part to allow light, circulation and ventilation) was itself a conspicuous, and excitingly scandalous waste of space. It created, in its great vaulted interior, the impression of an infinitely extended space, filled with an inexhaustible supply of commodities.

The atrium construction, with surrounding galleries, had already become an established principle of industrial architecture; in the factory, and most conspicuously in the prison (Foucault, 1977: 195–209). The panopticon design, pioneered by Bentham and taken up as the standard plan for all confining institutions (including schools), was the architectural realization of new types of social discipline. Social surveillance, the background to the adequate inculcation of self-control, required open interiors, and continuously observable workspace. The centre of the panopticon was an observation post occupied by a continuously watchful and authoritative eye.

The department store interestingly reverses this perspective. Its centre is hollowed out to accommodate the burgeoning commodity, so that all those wandering its galleries can observe its hypnotic forms. The object is at the centre; it fascinates and controls by liberating the wish, rather than through the imposition of a rational order of wants. In comparison to the 'primary process' of dreaming, the arrangement of galleries and circulating shoppers, which encourages the interaction of envious glances, and the activation of imitative wants, is of lesser significance.

THE PRIVACY OF DREAMS

The great age of the department store has passed. And in relation to them the new post-war shopping malls and shopping centres appear, for the most part, architecturally banal and psychologically regressive. This is not because shopping has become reabsorbed into a larger framework of rational activity. Far from it; we have learned the lessons of the department store, and no longer need to be educated in consumption. The larger propaganda aspect of display has been usurped by the more powerful, private and intimate form of television advertising. The shop window now opens directly into the home; the *flâneur* has become the somnambulist.

The physical isolation and morphological simplicity of the shopping mall reflects, together with the privacy of the dream world, the dominance of the motor car (Gosling and Maitland, 1976; Maitland, 1985). The first architectural principle of their design is specified in an exact relation between parking space and floor area. The internal design is primarily concerned with the flow of shopping trolleys, rather than the extravagant display of goods. All this quite adventitiously recreates the illusion of the 'rational' shopper determinedly exercising her or his (still more often her, but often his, and frequently their) 'choice' in the market-place.

But it is only an illusion. Both St Enoch Centre and Princes Square, along with innumerable similar developments throughout Europe and North America, in fact depend on the new psychology of wishing. We can see indeed, in these Glaswegian examples, the preservation of particular aspects of the dream architecture of the original department store. St Enoch Centre recreates something of the impression of enormity essential to the first stores, while in Princes Square, the psychological impact of the atrium has been rediscovered.

But, while the modern shopping mall, in isolating sheer size as the pre-eminent magnetic quality, oversimplifies and renders dull and lifeless the element of fantasy common to all the early stores, Princes Square has purified the 'rotunda design which was the hallmark of nineteenth-century department stores' (Benson, 1986: 39). At each level a variety of small shops minister to the sensuous and aesthetic needs of the body. Designer clothes, fashionable food and smart books predominate; there is nothing basic or necessary.

The central hall of the building, its floor slightly recessed, is covered with a colourful mosaic. Whether occupied by some 'performance' or not, this entertainment site is the building's central focus. Shoppers drift around the galleries, their gaze torn from the small window areas (restricted in size in order to preserve the 'feel' of the original Victorian stonework), towards the emptied-out interior. While for the department store it is the lure of the commodity itself which draws the shopper into the building, and, once inside, 'creates new states of mind' (Miller, 1981: 167), the interior design of Princes Square is itself the attractive spectacle and the commodity recedes modestly into the skin of the building. Compared to its original model, Princes Square is an empty structure.

Yet it is successful, people shop there. Princes Square in fact reveals, in its design and functioning, the wishfulness that bourgeois society had concealed within the 'classical' relations of desire. It is a kind of Foucault's Pendulum of the modern psyche. The limitations on consumption inherent in the older psychology of desire could be overcome only by transforming the ideal consumer into a different psychological world. But in the department store the wish had not been completely liberated from the rationality of desire. The customer had to be prompted by the extravagant contradiction of an external stimulus.

Princes Square is much smaller and more manageable than the classic store, or even the modern shopping mall. Within it the commodity has withdrawn, indeed, it has become almost invisible. And, without its distraction, the peculiarities of the modern commodity relation are made all the more evident.

The distinction between the rational market and the fantastic character of the modern shopping area might be pursued through a close examination of Freud's dream theory. We seek in the commodity a satisfaction which cannot be extracted by any mechanical or rational means. Every dream (commodity) simultaneously expresses and fulfils a wish. And the wish is a plastic image situated between two fundamentally dissociated 'worlds'. Freud portrays the psychic apparatus as having a certain depth. Towards its surface, representations of the outside world predominate, and are ordered according to rational norms, and towards its 'inner' edge images of spontaneously generated desire predominate.[5] Perceptions are registered at the surface, dreams at the deeper level. The outside world as a thing in itself is unknown, as is the central core of indifferent desire.

The design of Princes Square inadvertently reproduces Freud's architectural principle of the psyche. For the modern shopper, as for dreaming subjectivity, both outside world and inner reality are held at arm's length. The building is nothing but a sensitized skin;

a kind of primitive consciousness flickering to life in the perpetual flux of shoppers as they circle its galleries. From the outside it appears to be part of a city street, yet, entering through narrow passages, it opens into an abysmal interior. So that, just as for the dream world (whatever it represents), neither waking consciousness, nor unconscious desire, can directly enter its reality, so, for the shopper neither the 'outside world' of production – ordered and co-ordinated by strictly rational means – nor the hidden inwardness and depth of self-motivating desire, really exist.

The atrium which is also found at the centre of many refurbished office buildings, has become a commonplace of modern design. Less popular after better electric lighting, and air-conditioning, prompted architects to 'rationalize' shop construction and to economize on the use of space with through floors at every level (Benson, 1986: 39), its current popularity reveals a 'deeper' aesthetic appeal which outweighs narrowly economic calculation.

DISTINCTION AND INDIFFERENCE

The dream psychology of the modern relations of consumption is not fully realized in Princes Square, or in any other single development. The characteristics which it reveals, however, can be taken as representative tendencies. By imaginatively extending and inter-relating such tendencies the major characteristics of a more comprehensible 'model' of such relations can be outlined.

Infinity

Where the department store sought heroically to *contain* the commodity (*everything* was available within a single enormous building), in Princes Square a virtue is made of limitation in scale. It is made up of a series of small leased units whose contents, rather than appearing exhaustive, offer a continuously changing point of contact, with the ideally infinite, and therefore uncontainable, commodity world beyond it.

Incompleteness

The endless variety of commodities means that any actual display of goods can be no more than an arbitrary sample from an ideal set of infinite possibilities. Taken together all immediately available commodities do not constitute a 'totality' in the sense of a complete and finished world of objects.

Arbitrariness

The inner personal relation to the commodity is broken. It does not matter which commodity is chosen because each carries within it only the possibility, and not the promise, of thrilling excitement. The subjective satisfaction in consumption is, so to speak, arbitrarily distributed among commodities. In responding to a wish, rather than a want, any rational mechanism of choice has been abandoned. Shopping becomes the purest form of gambling in which the only 'rational' strategy is to maximize the probability of success through unconstrained and effortless consumption. Like dreaming, objects are lightly taken up and cast off. None has lasting value, and none become the *telos* of an inner process of self-realization.

Fragmentation

The consuming 'self', which expresses itself in arbitrary choices selected from an incomplete sample drawn from an ideally infinite set of commodities, experiences itself and the world in a fragmented fashion. Indeed, the self, as an integrated unity, is cast aside. It is as incomplete as the commodities fortuitously set before it, and can itself, therefore, be no more than sampled. Now we consume, not as an act of self-completion, but as a means of preventing the illusion of selfhood taking root in us.

Indifference

All commodities, as the unpredictable bearers of an arbitrarily distributed inner value, tend to become identical. This, in fact, is a simple consequence of mass production and the high levels of investment which it demands. Change is less extreme than it might be; variety symbolically infinite, but actually limited. Each commodity, like the spokes of a roulette wheel, is ideally like every other. The consumer is stimulated to a frenzy of acquisition, not by the certainty of gaining a known satisfaction, but by the hope that he or she will sooner or later be 'in luck'.

These general tendencies are to some extent limited and counter-acted by two other characteristics of the dream world.

Novelty

New commodities are usually thought to be more exciting than old ones. This is a type of 'superstition' commonly associated with gambling. The latest Premium Bond or lottery numbers are the most sought after, although, in principle, they carry no greater probability of winning. However, so long as novelty can be associated with 'glamour' in the sensibility of the consumer, it makes sense to 'keep up' with changing fashions. So that, even if the inner value of the commodity cannot be predicted from its external appearance, its newness can be relished.

Nostalgia

An apparently opposed strategy is to consume especially those things which are genuinely old, or, rather, those old things which we can associate with our childhood. Whereas underlying every want is the desire of and for the self, there is expressed in every dream, however varied and fleeting, the wish to recover the vanished sensuousness of childhood. The shameless nostalgia of Princes Square, recalling as it does the earliest days of the great department stores, is, thus, a wholly appropriate architectural style; an apt setting in which to discover that commodities have been transformed into toys.

It is, therefore, quite characteristic to find in the modern shopping centre, the old and the new placed side by side. New commodities imitate old designs, while 'genuinely' old items can be sold as 'originals'. The arbitrary nature of the distinction is already all too obvious, and the tendency towards indifference, towards the establishment of a continuous and infinite present of the commodity, renders insecure temporal, as well as all other, distinctions.

Neither in Princes Square nor in St Enoch Centre do we find exemplified in its pure form the psychological ideal type of the indifferent shopper. Such a type is no more than a tendency revealed in a consumer revolution which is now well over a century old. The mere fact of there being two such distinct shopping developments, with their different range of goods, and, more importantly their quite different *ambience* points to the persistence of organized social meanings in and through consumption.

Rather than simply contrast the individualistic model of the rational consumer with the mass character of modern indifference, any descriptive sociology of shopping would seem bound to focus on the relatively complex pattern of consumer groupings 'avid for distinction' (Saisselin, 1985: 6). Thus, in different ways, Douglas and Isherwood (1979) and Pierre Bourdieu (1984) have analysed consumption as a set of implicit signs, as part, that is to say, of the language of everyday culture. And, as social meanings can only be manufactured and transmitted through the perception of difference, the consumer, we might suppose, cannot become wholly insensitive to qualitative distinctions among commodities. Indeed, it seems wholly characteristic of modern society that consumers become far more discriminating than ever before, and the majority are now obsessively concerned over the smallest differences among the objects offered for sale. These distinctions convey a meaning, however, only because the basic elements of the system, commodities, are bereft of significance of their own. Significance is added to, and not discovered within, the actuality of things. It exists in the relations among, not the substance of, the objects which act as signifiers. Commodities are soulless and, because of this, superficial differences among them can be seized upon as a means of representing other, and possibly more significant, differences. Most types of commodities, thus, differ primarily by manufacturer's label, are identified by that label, and become associated with a particular price level. They bear a name as a totemic emblem. We purchase a 'Sony' or a 'Pentax', rather than a television set or a camera. And rather as novelty can acquire the 'added value' of glamour, so a particular brand name can arouse, quite independently of the object to which it is attached, an excitement of its own. Indeed, even in the absence of an arousing label, the price of a commodity can be used as a mark of distinction. And, similarly, something purchased in Princes Square may thus acquire, by virtue of the network of confirming architectural and cultural messages which are a permanent feature of the physical and social structure of the building, a different 'value' to an identical item bought elsewhere. It will absorb, in spite of being mass-produced and widely distributed, a certain glow of exclusivity, an association with the 'right' sort of place.

These and similar aspects of 'lifestyle' shopping are not opposed to the general drift towards indifference, they become possible, in fact, only because of it. The commodity can become a sign only because it has been emptied of intrinsic value. Its power to represent depends on its inner insignificance.

The tendency towards indifference should not be mistaken for lack of interest in consumption.[6] It is the indifference of the commodity which permits new meanings to adhere to the process of consumption. And while appetites may become jaded, and wants sated, wishes are endlessly alluring.

NOTES

1 The urban mall seems to be, in practice, a rather uniform structure with relatively few morphological variations. For an interesting attempt at formal description and classification of possible types, see Maitland, 1985: 109–25.

2 Glasgow hosted a number of international exhibitions of its own, notably in 1888, 1901 and 1911, which, in contrast to those held in Paris, were primarily celebrations of industrial production (Kinchin and Kinchin, n.d.). The International Garden Festival of 1988 was, therefore, a new departure, rather than an attempt to revive an older tradition.

3 It is wholly appropriate that the centre of a new shopping centre should have been, for many years, a rubbish dump. The French novelist, Michel Tournier, remarks, in an excursus intriguingly titled 'Aesthetic of the Dandy Garbage Man', 'After all, what is rubbish but the great storehouse of things multiplied to infinity by mass production?' (Tournier, 1981: 75).

4 Most elementary astronomy texts include some discussion of Foucault's Pendulum, (e.g. Payne-Gaposchkin and Haramundanis, 1970). In Princes Square, as elsewhere, the pendulum is allowed to swing freely above a clock face fixed into the ground. To keep reasonably accurate time, however, a hidden motor has to make continuous 'corrections' to allow for the effect of latitude, vibration, etc.

5 Freud's 'topographical' model of the psychic apparatus is outlined in Chapter 7 of *The Interpretation of Dreams*, which was a reworking of his earlier, failed, attempt at a 'Project for a Scientific Psychology' (Freud, 1954).

6 As, for example, Goran Ahrne, 'The increasing standard of living is mostly made up of a meaningless consumption, paid by useless toil'; in Otnes (ed.) (1988: 59).

REFERENCES

Benson, S. P. (1986) *Counter Cultures: Saleswomen, Managers, and Customers in American Department Stores, 1890–1940*, Urbana and Chicago: University of Illinois Press.

Bourdieu, P. (1984) *Distinction: A Social Critique of the Judgement of Taste*, London and New York: Routledge & Kegan Paul.

Bowlby, R. (1985) *Just Looking: Consumer Culture in Dreiser, Gissing and Zola*, New York and London: Methuen.

Eco, U. (1989) *Foucault's Pendulum* (tr. W. Weaver) London: Secker & Warburg.

Douglas, M. and Isherwood, Baron (1979) *The World of Goods: Towards an Anthropology of Consumption*, London: Allen Lane.

Ferguson, H. (1990) *The Science of Pleasure: Cosmos and Psyche in the Bourgeois World View*, London: Routledge.

Foucault, M. (1977) *Discipline and Punish: The Birth of the Prison* (tr. A. Sheridan), London: Allen Lane.

Freud, S. (1954) *The Origins of Psycho-Analysis* (ed. M. Bonaparte, A. Freud and E. Kris), London: Imago.

Freud, S. (1960) *Letters of Sigmund Freud 1873–1939* (ed. E. L. Freud), London: Hogarth Press.

Gosling, D. and Maitland, B. (1976) *Design and Planning of Retail Systems*, London: Architectural Press.

Hendrickson, R. (1979) *The Grand Emporium: The Illustrated History of America's Great Department Stores*, New York: Stein & Day.

Kinchin, P. and Kinchin, J. (n.d.) *Glasgow's Great Exhibitions: 1888, 1901, 1911, 1938, 1988*, Bicester: White Cockade.

Koyré, A. (1978) *Galileo Studies* (tr. J. Mepham), Hassocks: Harvester Press.

Maitland, B. (1985) *Shopping Malls: Planning and Design*, London: Construction Press.

Miller, M. B. (1981) *The Bon Marché: Bourgeois Culture and the Department Store, 1869–1920*, Princeton: Princeton University Press.

Otnes P. (ed.) (1988) *The Sociology of Consumption: An Anthology*, Oslo: Solum Forlag A/S and New Jersey: Humanities Press International.

Pascal, B. (1850) *The Thoughts on Religion and Evidences of Christianity* (tr. and ed. M. P. Faugère and G. Pearce), London.

Payne-Gaposchkin, C. and Haramundanis, K. (1970) (2nd edn.) *Introduction to Astronomy*, Englewood Cliffs: Prentice-Hall.

Rousseau, J. J. (1973) *The Social Contract and Discourses* (tr. G.D.H. Cole), London: J.M. Dent.

Saisselin, R.G. (1985) *Bricabracomania: The Bourgeois and the Bibelot*, London: Thames & Hudson.

Tournier, M. (1981) *Gemini* (tr. A. Carter), London: Collins.

Tournier, M. (1988) *The Golden Droplet* (tr. B. Wright), London: Collins.

Williams, R. H. (1982) *Dream Worlds: Mass Consumption in Late Nineteenth Century France*, Berkeley and London: University of California Press.

Zola, E. (1980) *Au bonheur des dames*, Paris: Editions Gallimard.

3

NEON CAGES
Shopping for subjectivity

Lauren Langman

Every historical epoch has distinct ways of organizing time, space, behaviour and subjectivity. These converge in its principal architectural sites and public spaces that articulate cultural texts of meaning, identity and power. Who may enter, what is done within, why do they do it and how do they think of themselves? The great cathedrals of Europe, built by and sustaining of earthly power structures, were temporal houses of an eternal God through which society might celebrate and sanctify itself as well as the birth, transitions and death of each person. Elites as well as commoners saw themselves as part of an organic unity held together by a higher authority. Social life transpired in times, places and ways deemed sacred or profane.[1]

In the contemporary world, the signifying and celebrating edifice of consumer culture has become the shopping mall which exists in pseudo-democratic twilight zone between reality and a commercially produced fantasy world of commodified goods, images and leisure activities that gratify transformed desire and provide packaged self-images to a distinctive form of subjectivity. A decentred selfhood has become a plurality of intermittent, disconnected, recognition-seeking spectacles of self-presentation. While the expressions of consumption-based displays of self provide gratifications and indeed realms of personal power and meaning, in so far as desire and selfhood have been appropriated to secure certain social arrangements, the costs may very well be a deeper malaise and abandonment of concern for collective good. Some fear that an enfeebled selfhood located in a fragmented social order may be disposed to an amusing techno-fascism.

THE CRITIQUE OF MODERNITY

How best can we understand the contemporary world and its signifying structure – the mall? While most buildings are improvements in technology, materials and techniques of construction, the mall is an unprecedented use of space for equally unprecedented forms of commerce and subjectivity. Amphitheatres have little changed from the open-air arenas of yore to sealed domes now oblivious to weather. Bazaars and markets are as old as cities. The crucial elements of malldom as a modern form are combinations of visually mediated commercialization, fantasy, artificiality of juxtaposition and the prior production of a subjectivity that finds identity, gratification and meaning in privatized consumption. This transformation of persons from workers into modern consumers in a global market-place may well have been the greatest social change since industrialization. Understanding the modern era rests on Marx's critiques of capitalist political economy, Weber's notion of rational domination, Freud's analyses of subjectivity and Simmel's observations of social interaction in a money-based rational urban world. But these critiques, rooted in nineteenth-century industrialization and its class structure, need elaboration and revision for an amusement society of extraordinary consumer carnivals that are located in malls.[2] Some suggest that a new postmodern era of globally transmitted visual images and linked computers *cannot* be understood within the classical frameworks of modernity.

From political economy to amusement culture

Historians of ideas may debate whether or not the contemporary cultural critique was the culmination of a classical paradigm or emergence of another. Rather than enter this debate, amusement society, even if 'postmodern', with all its goods, carnivals and spectacular images is still a production of capitalism, albeit in contemporary versions.[3] Nevertheless, the postmodern views need consideration and location within a critique of political economy. The outlines of this synthesis were laid out by the Frankfurt School of Critical Theory. This position has been well articulated by Kellner (1989b).

If the Gothic cathedral was the symbolic structure of the feudal era, and the factory of the industrial, the distinct structures of today are cultural sites or theme parks like the Centre Georges Pompidou of Paris or Disneyland, and the carnivals of consumption – the shopping malls. Indeed, the intertwining of consumption and carnival is now such that the differences between the two are ever harder to discern. Everyday life strategies and interactions in amusement society have become celebrations of never-ending fun, games and spectacles of privatized hedonism. The skies are filled with tourists going to new theme parks or older legacies now transformed into heritage theme parks. The expressways are crowded with cars; the land with private houses; the waters with boats, but most important, the malls are crowded with shoppers, lookers and exhibitionists.

From domination to hegemony

Domination through coercion, scarcity or even legitimacy was perhaps more typical of earlier eras. Within certain limits, themselves subject to negotiation and change, amusement society offers unprecedented opportunities for human agency. Following Foucault (1977), these realms can be seen as 'microspheres of power' and/ or, I might add, gratifications.[4] As shall be argued, there is now a dialectical relation of power and strategies of resistance. It is the very problematic and changing nature of hegemony that allows if not requires contestation – at least in those realms that leave unchallenged basic structures of privilege. This is often seen in the articulation of counter-hegemonic media and social movements. Everyday life offers opportunities for pluralities of interpretations and contestations about meanings over politics, sports or leisure practices.

Hegemony now depends on the affective gratifications provided by a mass-mediated popular culture whose themes express myriad deprivations, longings, satisfactions, aspirations and the desired experiences of particular taste cultures. There is love for the lonely, sex for the horny, excitement for the bored, identities for the empty and, typically, all are intertwined. There is a pop sociology that explains such megatrends and a pop psychology to soothe any remaining despair. Further, the culture of consumption creates realms of negotiation and empowerment in the consumption and interpretations of the goods and cultural productions that sustain the legitimacy of domination. Trends of protest in fashion, film and music, or even travel and leisure soon become mass-marketed for privatized consumption. Consider only jazz, blues, punk, rap or Madonna's sexuality. What this analysis suggests is that everyday life in amusement society proceeds within a dialectic of enfeeblement and empowerment.

Subjectivity and social life

Every historical era has not only its particular social structure, cultural forms and practices, but distinctive modes of subjectivity, ways in which individuals experience a socially constructed and mediated reality of their own actions, thoughts, feelings, images of self and appraisals by other people. The more or less conscious locus of various social activities, practices, strategies, plans, goals and understandings is the self.[5] It is expressed in self-presentations and/or contemplated in reflection. It is at the same time subject to evaluations and appraisals by others. Recognition and positive appraisals by others influence self-evaluations and in turn self-esteem. At the same time, the self negotiates reality, formulates goals and initiates social interactions to achieve certain plans and goals that may often bring about rewarding recognition. Particular expressions of self in its choices of cultural goods and practices, the kinds of social relationships in which it is expressed and its desires gratified, its modes of feelings and reflexive understandings are clearly located in history.

The concept of an autonomous self with its realm of private subjectivity – personal thoughts, feelings and desires – cannot be understood apart from the rise of capitalism in which public and private realms had become bifurcated to create the possibility of a personal life more or less free of public scrutiny, at least for the privileged (cf. Zaretsky, 1976).[6] Elias (1978) has called this the civilizing process in which manners and etiquette would establish guilt and shame over bodily functions. Internalized feelings of guilt and shame rather than direct surveillance would become the means to control interpersonal behaviour.[7] The differentiation of household and public realms, together with separate bedrooms for the young, fostered individualism, privacy and internalized controls over impulse. There would follow the recognition of childhood as a stage in the life cycle (Ariès, 1962).

The intertwined emergence of childhood, the psychological individual and the social construction of the rational person served important ideological as well as commercial functions. Individuated selfhood was part and parcel of the new capitalist culture in which inner subjectivity would be expressed in the newly required social relationships. The diffusion of romantic love from the courtly to the bourgeoisie was based on this new form of subjectivity and promise of its fulfilment in its private sphere. Thus while the relation of appearance and reality, truth and lie have been problematic since Cain's insouciance, with the growth of capitalism and its private realms outside public scrutiny, public displays of self became increasingly subject to manipulation and control and hence scrutiny by others to judge inner sincerity and moral worth.

Interaction and modernity

Georg Simmel's 'formal sociology' was concerned with sociation, what we now call interaction and subjectivity in the context of modernity. The growth of trade and urban life made for frequent contact with 'strangers' whose past life was unknown and current morality in the private realm was secret. By the early part of the century, the growth of bureaucratic capitalism had begun to make impression management as important as technical or entrepreneurial skills (this would eventually make Dale Carnegie the great trainer of social skills). Perhaps one's demeanour might be a clue as to inner worth and morality? Styles of interaction and self-displays of clothes or jewellery were now put on for the sake of the audience. Thus behaviour was seen as not simply oriented to the other, but seen revealing (or hiding) an inner or private subjectivity so that good manners, appearance and pleasant interchange was an indication of an inner self and in turn trustworthiness in business or personal life.

Simmel made preliminary attempts to understand the modern forms of social life such as the impartiality of the outsider, the playful eroticism of the coquette or role of professional dinner guest. He was among the first to note how sociation had situation-dependent elements. He also noted the relationship of feelings to situations such as the gratitude of a gift's recipient or the blasé indifference of the urban dweller. For various reasons – the political agendas of the Marxists or abstract quests for theoretical purity of functionalism – Simmel's work has had less attention than it deserves. For Collins and Makowsky (1989), when Simmel died, he was reincarnated as Goffman, who gave few citations to his predecessor.

For Goffman (1959, 1961a, 1967), social life consists primarily of ritualized theatrical performances, what he calls a dramaturgical approach. By that he means that we act as if on stages in such ways as to impress upon others the merit, sincerity and value of our performances – so as to reap interpersonal or material benefit. To control the definitions of situations, people use various settings, props and fronts, collude with others (team-mates) and, at the same time, deny information disconfirming of a performance, e.g. backstage secrets (Goffman, 1959). One of the more important insights of Goffman was to consider the role of region to perform-ance, especially the contradictions between the public or frontstage and the private or backstage regions, a bifurcation that was to a large extent the product of modernity (cf. Brittain, 1977).[8] For Goffman, the various uses of space, props, body language and rituals of interaction served to facilitate everyday social life, to make working and friendly relations easier (Goffman, 1967). But the value of Goffman's work is to situate self-presentation within the context of the larger society, now focused around amusement and consumption.

The routines of everyday life

Everyday life in the lived world can now be seen as situated in the institutionally required and rewarded activities where selfhood is realized and subjectivity experienced in typical routines, discourses and performances. Husserl's concept of *Lebenswelt* came to social theory in various ways through Lukács (1971), Gramsci (1971) and Schutz (1967). Schutz in turn influenced Berger, Luck-mann, Garfinkel and more recently Bourdieu's (1977) notion of the *habitus* as well as Habermas (1984–7) who sees the life world colonized by rationality. These various perspectives suggest that selfhood is expressed in everyday practices and typifications that also allow expression of identity(ies) drawn from elements of the culture as well as the person's earlier identifications. Thus in a differentiated society with a plurality of 'life worlds', there are specific regions for self-presentation where certain salient aspects of an identity may be realized. But identities may conflict between morality and gratification, between boring work and leisure fun. Some identities may give the person more gratification and recog-nition than others. The person is more likely to present these identities and experience them as more salient and authentic. The compartmentalization of conflicting aspects of selfhood is often adaptive.[9] The segregation of regions thus allows for diverse expressions of one's self and gratifications of desire.

Everyday life must be historically situated to see how arbitrary routines, strategies and tactics become normal for coping and often even empowering (cf. de Certeau, 1984). Ritualized manners, forms of politeness, deference and assertion of authority that facilitated the new forms of social and commercial life, first emerged in the royal courts and were later adapted by the bourgeois elites. This is the beginning of office politics, having instrumental relationships with co-workers or with those to whom we provide goods or services, but with whom we have few other ties like kinship or fealty. We may often dislike them, especially if they have authority, power and control over our lives, jobs, profits or commissions. We must act cordially and this is the function of manners.[10] This is the meaning of rationalization: everyday social and commercial life becomes predictable and without emotional considerations.

The quotidian of amusement society, its typifications of acts and feelings, its mundane routines of waking, bodily care, eating, dressing, going to work, lunching, returning home, and watching television has often been ignored as trivial. The routines of everyday life, like the commodity, appear at first to be quite simple. But closer scrutiny of these routines shows them to be like Marx's (1978) descriptions of commodities, 'very queer, to have strange metaphysical powers'. Everyday life, or at least its images and representations, have become a new realm of aesthetics (Featherstone, 1991). Today, most of the objects used or worn in everyday life are commodities existing within an ever-changing. Manichean range between the simulated Good of the hyper-real and the Evil of the mundane. Within these limits, selfhood, which always exists in relation to Other, real or imaginary, oscillates between spheres of domination and empowerment, roughly corresponding to the worlds of routine work on the one hand, and the shopping mall on the other. Most everyday-life routines fall somewhere in the middle.

Every society attempts to encumber everyday life practices with enough satisfactions (or feared deprivations) so that various routines become enduring components of the *habitus*. One result of socialization is the routinization or normalization of the arbitrary to become typifications from which deviance can evoke various forms of anxiety. Little anticipated by Freud, but indeed initiated by his nephew Edward Bernays, public relations and advertising infiltrated everyday life. Failures of 'proper' consumption have dire consequences. Fortunately, the consumption of a myriad of products provide appropriately desirable, albeit manufactured, self-images and gratifying emotional experiences.

Most of the items of everyday life, perhaps beginning and ending with designer toilet seats, are infused with symbolic values of desire as a new aesthetic; they are advertised with considerable hype and sold in malls. Everyday life has been transformed into an extension of consumer capitalism and the person rendered a consumer or spectator in whom the commodified meanings, the symbolic and affective values embedded in the sign system, have been interiorized as representations of reality. The ideology of consumerism promises the good life, good feelings and good selfhood. Emotional satisfaction and self-worth are dependent on the orderliness of your bathroom. Failure to use products that end foul odours or bathtub ring, or turn the water to blue, green, mauve or taupe can lead to a social fate worse than death. Various items from cigarettes to cosmetics to canned food yield emotional satisfactions from eroticism to grandiosity, with a bit of recognition and envy of your subjectivity from others thrown in. While particular models or styles change quite often, this seeming 'change' maintains the stability of a semiurgical society as the new model, fashion or fad are eagerly awaited. Annual changes in models maintain the underlying structure.

Just as work requires the worker to engage in impression management (Kanter, 1977) and render gratifications to others (Hochschild, 1983), the worlds of consumption allow alternative identities and provide gratifications to the self. Like the carnivals and fairs of old, these worlds are outside the ordinary, indeed may reverse its values and often mock and parody it. Everyday life has thus become the realm where ordinariness has been transformed into an unending series of mass-mediated fragmented 'spectacles' and carnivals that celebrate the universalization of consumption (Lefebvre, 1971; Debord, 1970). The routines of everyday life depend on commodified mass-marketing of goods and images to provide emotional gratifications to all consumers. *This* is the context of self-experience and social interaction in amusement society.

The new public sphere

The growth of mass-mediated culture was closely intertwined with the growth of national markets and brand-name products. The new cultural forms like pulp novels, magazines and records, would be available in every store especially the department stores which would become both the actual and symbolic sites of the convergence of urbanism, mass-produced goods and growing leisure time. The mass-mediated discourses of advertising would soon colonize the life world, or at least fill it with commodities and desires (Ewen, 1976: 1982).

After perhaps little more than half a century, global capitalism, now intertwined with the mass dissemination of visual images, would begin another metamorphosis – the coming of amusement society.[11] This is not to suggest that everyone spends a lot of time in malls or even goes to them with great frequency. Rather, they stand as symbols of and monuments to an entire amusement order in which carnivals and spectacles of consumption gratify desires and sustain images of self. Similarly, the great cathedrals were not the site of most everyday life for the peasants, but at the same time, daily practices and beliefs sustained the power structures that built the churches whose towering size and decor were texts of unquestioned submission to hierarchy. But whereas the laity is powerless in face of the clergy, mallers can find 'microspheres of empowerment' in the malls, from the products they get there and the meanings and pleasures the person can choose (Fiske, 1989).

The first defining character of a mall is that it is an enclosed aggregation more or less *isolated* from the larger environment.[12] Secondly, within its boundaries, everything from temperature to merchant displays are rigorously *controlled* in ways that sustain an ersatz world of fantastic images and displays. These ever more 'creative' images and representations constitute an unending stream of spectacles (Debord, 1970). Like prisons and cities, there is a 'panoptic' of design to control, but in malldom the control is not so much through surveillance as the organization of spatial settings and the allocation of fantasy and pleasure (cf. Foucault, 1977; de Certeau, 1984). Malls are not just places to buy goods, but one of the main sites of the intentionally produced simulations that constitute a new dream-like order of commercial reality as the promise of wish fulfilment in this new 'hyper-reality' of spectacular images and fantastic gratifications.

Thirdly, malls as dream-like *fantasies* are places of unabashed contradictions of time, place and subjectivity that exist as much in imagination as in reality. Although there have been historical antecedents in the distribution of goods, malls cannot be thought of apart from the mass-mediated images of television that stimulate and soothe at the same time. They exist as indoor worlds with atriums of plants and trees from faraway climes, marble fountains with multicoloured light shows with lasers, holograms and strobes with backdrops of chrome waterfalls. The design and layout of malls attempt to create a utopia of consumption situated between a mythical past of the pre-automobile Main Street of Smalltown where one walked from store to store, and the future high-tech world of neon, holograms, lasers and space travel as malls come to resemble the space station of *2001*, the Starship Enterprise or high-tech future cities. They create nostalgic memories of neighbourhood and lost community, or at least Christmas-card images of a past abundant with goods and social cohesion (Chaney, 1990). The appeal to an imagined communal past is especially clear when old churches, warehouses or factories are converted to malls and there are attempts to retain 'traditional' architectural features (wood beams, exposed brick) and sometimes even original names like Cannery Row, Faneuil Hall, Ghiradelli Square, Dearborn Station or South Street Seaport, etc.[13] Their restaurants are often designed to replicate the cabins of wood sailing-ships, colonial taverns (spelled with an 'e' and a 'ye olde' in the name), railroad dining-cars of the 1930s, nineteenth-century Italian villas or ancient pagodas. They simulate communities of memory as a means of encouraging privatization.

The unusual impositions and juxtapositions of unending spectacles already presuppose the habits of televiewing in which rapid changes of spectacular disconnected images are the norm. The adjacent positioning of contradiction need not be resolved. Thus a weight-loss centre may be found between an ice-cream shop and a large-size apparel store, a diamond merchant is next to a salami shop while across the hall may be a bank and video arcade and tax or legal service. This is little different from the media coverage of a war or disaster sandwiched between haemorrhoid relief and the new improved car (the latter causing the pain in the ass).

SHOPPING-MALL SELFHOOD[14]

Desire malled

The nineteenth-century emergence and shaping of subjectivity in a socially constructed childhood located within a warm but sexually repressed private sphere would create the social conditions and personal needs for Freudian psychoanalysis. This new science explained the development of the psyche and means by which hidden desires could be known. While his theories must be contextualized, and indeed many ideas such as the drive theory discarded, Freud's work is essential for understanding modern subjectivity, especially the means by which society appropriates desire, instils repression for social ends and becomes interiorized as values and lifestyles. But it also locates an inner life and private subjectivity that can become a realm of opposition.

Although a sociology of knowledge of psychoanalytic theory remains wanting, many have noted the relation of the theories, and subsequent elaborations, to specific times and places. Psychoanalysis as a psychology of affects, feelings and intentions, rather than drives and mechanisms may have been Freud's intent but he needed to articulate his text in the seemingly more 'scientific' discourse of forces and energy. His theory of erotic and aggressive drives may have been more suitable for the *fin-de-siècle* patriarchal bourgeois elite than the masses of suburban mall-rats and -bunnies of today.

To understand amusement society, desire can be considered as a socially constructed label imposed upon experiences of deficiency or lack. Through socialization and learning the affective *habitus* of the society, socialized desire fosters various actions, relationships, states of mind or feelings. A need for food is biological, to want fast food or French food is a desire and to consume same not only satisfies biological needs for food, but more important, confirms consumption-based selfhood. To say 'socialized' means that desire has been appropriated by society and instilled in early childhood as the representation of need. Just as every society has its norms and therefore types of deviance, it prescribes desires, evocations and controls how they may be satisfied and how they may become potential sources for opposition.

Psychoanalysis revealed the profound role of society in shaping and co-opting emotions and feelings to motivate and regulate behaviour and overt self-reflections. It is best seen as an *affective* psychology in which thoughts and behaviour, or more specifically their meanings, have ramifications for certain emotional gratifications – or deprivations, types of relationships and self-understandings. Its profundity is the revelation of feelings that impel behaviour and self-images. Feelings may not be overtly acknowledged, indeed denied, but they may nevertheless legitimate social relations, initiate behaviour and even cause psychic pain. While Freud was concerned with particular individuals and their unique biographies, the present essay is more concerned with the structures and contexts of socialization in amusement society and its constructions of desire.

Most of Freud's clinical work dealt primarily with unacknowledged or unrecognized emotions such as depression. His metapsychology of drives and forces leaves much wanting. There is an exception in his revised theory of anxiety as a signal or warning of a threat of which the person was not consciously aware (Freud, 1926). For Becker (1973) Freud's own character kept him from drawing out the implications of his revised theory. Anxiety was a warning of the ultimate human fear, death, and this *fear of death* is a basic affect that motivates a wide range of behaviour. There was a clear hierarchy of fears, loss of love of the object, loss of the object, threats to self-esteem, and threats of annihilation (in an amusement society we will note the importance of such anxiety-based threats to self, self-esteem or loss of love as motives for consumption). In so far as anxiety could *motivate* behaviour and/ or defences, the earlier theories of sexual and aggressive 'drives' as energic motivation became questionable. Further, while he noted the guilt-based sexually repressive features of society in general, he said little about the social aspects of anxiety that were especially characteristic of the bourgeois class (see Gay, 1984; Langman and Richman, 1987, and see below).

An alternative theory of anxiety and desire as socially transformed affects is possible. To summarize a very complex argument, humans, having evolved from lower mammals, are born with an inherent affect system that evolved to motivate behaviour and communicate with conspecifics. The fundamental emotional axis is the autonomic nervous system, sympathetic arousal being associated with fear and anger to motivate fight or flight, and parasympathetic arousal associated with sex and joy, stimulations of the pleasure centre, the limbic system. With inherent capacities for early bonding to caretakers, human societies could appropriate the primary affect system for purposes of socialization, social control and to motivate behaviour by amplifying or suppressing drives which are really quite weak for humans (Tompkins, 1984). While the mammalian affect system was established millennia ago, particular social arrangements are affectively secured and thus have a distinctive emotional hue: feelings are social (McCarthy, 1989).

The basic affective responses of anger, fear, grief, interest, surprise, joy, disgust, et cetera become subject to *social* and *cognitive* cues of elicitation. Social patterns of labelling, interpretation, modes of expression and gratification allow a wide range of emotional experiences. The ability of society to label, manipulate and appropriate emotion allows us to see their role as micro-regulators of social life. This is not so much through the intense experiences of joy or rage, as the everyday joys and frustrations that are sought or avoided. As a minimum, regular routines allay the anxiety of uncertainty (cf Giddens, 1984). Finally, emotions may then be experienced as conscious feelings and integral aspects of subjectivity. In so far as they become conscious, either as experienced or as states to be experienced, e.g. to plan for a thrill like a roller-coaster or go to a tear-jerker or go to the mall, emotions become subject to social elicitation, construction and negotiation. What is unique about humanity is the amount of time and effort a person will devote for a moment of joy, thrill or pride. Reading psychoanalysis as a theory of the historical contextualization of emotions that informs the emergence of selfhood makes it useful for understanding subjectivity in amusement society.

Preliminary understandings of the role of emotions can be found in sociological theories of self and self-presentation by Simmel (1950) and Goffman (1959), and understandings of consumption by Debord, Lefebvre or Baudrillard. Every society offers emotional gratifications or alleviations in the enactment of its required roles and everyday routines to sustain the affective underpinnings of the *habitus* as the site of social reproduction (see Langman, 1990).[15] Simply put, there is a degree of anxiety-based conformity in most societies. In cases where society may foster intense feelings that might be socially disruptive, it often provides various substitutes or 'detours', sublimations or defences for such expressions. Social strains or norms that evoke sadness, fear or anger, for example, are often associated with targets or rituals to alleviate adverse feelings or their consequences. This is what Durkheim (1965) called 'piacular rites' in mourning ceremonies. Witches, for example, were often targets of wrath and scapegoats to sustain other frustrations. But in amusement society, repressions and sublimations are appropriated so that socialized desires might initiate various gratifications in the performance of interaction rituals and patterns of consumption.

In all societies, there is a degree of anxiety about the security of early attachments; fears of abandonment and in turn annihilation are universal. Freud conflated attachments and libidinal gratifications. Some evidence suggests an inherent tendency for mammals to bond to caretakers. The theories of self psychology suggest that the recognition of emergent selfhood is as important as the provision of love and gratification of biological needs. Deprivations of empathy at this time so distort self-formation as to establish the core of narcissistic character disorders in which reparative efforts to merge with powerful others or attain grandiosity are ultimately self-destructive. When attachments to nurturing caretakers are gratifying, we have the foundations for positive identification with parents and a healthy sense of self. But failures of attachments, or attachments to depriving or frustrating caretakers fosters a 'false self' as a defence against further psychic pain. But that false self is often fragile and subject to a great deal of anxiety. Compensatory attempts for adult love and self-esteem to assuage the more basic insecurities often lead to a further range of pains and deprivations for the person and impairments in his or her relationships. Compensatory attempts at reparation in the seeking of wealth or power or other means of seeking love, approval and selfhood may inflict pain and suffering on others.

While Lasch's (1979) premise that narcissism is the basis of modern cultural practice is perhaps reductionistic, he nevertheless grasps a central truth of amusement society. The nature of school, work or other large-scale bureaucracies require many routine tasks that provide individuals with little recognition and acknowledgement of their unique selfhood and what they are like as persons. Those few who are noticed, not necessarily the most able, gain the promotions (cf. Kanter, 1977). Narcissistic pathology is then the extreme expression of normalcy in an amusement society where recognition from others has become problematic and often frustrated. But this emerges from the structure of the bourgeois family. Early parental regard provides emotional satisfaction and a stable core of selfhood. Brief consideration of an affective-based psychoanalysis of selfhood suggests that all societies depend on socialized feelings to motivate everyday life, maintain social control and reproduce themselves. But only in modern amusement society can gratification of desire and recognition of selfhood be found in the patterns of consumption and subjectivity realized in malldom.

What these perspectives on early selfhood and affectivity further suggest is that there are gender-based differences in early life and in turn gendered modes of attaining recognition and self-esteem (cf. Chodorow, 1978). Archaic aspects of gendered selfhood inform later identity and consumption. The early deprivations of privatized life become the raw materials for advertisers to exploit and promise good feelings (love or greatness) and desirable self-images through consumption.

Capitalism is not only unfair in the allocation of privileges that include consumption, but in emotional gratifications as well. How then does it succeed in seeing that most of its work, especially the routine tasks that *must* be done, get done? There even seems to be willing consent by subordinate strata to reproduce the society. The answer is simple. There are gratifications of solidarity and recognition in work settings so the satisfactions from tasks is secondary, but the income is necessary for amusement in other sectors.[16] In the extreme cases of the most menial of jobs, work provides money. But more important, save for the lower strata, those outside the mall carnivals of consumption, there are various gratifications to be found in strategies of empowerment by appropriating cultural practices (de Certeau, 1984). Feelings are now mass produced and distributed in the shops, theatres and food centres of shopping malls where much of the gratification is *without* cost. The uses of interpretations of cultural objects, or even creations of some practices ranging from children's games to adolescents' mall-roaming provide good feelings. The malls then are places to purchase the goods of gratification and/or to be something, to realize fantasies located outside of the usual constraints of time and place. Malling thus exists as a dialectic between doing something and being someone, a fantastic someone whose selfhood brings recognition and gratification.

This is the secret of modern hegemony: the dominant classes, via media, control norms of affective gratification and control in everyday life. The 'general good' that sustains class privilege in Gramsci's (1971) sense rests on the consumption of goods, fantasies and gratifying forms of self-presentation.[17] This is the key to understanding Goffman and presentations of self: the expressive aspects of role performances are intertwined with consumption to provide affective gratifications, and/or are themselves instrumental in securing them.

Subjectivity – from identification to consumption

The emotional constellations and attachments of privatized family life facilitate identification with the particular role models and general routines of everyday life in amusement society. The internalizations of early infancy become elements that are later melded with age-specific roles and cultural practices or elements that are recognized by others. These become one's identity. Identity consists of reflexive awareness of who one is, personal standards of evaluating situations and actions, a continually revised biography, goals for the future and plans to attain them. One's identity depends on the specifics of genetics, parental socialization values and practices. But it is also provisional and dependent on contexts of class, subculture and general environment of the particular group memberships where selfhood is recognized and confirmed.

In the writings of Freud, echoed by the Frankfurt School as well as Parsons, identification with parents took place later in life than the more archaic stages of emergent selfhood described above. These early attachments and internalizations are now seen as the initial stages of the cultural shaping of subjectivity. In the classical writings, identification, as a defence against abandonment or aggression, was as much with the parental personality as with their role expectations, the warm love of mother or instrumental (rational) achievement of the father. But these writings were reflections of an earlier time of patriarchal families headed by powerful, if remote, fathers. The decline of patriarchy in the face of rationalization, increased education and female employment in the society of consumption, changed parental roles from models of worker and production to leisure and consumption. There have also been changes in socialization practices with less stress on classical obedience and gender bifurcation.

The classical models of identity based on internalization of parental role models ignore three important factors besides the earlier pre-Oedipal developments described. First, to a large extent television heroes have become models for imitation.[18] In amusement society, most of the heroes and heroines of today are more likely to be stars of manufactured fame who are more likely to live affluent, exciting lives rather than doing good or brave deeds without reward. Second, adolescent peer-group experiences are *crucial* in the consolidation of an identity, and this age is especially targeted by advertising and subject to the forces of marketing that provide consumption-based identities. Third, the unity of a core self, if not problematic, may encounter a great deal of stress in amusement society where pluralities of contradictory self-presentations become typical.

Mead began to write about the role of the general Other at about the same time as the commercial was becoming an important means of socializing consumption. With the intrusion of television into the socialization process, the relation of self to Other has taken on a new quality, what I would call the *Other of the Imaginary*. In the age of television, we learn to see Others as if our eye were a camera. Role-taking and -making are less based on words than images. Taking the role of the Other is now to imagine that we are being seen via camera by the larger audience of home viewers. The audiences, persons or groups to which self-presentations are now directed may not exist in reality, but in hyper-reality. This anonymous audience of viewers constitutes the Other of the Imaginary. In the classical formulations of reference group behaviour, anticipatory socialization was seen in comparison to and/or preparation for inclusion into an *actual* group. But now, consumption-based selfhood sees itself as the key figure of a TV program, movie or commercial. Thus the use of a product, driving a _____ car, drinking a _____ beer or wearing _____ clothes brings recognition not only by those in clear view, but by millions of viewers out there in television land. Being seen brings gratification through recognition of self. In amusement society we act not so much by taking the role of the Other but as if the camera is on us and Other is watching.

Television socializes the positive emotional reactions gained from being recognized by Other, by transforming the *passivity* of viewing into the *activity* of looking at the Other. The socialization of Hegel's dialectical quest for recognition, now understood as voyeurism-exhibitionism, while historically emergent with capitalism, establishes the psychological foundations for a consumption-based identity sustained by recognition from Others. The very existence of self cannot be thought of apart from recognition by the Other. For Hegel the master-slave struggle for recognition under conditions of domination was essential for the very existence of self as recognized and confirmed. This has been clear to most theories of socialization (see Benjamin, 1988). Conversely, to look at Others, even if only representations that appear as screen images, is to have power over them and in turn emotional satisfaction. This was why Hegel's slave had power over the master. For Sartre (1956) the gaze of the stranger was his power over one's subjectivity. For Foucault (1973) the doctor's gaze gave him the power of life and death.

What is unique about television is the extent to which the relationships and imagined interactions with characters and images leads to identifications with them. Consumption then becomes a means of identification with fantastic role models and the means of finding relationships of love, friendship, or adventure et cetera, with these simulated personas of mass media.[19] Television not only socializes consumption, but predisposes later mall-based seeing and being seen as central for modern subjectivity.

The public expressions and presentations of socialized selfhood, the persona, are supposed to be the surface manifestations of an underlying unified core of the person. But with the influence of so many models in diverse realities, and the unending bombardment of media images, it seems more likely that identity is expressed in a variety of provisional identities or self-images that may serve as templates or strategies for self-presentations in *specific* situations. While the person has a more or less stable temperament, memories of selfhood across various times and activities, and has learned and internalized the socially constructed *habitus* of their society which includes a notion of selfhood, the trans-situational stability of identity may be more imputed than real.

Subjectivity, as identity experienced and seeking confirmation and recognition by Others, is expressed in various discursive practices that utilize cultural elements as badges of identity and group membership. People use cultural objects and meanings to fashion their subjectivity. This begins in infancy when cultural practices shape the structures and contexts of early experience. In amusement society, the visual fantasies of marketing impinge on childhood to socialize and appropriate desire, condition emotional satisfactions and establish identities through consumption. Somewhere between walking and talking, toddlers learn to operate the television, the gifted ones the VCR. Socialization to consumerism thus begins early. It is seen every day when little children shout 'buy me' when passing the 'tele-familiar' sugar-laden boxes called cereals, or candy counters. By the end of childhood – and constant exposure to the backstages of life may even erode childhood – the ideologies and cultural practices of consumption become interiorized modes of subjectivity. By the age of five, many, perhaps most, children can name malls, identify brand names and recognize their place in the status hierarchy. Possessions of certain brands of clothes can be the basis for peer-group inclusion or exclusion. When children reach the ages in which they can spend their own money, they constitute a major market for various brand names of clothes, popular culture stars and leisure products or services. They control about 10 per cent of the GNP in the western core nations.

Coming of age in shopping malls[20]

In societies with a disjunction between childhood and adulthood, adolescence emerged as a stage in the life cycle that coincided with generationally based subcultures, typically located in the high schools and neighbourhood corners. In amusement society, especially the suburban enclaves, many adolescent subcultures are found in malldom – free of scrutiny by parents or teachers. Many youths spend almost as much time in malls as in school or at home. As the mall has become one of the major hangouts where many youths try to locate their communities of peers, it is also the space where the production of mass-mediated heroes and goods can be utilized in the establishment of provisional identities that may often conflict with each other or those required in work, school or family life outside of malldom. The malls have become a primary hangout and site of such truly significant life events as first use of a charge card, driving a car (to the mall) and losing one's virginity in the parking lot.

Androgynous teenaged mall-jammers, doing more looking than shopping, go to the malls to kill time, an apt notion in a society that destroys history and replaces it with a high-tech dystopia. Malling confirms consumption-based lifestyles and identity; teenaged mall-rats and bunnies may be the prototypical group of amusement society.[21] This is all the more the case as television, having hurried if not destroyed childhood, has created the grown-up child and immature adult as the whole of a life course sandwiched between infancy and senility.[22] Many of the characteristics of 'children', egocentrism, simplistic reasoning, belief in the 'reality' of television images, and the inability to defer hedonistic gratification, seem to be ever more typical in amusement society. Indeed, modern hegemony depends on the hedonistic and magical logic of children. This plays no small part in the elections of comic-book presidents.

Three major tasks of adolescence are establishing autonomy from parents, testing and consolidating one's identity(ies) and learning to cope with newly emergent sexuality. Today, automobilized mallers form distinct subcultures of consumption located in mallworlds free from the surveillance of parents or teachers. Malls become stages in which the identities gleaned in earlier socialization by parents or media are expressed and recognized. Those identities that get approval become more salient and recur. Often, going to a mall on a weekend night involves elaborate preparations for transportation and, for young women, extensive rituals for make-up and costume selection to insure the proper image and impression management for group inclusion and initiating relationships that might become sexual. Males practice walks, looks and hair styles of various ranks of cool in hopes of 'scoring' – one of the primary means by which adolescent males gain self-esteem. And with the erosion of age grading – some men never grow up – teenaged malling can be considered anticipatory socialization for later life and singles-bar rituals, especially for the college-bound (cf. Deegan, 1988).

These are the ages when people are most open to changes in the styles and fashions of clothes, popular culture and advanced consumer goods.[23] This is especially the case for those trend-setting mall-jammers the marketing research people call 'alphas'. Thus many malls, especially those with theatres, video games and food courts, have become centres of social life and pseudo-community. Each region or type of store is staked out as a particular turf for the members of communities of consumption. The various subcultures of adolescence confirm not only those self-presentations constitutive of an emergent identity, but integrate the person into particular groups that affect subsequent life trajectories. Adolescent groups with common cultural capital become the socialization agents for, and models of, what Bellah (1985) has termed lifestyle enclaves that reflect current life chances and subcultures of particular consumer tastes which offer identity packages that typically endure through subsequent life careers. But these are really more

59

'proto-communities' of shared patterns of cultural consumption and communication through shared tastes and fashion than the more traditional forms of community and face-to-face verbal communication (Willis, 1990). By the time most young people have finished high school or college, their lifestyles and self-images expressed in consumption-based self-presentations have been crystallized. (For those who do achieve upward mobility, there are a number of image consultants to resocialize the gauche consumer tastes of previous class membership and mall patronage, e.g. replacing Elvis posters with Warhol lithographs or Miro originals.)

The various subcultures of jocks, brains, nerds, popular kids, gangbangers (rappers), greenies, preppies and/or prissies, are clearly differentiated by the styles, fashions and tastes of particular stores, brands or regions of malldom in which membership is indicated in self-displays of identity such as the athletic shoes and outfits of the working strata, the 'outdoor' or 'natural' look of preppies, the black leather and chrome chains of punks or the jeans and Greenpeace T-shirts of the socially conscious whale-loving greenies. It seem as if most mallers wear some kind of statement to express a consumer-based identity of brand name, radio station, exotic place or to simply outrage, 'gross out', the viewer. In some groups, the wrong designer label or athletic shoe, or even disdain of fashion, can turn one into an outcast ranging from the computer geeks hanging around computer or software stores to the bookstore dweebs. There are a few who reject commodity-based selfhood but can't stop looking at the Others.

Malls allow not only incorporation into the worlds of consumption-based lifestyles and identities but as spatial sites of modern hegemony, shopping centres allow a degree of contestation, reinterpretation and often mobilization, if not in fact, in fantasy. For many youth, the school has become the world of submission to boring routine, the mall offers empowerment through hyper-real gratification – for example having the attitudes toward school that characterize Bart Simpson or Pink Floyd.[24] This is especially the case given the relative stagnation if not decline of the capitalist countries where only a few young can look forward to rising standards of living. A number of cultural studies, from Hoggart (1967) to Willis (1990), have shown how disempowered youth uses and transforms received cultural practices in ways to find empowerment and meaning.

Those groups that are destined to remain peripheral to the

spheres of real power and affluence are most likely to embrace the empowerments allocated by popular culture and the commodities of malldom. This is the meaning of counter-cultural practices from punk to rap, or the 'wanna be' attempts to mimic Madonna, Bono or George Michael. Such teenagers are simply honest expressions of appropriating subjectivity through sympathetic magical rituals. Like the primitive who dances like a wolf to gain bravery, the maller imitates the fashions, gestures and speech patterns of stars to gain an identity and glean recognition from Others. Identification with the simulacra of mass media offers 'microspheres of empowerment' and/or gratifications of recognition and dignity that compensate teenagers for exclusion from the ever more distant worlds of bourgeois affluence.

The simulacrum of self in everyday life

In 1844 Marx saw how work affected the subjectivity of the worker. When he described the glorious markets of London, he could not imagine an entire world as a bazaar, or that in that world, goods would become integral aspects of self-expression.[25] We have seen how commodification has colonized childhood. In a most prescient analysis, Fromm (1947) saw the phallic aggressive personality as a 'marketing' character who sold himself as a commodity, to sell others his products. Arthur Miller's character Willie Loman would become the archetypical expression of the salesman whose worth is the latest commission and his person easily expendable. C. W. Mills (1951) would discover that the sales clerk would find subjectivity by identifying with her customers. In this tradition, Hochschild's 1983 study of flight attendants can be seen as the culmination of the process by which capital first appropriated the body of the labourer and now co-opts the emotions of the worker. The distinctive feature of amusement society is its appropriation of the body and transformation of feelings and images into commodified signs of self. Fashion as a sign of self is no longer just clothes but body shape, style and colour or hue – all of which can be purchased in stores, beauty parlours, spas and hospitals or at least cosmetic-surgery mills.

Commodified self-presentations and interaction rituals of work or leisure in an amusement society are now intertwined with many of the other commodities and fantastic images of amusement society. They can be seen as simulacra, intentional productions constitutive of the new semiurgical order. Thus Simmel and Goffman can be seen as laying the groundwork for a postmodern social psychology that deconstructs the expressions of self and inter-action. When these are seen from an affective perspective, we can join a critical depth psychology with a critical dramaturgy to understand subjectivity in everyday life practice (cf. Deegan, 1988). One of the most important linkages of recent depth psy-chology to social interaction was to suggest that affective recog-nition is a basic human motive; to be noticed, as well as loved, provides pleasurable emotional experiences. And even if not loved, to at least be noticed has become a powerful motive sustaining the self and encouraging consumption. As late capitalism has become an amusement society, personal conduct has itself become a spectacle, a performance to bring attention to the person for the sake of attention or means to another goal.[26] These are the pseudo-events or simulacra at the personal level: selfhood as spectacle to gain the 15 minutes of fame that guarantees immortality.

Commodified selfhood is a simulacrum of a personality structure that no longer depends on defences and repressions of desires that are now appropriated and controlled by amusement society. Rather, it is an expression of a shell who does 'emotion work' or expresses the now appropriated desires without an interior to hide. Such exteriorized expressions of selfhood involve consumption of commodities to produce interpersonal rituals as commodities. The various props of appropriated selfhood such as clothes, car, home, leisure and cultural tastes are ever more synonymous with the self. One of the best critiques of such appropriated identity, not often realized, was the movie *Invasion of the Body Snatchers* in which the alien beings appropriated human bodies who still maintained their usual lifestyles including suburban mentalities and shopping malls (cf. Kroker *et al.*, 1986; Kroker and Cook, 1989). Think of the aliens as consumers shaped by advertisers and marketers.

The production of recognition-seeking spectacles of self is expressed in the language and forms of commodities and signifi-cation rituals that elicit recognition to provide affective gratifi-cations as parasympathetic arousals that go directly to the limbic system (pleasure centres). In an amusement society of unending, disconnected simulacra, the presentations of self and interaction rituals, regulated by commercial codes and affective cues as surface manifestations of socialized desire, intersect in the routines of everyday life. Commodified desires and images are the strings regulating a puppet show of self. Selfhood, having shifted from institutional roles to consumption-based lifestyle displays of selfhood, is presented in those simulated forms that are typical of amusement society. The objects of daily life provide gratifications, meanings and statements about the user's social status and identity, if they are not one's very identity. In the United States, the language of commercials becomes everyday parlance; within days of broadcast, the commercial jingles are hummed everywhere. Indeed many of the products and experiences of a consumption society are primarily laden with affective symbolic value. In a society of the simulacra, the presentations of self, and qualities of its relationships, have themselves become commodified spectacles seeking recognition.

The expressive features of interaction can be seen as productions of commodified spectacles at the interpersonal level.[27] As a commodity, social interaction is appropriated by the market. In an amusement society, self-presentations stand as dramaturgical simulacra of social life, hyper-real expressions of selfhood in fragmented social life. Self-presentations are increasingly intertwined with popular imagery, at times becoming parodies of media images and celebrities. Life, or at least subjectivity, imitates mass-produced art. But since most people work in organizations, expressions of more intrinsically gratifying selfhood are most likely seen in the private worlds of amusement. The myriad forms of personal self-display and media fantasy are ever less clearly differentiated. The centre of front stage has moved to the malls that now provide training, provisional selfhood, props and audiences for self-presentation.

Empowerment

For Marx, factory-based capitalism was a system of domination. In so far as mall-based hegemony provides, if not requires, a plethora of gratification spectacles, from video and computer images to the self-presentations of everyday life, there are a number of ways that people experience freedom, power and control that mask a deeper powerlessness. As Baudrillard observed, to flip a light switch is a God-like act: let there be light. But this act is at the end of a complex technological chain of dependency on fuel, generators, transformers, distribution lines and the manufacture of light bulbs. In this way the *habitus* of amusement society provides experiences of domination and control over technologies which most individuals little understand or control but which seemingly empower the users. At the same time many of the mundane routines of high-school learning and much of the work of the lower strata – routine production, technical or personal service jobs – are more and more de-skilled and disempowering. Thus the popular culture and worlds of malldom offer realms of defiance and refusal, contestation and negotiation, that sustain the fundamental arrangements. We have seen that, for young adolescents, malldom becomes a site of communities of resistance and dignity outside of school or work. Thus we can suggest that the consumption of goods and experiences that inform self-presentations provide experiences of power and dignity outside the realms of work.

Many of the managerial cadres of global corporations, despite being a privileged class, ask questions about the incessant demands of work, problematic job security and the power politics of the corporation in which temporary friendships exist primarily for instrumental ends such as commissions, bonuses and promotions. Many managers complain of high stress and little gratification. As Brian Palmer, one of the subjects in Bellah's study (1985) found out when his first marriage failed, being 'up there' isn't all it's cracked up to be. But such managers have the compensations of income, status and a sense of dignity. Among blue-collar workers, an extensive knowledge of professional athletics, players and owners, records and strategies, provides realms of competence which provide both a sense of empowerment and dignity (Aronowitz, 1973). In the same ways, their wives read the weekly tabloids and find that the famous may have wealth, but still have problems of drugs, alcohol, infidelity and other family problems. Further, having the inside scoop on alien sex fiends and the location of Elvis's spirit gives social advantage and a realm apart from the real problems of dealing with limited means (cf. Rubin, 1976). But while there are a number of cultural practices that give dignity and recognition, none do it with as much fun and panache as the ever more fantastic malls.

> Shopping malls are the real postmodern sites of happy consciousness. Not in the old Hegelian sense of a reconciled dialectic of reason, but happy consciousness, now in the sense of the virtual self. A whole seductive moment, therefore, between a willed abandonment of life and a restless search

for satisfaction in the seduction of holograms. Or, is it that the self now is a virtual object to such a degree of intensity and accumulation that the fascination of the shopping mall is in the way of homecoming to a self that has been lost, but now happily discovered. The postmodern self as one more object in the simulacra of objects. Shopping malls, therefore sites of possessive individualism *par excellance . . .* Shopping can be the primary leisure time activity of post-modern culture because it is *nouvelle* play, this time in the voyeuristic form of the hyper-real, the look which fantasizes, appropriates, and discards, and all this at a seasoned glance.

(Kroker and Cook, 1989: 208–9)

In sum, most subcultures of age, gender or class of amusement society find a number of pathways leading to emotional satisfactions. These pathways converge in the mall.

The enfeebled self

For Freud, the ego was the weak slave of three masters. For Goffman (1959), self is annihilated and all that is left is an ephemeral situational reality that emerges in interactional rituals. It is like the smile of the Cheshire cat. It exists only when observed in performance or when observing the Other. In the Hegelian struggle for recognition, now the plight of everyman, everyman is losing the struggle. Amusement society has become less stable and predictable. Its norms are more problematic and subject to revisions as frequent as Paris fashion shows or new car debuts. The modern danger to the self is its weakness in face of an ever more fragmented social order (cf. Horkheimer and Adorno, 1972; Wexler, 1987). At the same time, with the demise of stable anchorings, a continuous sense of self has waned. If Nietzsche announced the death of God, Goffman's work announces the death of the soul, or at least the terms of its sale. But the corpse of decentred selfhood doesn't know it's dead and stays on stage seeking confirmation from its audience. And failing that, it seeks some other kind of commodified experience, perhaps in the presentations of commodified simulations of selfhood to confirm to itself its own existence as reflected in the gaze of the Other. That Other may be present and within view or what was called the 'Other of the imaginary', the anonymous viewers that inhabit malldom or all those folks out there in the television audience.

There are several reasons for the enfeeblement of selfhood. The various critiques of lost community, bureaucracy, rationality and interdependency in amusement society have been commented on by almost every sociologist from Weber to Habermas. But, in terms of what has been said, several points can be made. First, the loci of selfhood have become more numerous and fragmented, given the nature of modernity as differentiation, and amusement society as ever faster social change. Second, there has been a gradual withdrawal of the subjective life and selfhood from the public to private realms, what Sennet (1977) called the fall of public man. The commodification of everything that began with capital's appropriation of wage labour, has now culminated in appropriated selfhood and feelings.

Identity is especially problematic in a society in which the kinship and community ties no longer bind the self into stable social networks. Instead, identity depends on sporadic recognition in work or, increasingly, in mall-based expressions of consumption. There are increasing disjunctions between such situationally specific expressions of selfhood. Some go so far as to question the very possibility of selfhood as transitional, self-reflexive image and practice. The postmodern consumer culture has witnessed a pluralization of life worlds and ever greater multiplicities of feelings, gratifications and self-images provided by mass-mediated imagery. These trends have paved the way for subjectivity as an intermittent series of fragmented performance spectacles. Zurcher (1977) put forward the notion of a mutable self, easily adapted to whatever the situation. Gergen (1986) goes so far as to argue that there is no stable core of selfhood but rather a situational self that emerges in response to various social cues. Given the plurality of life, worlds with multiple and often contradictory and hyper-real practices of everyday life, selfhood has become more enfeebled and thus seeks more and more mall-based empowerment and recognition.[28]

In amusement society, greater mobility and transitory memberships in institutions and the fragmentation inherent in a plurality of social worlds colonized by impersonal forces, has encouraged the marketing of a popular psychology with a 'jargon of authenticity' or therapeutic ethic that extols self-realization as a *personal*

problematic. As the public sphere has become increasingly fragmented and less gratifying, individuals have become more likely
to withdraw into their own private realms to seek self-confirmation,
gratification and even express counter-hegemonic practices and
contestations. Goffman (1961b) coined the term role distance to
describe the separation of self from its performances. Curiously,
he based this idea on observations at an amusement park. Turner
(1976) has demonstrated a secular trend that people are less and
less likely to locate selfhood in formal organization and networks
that are more or less stable. They are now more likely to find
their feelings, impulses, personal qualities, subjective experiences
and leisure pursuits as the locus of a selfhood that is more variable
and provisional. Privatized consumption has thus become the contemporary locus for a hedonistic subjectivity that has withdrawn
from the public realms.[29] But this withdrawal lets the social order
become more powerful with an ever more enfeebled privatized self
less likely to contest major issues – as the recent Persian Gulf war
showed. When the going gets tough, the tough go shopping – and
at malls. It is of course no accident that after the Nintendo war,
malls all over the country had celebrations of consumption for the
'heroes' of Desert Storm.

THE COSTS TO THE SELF

At the beginning of the twentieth century, a new form of dealing
with bourgeois malady had emerged: psychotherapy (Langman
and Richman, 1987). But the same forces of rational capitalism
that gave personal angst its distinctive hue would undergo subsequent metamorphosis and appear as amusement society in which
bourgeois consumption would be universalized. Yet this mall-based
allocation of goods and dreams, gratifications and identities, provides no more than intermittent palliatives for underlying anxiety
and appropriation of, if annihilation of, subjectivity.

If the subject is not dead, s/he is more likely decentred, fragmented, and differentially expressed and experienced depending
on context. On slow nights, the local news often does a feature on
the socialite hooker, banker rock singer or jock who crochets.
These incongruities of selfhood legitimate the reality that we are
all more likely to have clusters of often contradictory identities and
biographies available for specific situations rather than an enduring sense of self. But this also suggests a good deal of strain in a

world without stable social anchorings where the self needs constant affirmation. Modern subjectivity, needing and seeking recognition, confirmation and emotional gratification in everyday routines located between the boring mundane and the fantastic hyper-real, experiences a dialectic of enfeeblement and empowerment as it weaves among plural and often contradictory life worlds that converge in malldom.

The mall-rat or -bunny, prototypical forms of ageless postmodern every person, needs and seeks confirmations of selfhood and feelings of a subjectivity that has now been appropriated and turned into carnivalesque displays. The fragmentation of every day life where the commodified fantasies of hyper-reality exist alongside mundane ordinariness induces huge strains and costs for the compartmentalization, decentring and enfeeblement of diverse expressions of selfhood. While modernity differentiated life worlds, the regions of aesthetic, cultural and touristic consumption reproduce the very fragmentation and isolation they would alleviate. What must we pay for the perpetuation of amusement society? Panic, envy, loneliness, inauthenticity and imprisonment.[30] Cheap!

The shopping-mall self seeks substantiation if not salvation in consumption to buy more gratifying subjectivity but finds instead a lonely, voyeuristic, 'micro-circuitry of desire, ideology and expenditure for processed bodies drifting through the cyber-space of ultra-capitalism . . . where what is truly fascinating is expenditure, loss and exhaustion' (Kroker *et al.*, 1989: 208). Like a B-grade sci-fi, the mall emanates signals called commercial fantasies. 'Normal' beings, as if suddenly in a trance, head to the mall, consume and depart – but only to return again in mutated forms. And this is the very theme of George Romero's *Dawn of the Dead*: the graves give up their dead, zombies are born again to go to the mall to shop. This was the most important place in their earthly lives and what heaven is like in the next.

Panic and envy are the feelings from the dark side of the force of amusement society. If classical capitalism engendered anxiety over salvation and guilt-ridden sexuality, amusement society fosters panic and provides commodified means for its alleviation in ever more consumption. The commodified simulacra of self or commodified gratifications can only momentarily mask underlying terrors of emptiness and loneliness that culminate in *panic*, the intense form of anxiety that seems without end.

Weber located the anxiety described by Kierkegaard and Freud in uncertainty over salvation that in turn motivated work. Success gave one esteem in the eyes of one's peers, and was maybe a sign of God's blessing. But in amusement society, one's status is more often based on lifestyles of consumption. Esteem-based security is more transient and ephemeral. The rise of individuated selfhood and the attenuation of cohesive groupings that were first associated with the rise of a market economy reached culmination in the presentations of shopping-mall selfhood as simulations within 'proto-communities' of taste and style without real interaction or enduring social relationships. Ever more fragmented selfhood needs ever more confirmation of its existence by Others. Failures of confirmation recapitulate the anxiety and vulnerability of early infancy in which parental recognition was so vital for the establishment of a cohesive self that became differentiated from caretakers. The enduring anxieties of this early fragility are assuaged by the offerings of amusement society with unending visual spectacles and abundant goods that converge in fantastic malls. As styles of cultural productions, goods, selves or relationships change and become obsolete, the self becomes obsolete and there are new anxieties to renew the vicious cycle.

At the same time that status-based selfhood is more prone to anxiety, intimate relationships, the bourgeois answers to fragmentation and inauthenticity, become more tenuous. 'Family' used to be defined as those to whom you were permanently attached. Such ties are weaker today. Anxieties about relationships, while universal, have in amusement society become intertwined with one's problematic social status that must be ever renewed. Marriages promise more than they can deliver, friendships are more fleeting (especially for males) and suburbia more anonymous than cohesive. Thus the longings for human connection, momentarily satisfied in mall-based illusions of community, become repressed and indeed denied.[31]

Modern women are subject to additional pressures of familial disempowerment. Corporate wives once gave up their own identities for the sake of their husband's career (Kanter, 1977). Now turned professional, these women come home not to intimacy and fulfilment, but to a 'second shift' of housework and childcare (Hochschild, 1989). Blue-collar women often thought their marriages would provide the joys and love that were absent in their own families, but were continually seen in the hyper-real images

69

of a happy family *circa* 1950. These media-based fantasies created expectations that were bound to be frustrated (cf. Rubin, 1976). Their domestic life is more bleak, and if they work, it is likely to be in the more routine lower-echelon jobs. Thus it is not surprising that women are much more likely to spend time in malls than men. In the mall they can have and be the advertised and com-modified fantasies of beauty, glamour and empowerment that is gained in choosing meanings and interpretations. The inegalitarian social reality denies women the pleasures of empowerment (cf. Fiske, 1989).

Panic, as the extreme expression of anxiety, is ultimately based on the fear of death that lies deep in phylogeny and ontogeny. The earliest threats to selfhood are the vagaries of early survival and fears of abandonment by Others that they may not grant nurturance or recognition. These early fears are evoked by the structure, or lack thereof, in amusement society. Panic has thus become the mood of postmodern subjective helplessness in face of the new semiological order without assured ties of family and friends that guarantee social solidarity and provide an identity. The fervent embrace of the simulacrum of selfhood and spectacles of commodified interaction is the indication of the very failure of the simulacra of malldom to provide lasting identities, compensations and gratifications. This leads to a panicky oscillation between ecstasy and fear in the sequential spectacles of the modern amusement culture; panic lies between delirium and anxiety, between the triumph of cyberpunk and the political reality of cultural exhaustion . . . the oscillating *fin de millénium* mood of deep euphoria and deep anxiety. It is a response to the breakdown of standards of public conduct and the loss of the internal self (Kroker *et al.*, 1989). The fragmented inner life and its expressions in overt momentary rituals and purchases in a plurality of social worlds leads to ever more desperate searches for gratification. But the quest is ever more anxiety-evoking.

The other distinctive emotional quality of today is envy. The Ulanovs (1983) suggest that envy is one of the causes of modern misery. They argue the universal popularity of Cinderella is based on its message that the envy of the Other destroys the self that envies.[32] Like panic, envy is rooted in earlier experiences. Freud thought it had something to do with the woman wanting a penis, his way of legitimating submission to patriarchy. The major theorist of envy was Melanie Klein who saw envy as a primitive form of oral and anal sadism. While some of her suppositions are dubious, what is important is her insight on how envy wants to destroy the goodness of the Other, and in terms of this analysis, that goodness is the subjectivity imputed to exist behind the appearance of the Other. Postmodern envy is not so much in wanting your neighbour's spouse or even wanting his/her various possessions (lawnmowers or pasta makers), leisure and travel pursuits. Envy is a comparison of one's own subjectivity to that of the Other. This creates what might be called a relative deprivation of selfhood. Comparisons to the Other make one's own subjectivity feel discredited or degraded and the self becomes envious of the Other's being (cf. Garfinkel, 1956; Goffman, 1963).

What is distinct about postmodern envy is that the envied subjectivity of the Other is itself likely to be a commodified fantasy, a simulacra of selfhood no more substantial than that of the envier. Or, commonly, the envied is a character of media or the manufactured star of the 'unreality industry' who plays him or her (cf. Mitroff and Bennis, 1989). In so far as the commodified images of the hyper-real characters of movies, TV and the commercials seem to have more recognition and gratification than we do, we feel especially envious. This is evident among the pubescent, mall-rat 'wanna-bes' who dress and act like a simulacrum of the culture industry. We now see the other side of gratifying empowerments is an emptiness of a degraded self that needs to appropriate the subjectivity of the Other.[33] The various jokes of deprecation so common today can thus be seen not so much as hostility, but compensatory for impaired self-esteem. Thus to envy is to want to be like the Other, whose subjectivity is seen to be more valued than one's own and must hence be degraded. The Other's subjectivity must be destroyed so it is turned into an object that can be appropriated. What is envied today is not the possessions and lifestyle of the Other but the subjectivity that these would seem to indicate. Thus it is only in amusement society that subjectivity can be reified as if it were the objects it possesses. But given what we see as the more fundamental dialect of recognition, to envy the Other is to destroy the recognition s/he provides and to become the Other is to be without his or her recognition. Just as panic cannot be alleviated by consumption, neither can envy be overcome in the possession of objects in lieu of substantiated selfhood.

Goffman's *Asylums* (1961a) can be read as a critique of domination (Fine, 1990). While the idea of total institutions as the 'iron cages' described by Weber may be apt for the industrial society of his era, today that imagery is a bit stark. Malldom is better seen as a modern 'panopticon' in which the search for subjectivity locks people into 'neon cages' of consumption, sentenced to life-times of shopping for subjectivity. Nevertheless malls share some features with jails and asylums. Goffman noted how total insti-tutions degrade the prior status of the person and eliminate prior notions of individuality and privacy (cf. Garfinkel, 1956). Eating *en masse*, the wearing of uniforms and constant surveillance of personal behaviour insure the loss of freedom, subjectivity and integrity. The mall generations have now eaten almost 100 billion identical burgers and express their pseudo-individuality in the mass-produced fads and fashions of 'The Gap' or 'Limited' brand clothing. They experience not degradation but celebration. They flock to the malls or other carnival sites to seek the surveillance, scrutiny and recognition by the Others who share their tastes. When they grow up and work for the administrative apparatus of amusement society, the corporations, they will have been well socialized, malled, to deny any genuine individuality or any kind of critical consciousness.

If iron bars keep us from getting out of prisons, neon lights, lasers and hologram images keep us from wanting to get out of the fantastic world of malldom. Like force fields of sci-fi, the barriers are invisible and impermeable. The similarities of malls with images of totalitarian dystopias is striking; consider only the sets from *Metropolis*, *The Shape of Things to Come*, *Logan's Run* or *THX–1138*. In this way, the neon cages of malldom as total insti-tutions are reflections of amusement society as a concentration camp (Brittain, 1977), the person as an inmate (Horkheimer and Adorno, 1972), and the chains forged of commodified signs and narrative texts that make oppression opaque. Conformity to simul-acra is the freedom of interpretation. While the Holocaust would destroy the bodies of Jews and other enemies of the *Reich*, amuse-ment society would appropriate the subjectivities of all through consumption-based gratification. Its everyday life is fun, its com-modities are benign. The guards are sponsors and talk-show hosts. Big Brother is not watching, he's the lead guitar in a rock group.[34] Those whose subjectivities the Gods would destroy will first go shopping in malls. As Postman (1985) argues, the modern dystopia is the brave new world where everyone is happy through consumption. Amusement society functions best when the inmates willingly accept it as normal and desirable and remain oblivious to its psychic and social costs.

CONCLUSION

In the 1844 manuscripts, Marx argued that commodification of labour was the basis of an alienation that distorted subjectivity and social relations. So convinced was he of the demise of capitalism, he failed to anticipate bureaucratic mass production, consumption and a global media of visual images that would converge in the fantasy realms of malldom. These sites of hyper-reality, not the factories, would be the locations where amusement society would reproduce itself. To understand hegemony embedded in the commercial spectacles of everyday life would require a critical social psychology to deconstruct a subjectivity transformed to seek willing if not somewhat gratifying assent. Starting with the penetrating observations of Simmel and Goffman and a depth psychology of feelings, we noted how a postmodern society of spectacles colonizes childhood to appropriate desires and images of self to be realized in the intertwining of hyper-real consumption and mundane routines of everyday life in the pluralistic life worlds of amusement society. These everyday routines, rituals and interactions that are located in concentric circles around malls are sources of partial satisfaction that co-exist with and in part assuage more fundamental frustrations and malaise (cf. Deegan, 1988).

Contemporary psychoanalytic practices have shifted from conflicts over repressed desires to concern with self pathologies in which an enfeebled character structure pursues recognition to sustain self-esteem and, failing that, experiences anger, rage, feelings of emptiness et cetera. Kohut (1977) suggests that Freud treated Guilty Man tormented by unacceptable desires; today's patient is Tragic Man, an empty façade seeking ever more problematic confirmation of a fragmented selfhood that anxiously experiences itself as without cohesion from either within as legacies of infancy, or from without in the pluralistic life worlds. It seeks recognition in grandiosity or merger with those who have it. Behind the dialectic of voyeurism-exhibitionism in everyday self-presentations are the high emotional costs of appropriated desire and commodified selfhood that are constituted as signs of a consumption-based ideology in which the destruction of the subject is all but completed.

What early sociologists hailed as modern differentiation and progressive rationality, we see as a breakdown of cohesive community and fragmentation of subjectivity. The pluralistic life worlds with strains of panic, envy, and quests for authentic selfhood that first emerged with modernity have been intensified by amusement society. Horkheimer and Adorno (1972) noted how the legacy of the Enlightenment project would be fear and panic that would lead people to embrace fervently the very world that is the source of their malaise. Today, to assuage the horrors, to overcome the loneliness of modernity, people flock to malls where 'proto-communities' of strangers seek clothes, cultural products and techno-gadgets that promise gratification or at least recognition through possession.

But wait! What's that dust on the horizon? Is it the cavalry, a posse, or are they breaking ground for a new hypermall? No, it looks like economic contraction and a fate worse than death or nuclear war: the closing of malls.

The political economy of amusement society has itself become a simulation, that is its sycophants and public relations specialists cheer its abundance while in the US and western countries, the low overall growth masks long-term structural features of increasingly 'normal' levels of unemployment and a greater disparity of the haves and the have-nots. In the US, four-fifths of the population have less disposable income today than they did 15 years ago. But the collusion of television and marketing that destroyed childhood and infantilized adulthood make the necessary remedies – deferred gratification – intolerable. No child likes bitter medicine.

The emotional consequences of today have a particularly odious hue. Sixty years ago, when the foundations of amusement society were being cast, the contradictions of capitalism would usher in the most barbarous epoch in human history. The breakdown of outer control and inner subjectivity then disposed fascism (Horkheimer and Adorno, 1972). But today such conditions are less likely to take the form of mass rallies than visual entertainments by a techno-fascism of Robo-Cop terminators, Mad Max warriors and Nintendo wars of sanitized destruction that aestheticize violence (Kellner, 1990). While the various expressions of proto-fascism in punkers, skinheads, bikers and reactionary Christian fundamentalism are little more than sociological curios, we must recall that,

74

before the economic collapse of the 1930s, they laughed at the Nazis. To develop more fully the implications of this argument could become a bit gloomy. And besides that, there is a big sale at the mall and then we could catch the new flick at the multiplex. It's called *Scenes from a Mall* and stars Woody Allen and Bette Midler. Fantastic!

NOTES

1 While this analysis follows Durkheim (1965), we would add that while religion may serve solidarity functions, it can also vouchsafe authority relations and class structures. It seems as if Durkheim's discussions of sacred places as sites of the power of society informed Foucault (1977) and others who examined in detail how secular places like factories, asylums, hospitals and prisons were organized for the sake of power and control.

2 The concept of carnival as extraordinary reversals, gratifications of the forbidden and aetheticization of the grotesque has a special meaning for the analysis of consumer society. See for example, Featherstone, 1991.

3 In this paper, 'spectacular' and 'fantastic' have specialized meanings, spectacles are staged and produced events or symbols that appeal not only to realities but fantasies based on cultural myths and/or unconscious desires that like dreams may fulfil frustrated longings.

4 There have been similar notions such as 'repressive desublimation' in which sexual freedom secures consumerism, or 'repressive toleration' in which legal or political struggles are encouraged in so far as they do not really change structural conditions.

5 The relation of self to identity is often not very clear, and often depends on the author. Thus, for Freud, there were unconscious aspects of the self. More recent works of self psychology, for example Kohut (1971, 1977), emphasizes unacknowledged rage, feelings of inadequacy and desires for gradiosity as crucial elements of selfhood that are not simply due to libidinal or aggressive needs, concepts that are a bit dubious. Rather, as shall be argued, self psychology is better located within an affective framework than a drive-based theory of motivation.

6 This privatization would also allow realms of thought or feeling apart from scrutiny from which social criticism might emerge, especially among the educated with time to read and write. This realm would also permit a sphere of aesthetic experience outside the everyday realm. While this is central for the aesthetic theories of Adorno and Marcuse, later we shall suggest the realm of aesthetic freedom is not simply limited to Bach, Brecht, Berg and Baudelaire.

7 How manners would do so is a complex issue. For sake of simplification, the control of impulse, as noted by Nietzsche, Freud and Weber would foster the feelings and motives required for capitalism,

for example, capitalism depended on anxiety over impulsivity and salvation to motivate work. But such feelings and motives were part of a complex that included printing, the construction of childhood and individualism. No single factor has clear primacy, but Habermas (1979, 1984–7) suggests that the economic determination of social life and culture has the most efficacy at times of transition.

8 This is not to ignore the extent to which the elites had backstage realms in which various plots and intrigues were planned. At the dawn of modernity, Machiavelli counselled the Medicis on the role of frontstage impression management. Rather, what is important is the extent to which the bulk of the population has private realms of life, secrets, free from surveillance. These would be created by capitalism and destroyed by television.

9 Thus for example Goffman (1959) noted the priests who went to the beaches in other parishes so as not to be seen in a discrepant role. Today, we find some raping their secretaries or paying hookers to watch them masturbate. The secret identities that disconfirm a public one are increasingly likely to be revealed as exposé has been increasingly commodified since the trysts of JFK (cf. Meyrowitz, 1985).

10 Among the earliest comments on the role of 'personality' in modern commerce would be Fromm (1947), Mills (1951) and Marcuse (1964). Elias (1978) suggested that civilization was made possible when manners came to control impulses and people began to feel shame over bodily functions and sexuality.

11 This is a clear reference to Bell's announcement of industrial society where ideology is passé. Rather, as is argued in this paper, an ideology of consumption that sustains dominant class privilege is embedded in the myriad of everyday life practices that are shaped by this consumption that in turn reproduces that political economy.

12 There are overlaps between the more simple shopping centres that often include supermarkets or hardware/lumber stores that provide goods more necessary for everyday life subsistence. The mall is more likely to have specialized 'gourmet' exotica and high-tech doodads.

13 The importance of commercially produced and marketed nostalgia, temporal escapes from the toils of modernity – including commercialization and fragmentation – to a more gratifying mythological past has been noted. See for example, Stauth and Turner (1988). This attempt at restoration can be seen in such diverse cultural forms as the layout of malls, fads in fashion (back to 'elegance' or 'basics' depending on last year's pitch), films and TV series (*Back to the Future, Quantum Leap*) and political movements from fascism to fundamentalism to the made-in-Hollywood fantasy called Reagan's America (see Wills, 1987, for an analysis of fantasies of nostalgia as politics).

14 The reader should be reminded that the focus on mall-based consumption is an ideal type to inform the nature of subjectivity. There are a number of other factors such as family, status and, to be sure, there are large numbers of people whose incomes have fallen to levels that permit little discretionary surplus for self-indulgent displays of consumption. But growing poverty is part of a totality where mall-jam-

mers place more priority on designer jeans than dealing with the growing poverty.

15 McCall and Simmons (1966), using exchange theory, and J. Turner (1988), using emotion, have previously argued that self-presentations provide gratifications. Collins and Makowsky (1988) suggest that self-presentations as collective rituals provide gratifications to the person and solidarity to the society. My position sees these gratifications serving hegemonic functions, and as an unrepentant Freudian, finds these psychologies not just simplistic, but without a dialectical sense of tragedy.

16 There is some literature suggesting that those who are most likely to enjoy their work are those with the most freedom and responsibility, self-control over activities, creativity and use of symbols, e.g. sciences, professions, artistic/intellectual work, etc.

17 Of course the dysfunctions of unequal access to such gratifications are seen in urban crime and drug addiction. But ghettos don't encroach upon the good life of suburban malldom. Save through rap music or urban crime movies, these are not part of fantasy land. To situate this paper, it was written at the time of controversy concerning 2 Live Crew's *As nasty as they want to be*, a collection of lyrics consisting primarily of variations of 'fuck', and '*New Jack City*', Mario Peebles' movie of drug gangs. But we should note that there are a number of inner-city people that do work in the backstages of malls, in janitorial, custodial, security or fast-food preparation.

18 This is not to ignore the many other functions that parents or caretakers may serve, from providing security and comfort to instilling morality and values, and providing cognitive stimulation and cultural tastes. Rather, the extent to which parents/caretakers serve as undiluted role models is being questioned.

19 Television junkies may remember 'Fantasy Island', the postmodern programme in which traditional distinctions of reality and fantasy no longer applied or even mattered. Ricardo Montalban granted wishes, always gratified in lavish consumption. There were always two stories; in one the person found love, in the other, recognition of his/her narcissistic heroics.

20 The author is grateful to one of his graduate students, Carol Gagliano, who suffered the horrors of malldom for the sake of sociology. Many of the observations reported are her's and not the author's.

21 It should be noted that not all malls attract mall-rats. The glitzy galleries of haute couture in which stores with French and Italian names sell clothes from Asia are out of the price range for most teens.

22 There is a large literature suggesting that television subverts the value of words in favour of images and these images include the backstage realms from which children were excluded, namely sexuality, violence and war. If, as Meyrowitz (1985) claims, there is no more sense of place as backstage or front, we might add nor of time, age and childhood. See, for example, Postman (1982). The study of the adult life course emerges as the phenomenon fades.

23 Surely many readers over thirty-five have had the embarrassing experience of a teenager straightening out a computer mess or showing you

how to operate your VCR or CD player. It is especially painful when that whiz is your own child!

24 There are of course a few teenaged deviants who still believe in education and hard work as means to, if not grace, a successful career. But most of these recent Asian immigrants have parents who were not fully socialized into an amusement society.

25 In his discussion of the power of money to buy beauty, health or intelligence, Marx (1844) seemed to anticipate the present analysis. I would suggest, however, that were he writing now, he might well note the 'commodity fetish' as not only mystifying the social relations of production, but that selfhood as a commodified expression or advertisement has itself become such a fetish.

26 A long literature, both sociological, e.g. Kanter (1977), or popular such as Ringer (1976) *Winning Through Intimidation*, has shown how getting noticed and projecting an image of either efficacy, power or both has become more important in business or corporate life than actual competence.

27 This reading is similar to Collins and Makowsky (1988) who read Goffman as a legacy of Durkheim; solidarity emerges from the millions of ritualized performances that characterize everyday life. But what the critical reading adds is that these ritualizations have been shaped by the commodity form and are part of hegemonic process.

28 Jameson (1988) has argued, however, that the notion of the powerful bourgeois self now weakened may itself be an ideological mystification.

29 It is perplexing to the Democratic party in the US that two-thirds of people between 18 and 30 prefer Republican candidates that articulate private greed rather than social concerns. It's simple: mall-rats vote for personal consumption not social justice – nor do they believe that poverty, world peace and environmental pollution are any more real than Bart Simpson or Mutant Ninja Turtles.

30 But we must not ourselves succumb to the commodified nostalgia that once upon a time things were better or the naive Marxism that someday there will be a socialist Utopia where things will be better. Rather, as we have argued, amusement society has destroyed the past and *is* the future.

31 It is interesting to note that at the time of this writing, Slater's (1970) *Pursuit of Loneliness* has just been republished. It remains a classical statement of the fragile psychic underpinnings of amusement society.

32 Then again one might argue that Cinderella's magical transformation from a charmaid to a commodified beauty married to a dippy prince was just a changed form of domination in which castle life was at least more amusing. NB, in the sequel, she comes out, divorces the prince and works for feminist causes.

33 One of the reasons for the popularity of Woody Allen is that his films are generally variations on the theme of a search for subjectivity; *Zelig*, *Alice*, *Hannah* and *Danny Rose* are but variations on a theme that can be seen as humour. But we recall what Freud said about 'jokes'.

34 Some of my cohort may remember Janis Joplin's band was called Big Brother and the Holding Company, a veiled allusion to domination

by pleasure-generating drugs, which like mass-marketed goods provide a temporary high, albeit addictive and whose ultimate cost is one's very subjectivity.

REFERENCES

Ariès, P. (1962) *Centuries of Childhood: A Social History of Family Life*, New York: Vintage.

Aronowitz, S. (1973) *False Promises: The Shaping of American Working Class Consciousness*, New York: McGraw-Hill.

Baudrillard, J. (1975) *The Mirorr of Production*, St Louis: Telos Press.

Baudrillard, J. (1981) *For a Critique of the Political Economy of the Sign*, St Louis: Telos Press.

Baucrillard, J. (1983) *Simulations*, New York: Semiotexte.

Becker, E. (1973) *The Denial of Death*, New York: Free Press.

Bellah, R., Sullivan, W., Swidler, A. and Tipton, S. (1985) *Habits of the Heart: Individualism and Commitment in American Life*, Berkeley: University of California Press.

Benjamin, J. (1988) *Bond of Love*, New York: Pantheon.

Boorstin, D. (1962) *The Image*, New York: Atheneum.

Bourdieu, P. (1977) *Outline of a Theory of Practice*, Cambridge: Cambridge University Press.

Brittain, A. (1977) *The Privatized World*, London: Routledge.

Chaney, D. (1990) 'Subtopia in Gateshead: the MetroCentre as a cultural form,' *Theory, Culture & Society*, 7: 49–68; London: Sage.

Chodorow, N. (1978) *The Reproduction of Mothering*, Berkeley: University of California Press.

Collins, R. and Makowsky, M. (1988) *The Discovery of Society*, New York: Random House.

de Certeau, M. (1984) *The Practice of Everyday Life*, Berkeley: University of California Press.

Debord, G. (1970) *The Society of the Spectacle*, Detroit: Black and Red.

Deegan, M. J. (1988) *American Ritual Dramas*, New York: Greenwood Press.

Durkheim, E. (1965) *Elementary Forms of Religious Life*, Glencoe: Free Press.

Elias, N. (1978) *The Civilizing Process*, New York: Pantheon.

Ewen. S. (1976) *Captain of Consciousness*, New York: McGraw-Hill.

Ewen, S. (1982) *Channels of Desire*, New York: McGraw-Hill.

Ewen, S. (1988) *All Consuming Images*, New York: Basic.

Featherstone, M. (1991) *Consumer Culture and Post Modernism*, London: Sage.

Fine, G. (1990) 'A partisan view: sarcasm, satire, and irony as voices in Erving Goffman's *Asylums*', *Journal of Contemporary Ethnography*, 19 (1): 89–115.

Fiske. J. (1989) *Reading the Popular*, Boston: Unwin Hyman.

Foucault, M. (1973) *The Birth of the Clinic*, New York: Pantheon.

Foucault, M. (1977) *Discipline and Punish*, New York: Pantheon.

Freud, S. (1926) 'Inhibition, symptoms and anxiety', in *Collected Papers*, London: Hogarth Press.

Freud, S. (1961) *Civilization and Its Discontents*, New York: Norton.

Fromm, E. (1947) *Man for Himself*, New York: Rinehart.

Garfinkel, H. (1956) 'Conditions of successful degradation ceremonies', *American Journal of Sociology*, 61 (5): 420–4.

Gay, P. (1984) *Education of the Senses: Victoria to Freud*, New York: Oxford University Press.

Gergen. K. (1986) *Social Psychology*, New York: Springer-Verlag.

Giddens, A. (1984) *The Constitution of Society: Outline of a Theory of Structuration*, Cambridge: Cambridge University Press.

Goffman, E. (1959) *The Presentation of Self in Everyday Life*, New York: Anchor.

Goffman, E. (1961a) *Asylums*, Chicago: Aldine.

Goffman, E. (1961b) *Encounters*, Indianapolis: Bobbs-Merrill.

Goffman, E. (1963) *Stigma*, Englewood Cliffs: Prentice-Hall.

Goffman, E. (1967) *Interaction Ritual*, New York: Doubleday.

Gramsci, A. (1971) *Selections from the Prison Notebook*, New York: International Publishers.

Habermas, J. (1979) *Communications and the Evolution of Society*, Boston: Beacon Press.

Habermas, J. (1984–7) *The Theory of Communicative Action* (2 vols.), Boston: Beacon Press.

Hochschild, A. R. (1983) *The Managed Heart: Commercialization of Human Feeling*, Berkeley: University of California Press.

Hochschild, A. R. (1989) *The Second Shift*, New York: Viking.

Hoggart, R. (1967) *The Usage of Literacy*, London: Chatto & Windus.

Horkheimer, M. and Adorno, T. (1972) *The Dialectic of Enlightenment*, New York: Herder & Herder.

Hsu, F. (1963) *Caste, Clan, and Club*, Princeton, New Jersey: Van Nostrand.

Jameson, F. (1988) 'On habits of the heart', in C. H. Reynolds and R. V. Norman (eds) *Community in America*, Berkeley: University of California Press.

Kanter, R. (1977) *Men and Women of the Corporation*, New York: Basic.

Kellner, D. (1989a) *Critical Theory, Marxism, and Modernity*, Baltimore: Johns Hopkins University Press.

Kellner, D. (1989b) *Baudrillard*, Stanford: Stanford University Press.

Kellner, D. (1990) *Television and the Crisis of Democracy*, Boulder: Westview Press.

Kohut, H. (1971) *The Analysis of Self*, New York: International Universities Press.

Kohut, H. (1977) *The Restoration of the Self*, New York: International Universities Press.

Kowinski, W. S. (1985) *The Malling of America: An Inside Look at the Great Consumer Paradise*, New York: W. Morrow.

Kroker, A. and Cook, D. (1989) *The Postmodern Scene*, New York: St Martins Press.

Kroker, A., Kroker, M. and Cook, D. (1986) *The Panic Encyclopedia*, New York: St Martins Press.

Langman, L. (1990) 'The experience of feelings in everyday life', paper presented at American Sociological Association, Washington, August.

Langman, L. and Richman, J. (1987) 'Psychiatry as a vocation: from the moral milieu to healing through feeling to pills pay bills', in H. Lopata (ed.) *Current Research on Occupations and Professions*, Greenwich, Conn.: JAI press.

Larsen, N. (1990) *Modernism and Hegemony*, Minneapolis: University of Minnesota Press.

Lasch, C. (1976) *Haven in a Heartless World*, New York: Norton.

Lasch, C. (1979) *The Culture of Narcissism: American Life in an Age of Diminishing Expectations*, New York, Norton.

Lears, T. J. J. and Fox, R. W. (1983) *The Culture of Consumption: Critical Essays in American History, 1880–1980*, New York: Pantheon.

Lefebvre, H. (1971) *Everyday Life in the Modern World*, New York: Harper & Row.

Lukács, G. (1971) *History and Class Consciousness*, Cambridge, Mass.: MIT Press.

McCall, G. and Simmons, J. L. (1966) *Identities and Interactions*, New York: Free Press.

McCarthy, E. (1989) 'Emotions are social things', in D. Franks and E.D. McCarthy (eds) *Essay in the Sociology of Emotions*, Greenwich, Conn.: JAI Press, 51–72.

MacIntyre, A. (1981) *After Virtue: a Study in Moral Theory*, Notre Dame, Ind.: University of Notre Dame.

McLuhan, M. (1964) *Understanding Media*, New York: McGraw-Hill.

Marcuse, H. (1955) *Eros and Civilization*, Boston: Beacon Press.

Marcuse, H. (1964) *One Dimensional Man*, Boston: Beacon Press.

Marx, K. (original edn. 1844) *The Economic and Philosophical Manuscripts of 1844*, in R. Tucker (ed.) *The Marx-Engels Reader* (2nd edn.), New York: Norton (1978).

Marx, K. (1867) *Capital* in R. Tucker (ed.) *The Marx-Engels Reader* (2nd edn), New York: Norton (1978).

Masson, J. (1984) *The Assault on Truth*, New York: Pinquin.

Meyrowitz, J. (1985) *No Sense of Place*, New York: Oxford University Press.

Mills, C.W. (1951) *White Collar: The American Middle Classes*, New York: Oxford University Press.

Mills, C.W. (1959) *The Sociological Imagination*, New York: Oxford University Press.

Mitroff, I. and Bennis, W. (1989) *The Unreality Industry*, New York: Lyle Stewart.

Postman, N. (1982) *The Disappearance of Childhood*, New York: Delacorte Press.

Postman, N. (1985) *Amusing Ourselves to Death*, New York: Viking.

Ringer, R. (1976) *Winning Through Intimidation*, New York: Fun & Wagner.

Rubin, L.B. (1976) *Worlds of Pain: Life in the Working-Class Family*, New York: Basic.

Rubin, L.B. (1983) *Intimate Strangers*, New York: Harper & Row.

Sartre, J.-P. (1956) *Being and Nothingness*, New York: Philosophical Library.

Schutz, A. (1967) *The Phenomology of the Social World*, Evanston: Northwestern University Press.

Schutz, A. (1973) *The Structures of the Life World*, Evanston: Northwestern University Press.

Sennet, R. (1977) *The Fall of Public Man*, New York: Knopf.

Simmel, G. (1950) *The Sociology of Georg Simmel*, Glencoe: Free Press.

Slater, P. (1970) *The Pursuit of Loneliness*, Boston: Beacon.

Stauth, G. and Turner, B. (1988) *Nietzsche's Dance*, Oxford: Blackwell.

Tompkins, S. (1984) 'Affect theory', in K. Scherer and P. Ekman (eds) *Approaches to Emotion*, Hillsdale, N.J.: Lawrence Erlbaum Associates.

Turner, J. (1989) *The Theory of Social Interaction*, Stanford, California: Stanford University Press.

Turner, R. (1976) 'The real self: from institution to impulse', *American Journal of Sociology*, 81 (5): 989–1016.

Ulanov, B. and Ulanov, A. (1983) *Cinderella and Her Sisters*, Philadelphia: The Westminster Press.

Veblen, T. (1934) *The Theory of the Leisure Class*, New York: Modern Library.

Weinstein, D. and M. (1990) 'Simmel and the Theory of Postmodern Society', in B. Turner (ed.) *Modernity and PostModernity*, London: Sage.

Wexler, P. (1987) *Social Analysis of Education*, London: Routledge & Kegan Paul.

Willis, P. (1990) *Common Culture*, Boulder, Colo.: Westview Press.

Wills, G. (1987) *Reagan's America*, Garden City, NY: Doubleday.

Zaretsky, E. (1976) *Capitalism, the Family and Personal Life*, New York: Harper & Row.

Zurcher, L. (1977) *The Mutable Self*, Beverly Hills: Sage.

4

STONEHENGE AND ITS FESTIVAL

Spaces of consumption

Kevin Hetherington

INTRODUCTION

On 1 June 1985 a slowly moving convoy of vans, lorries and buses in various states of repair, from the barely roadworthy to almost vintage status, travelling on their way to Stonehenge in Wiltshire, were forced off the road by the police and into a beanfield where a rather one-sided 'battle' between the police and travellers then ensued. Many convoy vehicles were damaged and over 500 people were arrested, others managed to flee into the depths of the sur-roundings of Savernake Forest. The so-called 'peace convoy' as it had been dubbed after a visit to Greenham in 1982 had become the most visible manifestation of an annual summer ritual for many people to gather at Stonehenge, an ancient megalithic site, in order to celebrate the summer solstice and participate in a rock festival that had taken place annually in an adjacent field since 1974.

The so-called Wallies as they had styled themselves and notably Phil Wally (also known as Phil Russell) had started the festival at Stonehenge then, originally as a form of sun worship on the longest day of the year. Infused with hippy music and drug culture, an eclectic mixture of religious beliefs and the ideal of the medieval fair, free festivals had been revived in Britain in the early 1970s. But it was only after the destruction by the police of the Windsor free festival in 1974 that Stonehenge became the site of the major summer festival (Clarke, 1982). While attendance at the early Stonehenge festivals was small and limited to a few dedicated supporters, it grew steadily bigger each year (despite a temporary lull in the late 1970s) until 1984, the time of the last festival proper, when it was estimated that upwards of 30,000 people attended. By then the early enthusiasm and dedication had been lost. Problems with outside drug-dealers, theft, damage to the site and large amounts of accumulated garbage were beginning to cast a shadow over the original ethos of the festival as a spiritual renewal and coming-together of people in an atmosphere of freedom and mutual trust. Perhaps the one unifying feature over the years of the 'free' festival had been its commercial side. As a commercial centre for this counter-culture, Stonehenge was a place in which the atmosphere provided a sense of carnival, intoxication and neo-pagan spiritual revival within the ethos of the 'New Age'.

Then of course there were the travellers – dedicated festival people unlike the majority who only attended festivals during college holidays or when they could get time off work. The travellers, although not the original festival organizers were people who lived on the road all summer, opting only to park up or return to city squats during the winter. They have subsequently become identified with Stonehenge and the festival. They took the brunt of police hostility in 1985, the year the festival was suppressed. In 1986 the convoy spent May and June being split up, forced from one site to the next by the police, magistrates, landowners and local authorities who refused to allow these people to congregate and hold anything representing a free festival. Farmers blocked their fields with tractors and agricultural machinery, vehicles were impounded, arrests made, children taken into care and pets put down. In 1987, English Heritage tried to compromise: an all-ticket festival, with a meagre 500 tickets in total, was organized. Some went and managed to reach the stones, others stayed away or went to the now fully commercial festival at Glastonbury instead. In 1988 many more tried to get to Stonehenge; a riot occurred with many arrests and a number of injuries.

In subsequent years, things have so far been more quiet, partly due to the four-mile exclusion zone around Stonehenge at solstice time, the ban on more than twelve vehicles travelling in convoy (made possible by the 1986 Public Order Act), coupled with miles of razor wire, road blocks, police dogs, helicopters with searchlights and in some years thousands of police. The travellers, however, have not disappeared; many who know them say their numbers are growing; some estimate that there are currently 10,000 'New Age travellers' living on the roads in Britain. Many are there by choice, unable to accept a more settled way of life; others, mostly young people, have taken to the roads partly because of the notoriety and glamour they attach to the traveller lifestyle and partly due to changes in social security rules or to avoid paying tax. While the Stonehenge summer solstice festival has not taken place since 1984, the travellers and other festival-goers have been resourceful, they have gone instead to other ancient stone circles, or tried to go to Stonehenge for the winter solstice or at the spring/ autumn equinox; some have travelled abroad, to Germany, to France; there are even some who have taken up living in caves in Spain.[1]

What seems so bizarre is not so much that people should want to live as travellers, but the extremity of the hostility towards them. Why the travellers? Why Stonehenge? In attempting to answer these questions, I shall make a number of related claims; that Stonehenge is a *modern* site and significant because of the way it draws out the different modes of living that have attached themselves to it. The 'neo-tribal' (Maffesoli, 1988) form of lifestyle associated with the travellers is perhaps only one of the most visible manifestations of a seemingly ambiguous aspect of modern life; increased de-individualization and affective, intensified forms of sociation that are the outcome of the process of individualization and the decline of more ascriptive bases for lifestyle, notably that of class. I shall argue that the travellers are one of the more obvious forms of such groupings whose identities are formed around the *risks* associated with this process. These elements may be brought together under the rubric of lifestyle consumption, in this case that which is associated with festival, which is at the centre of the symbolic production of the traveller lifestyle.

STONEHENGE AS A SITE OF CONSUMPTION

Festivals have always been associated with markets and the Stonehenge festival has been no exception. Almost anything could be bought at Stonehenge: drugs, New Age paraphernalia, health remedies, old bits of tat, scrap, vehicle parts, food, services; one person used to provide hot baths in an old tub in the middle of the field (surrounded by a screen), somebody even had the enter- prising idea of selling people breakfast in bed, strawberries and Champagne if it was your birthday, otherwise fried-egg sand- wiches! And yet the festival promoted the idea that it was free with no admission fees (except when some tried and succeeded in collecting entrance fees from the gullible and uninformed). The music was free, bands such as Hawkwind and many others would just turn up and play, often over ropy old public-address systems. There were also 'traditional' entertainers like the Tibetan Ukrainian Mountain Troupe, assorted jugglers, clowns, performers and festival-goers in various states of intoxication just having a go. The fact that such a festival should be associated with a solstice ceremony of sun worship, even if only by a minority of festival-goers, provides us with a good example of what Bakhtin describes as the carnivalesque, a heterogeneous, playful inversion of acceptable modes of behaviour, a world turned upside down, the mocking of authority, the exclusion of policing agencies from the site, the celebration of dirt, mess, abandon, intoxication, excess and waste (Bakhtin, 1984).

The festival was not only a place for large numbers of people to congregate for several weeks of festival but it was also a market for the New Age travellers, at which they could make some money, meet up with old friends and acquaintances, swap stories, reminisce and take part in the festival. Many of the goods and services were provided by the travellers to the others at the festival who led more sedentary lives but went to festivals like Stonehenge and Glastonbury during the summer months. The Stonehenge festival was itself part of a 'season' of summer free festivals. Like the periodic markets of medieval times, travellers would move on from one fair to another, earning money, selling goods, offering and exchanging services. The carnival element was present at the other festivals, even the more 'commercial' ones like Glastonbury, where admission fees were charged and the commercial and festival entertainments were more organized, licensed and regulated. But Stonehenge was special to those who went there; the ambience of the site, the myths and legends associated with it were stronger and it generated more hostility from its detractors.

The ambivalent nature of Stonehenge, a *topos* associated with carnival and markets, make it a good example of what has been described as a liminal zone, a margin or boundary, the crossing of which involves ritualized forms of transgression (Turner, 1969). The transformative potential of such a site is represented not simply in terms of carnivalesque rituals, pagan ceremonies and drug-induced states, but significantly by commercial activities whose meaning takes on transformed significance when associated with such liminal spaces. Consumption at Stonehenge when related to festival is highly ambivalent. It is both spontaneous and organized, monetary but with a strong emphasis placed on gift exchange; it is removed from all associations with rational consumption (licensed, taxed and regulated) but the sense of reciprocity is strong. Consumption in a liminal space reveals its archaic 'sacrificial' character: as an act of destruction, devouring, consuming, fetishizing, destroying, transforming the product of labour into waste. Consumption in such an unregulated manner led to the accumulation of filth and garbage. It is consumption primarily associated with satiating bodily desires, through food, alcohol, drugs and ritual adornment. There is a strong element of idealizing the transformative potential of consumption here; that which is 'devoured' gives the destroyer powers, whether they be associated with hallucinatory experiences, states of relaxation, beauty or sexiness. The outcome is waste and decay, the bad trip, the hangover and excrement.

Stonehenge as a festival of consumption was a destructive event that left the destroyer surrounded by the waste and decay; it represents a lifestyle of excess, liminally constituted and a deliberate challenge to the established order of things. The transient nature of social activities is revealed through festival, that things cannot last or that the consequences might be unpleasant. Festival after all has often been associated with death, as a release from the anxieties associated with one's ultimate demise.

The travellers and other festival-goers celebrate their marginal lifestyle not simply in terms of what they consume but through the inversions and rituals of festival. Consumption under these conditions becomes an *enactment of lifestyle* rather than simply the means to a lifestyle, with the site, or topos, in this case Stonehenge, providing the dramaturgical stage for these liminal practices. As such the performance has a dual role, as a practice through which identity and solidarity are held together and as a means of distanciating the proponents of such a lifestyle from the routine and mundane of everyday life. What is significant to both is the spatiality of this enactment. Such activities only have significance if they are visible, while at the same time being closed off from 'non-members'. It is this visible enactment of an alternative lifestyle that has been the source of much of the conflict surrounding the Stonehenge festival, a conflict that has its source in the problematic status of the visible transgression of the accepted conventions of what should be open to public view. While it is drug-taking, sexual licence and an appearance that seems strange that are often the source of concern, their visibility makes the space in which they occur the source of conflict as much as the practices themselves. This conflict over space and the types of lifestyle that exist therein *together* form the basis of this particular lifestyle. In order to understand that lifestyle more fully and therefore the significance that consumption plays, one first has to understand the significance of the context in which it arises.

SPACE AND SOCIAL ORDER

Stonehenge is a prime example of a social spatialization. '[The] ongoing social construction of the spatial at the level of the social imaginary (collective mythologies, presuppositions) as well as interventions in the landscape . . .' (Shields, 1991a: 31). It is a site with many conflictually produced and contested meanings, but they centre around two fundamental social spatializations: that of *heritage* and that of *festival*. The creation of meaningful, competing contemporary social spatializations can be seen in the descriptions of Stonehenge as an important archaeological site, a temple, an ancient astronomical instrument, a tourist attraction, a symbol of ancient Britain as culturally and technologically skilled, a New Age site of worship, part of England's cultural heritage, a node in a system of powerful ley lines and the site of an annual rock festival (Chippindale, 1983; Chippindale *et al.*, 1990). It is the latter and its connection with New Age religious meanings that provide us with the example of Stonehenge as a site of festival embodied in the celebration of the solstice and through forms of popular culture. The other examples, although diverse, provide us with the view of Stonehenge as a site of heritage.

As a site overburdened with meaning it has become policed, both literally in the form of thousands of police officers at the time of the now banned festival, with the use of perimeter fencing, admission fees, and symbolically through the way meanings are given to such a space. Despite its ancient origin, the host of meanings given to Stonehenge are all modern. Even the Druids who hold their own ceremony during the solstice are a modern phenomenon founded at the beginning of the eighteenth century, despite their claims to be able to trace an unbroken lineage to the ancients (Piggott, 1985). Stonehenge is more than just a contested space, it is a modern site at which some of the fundamental features of modernity come into conflict. This is not however a contest between modernity and tradition, between new and old interpretations of the significance of the stones, but *reflexively* the conflict between modern and counter-modern tendencies using an ancient site to legitimize different sets of practices and individualized lifestyles.

Both the concepts of heritage and festival are related to fundamentally opposing conceptions of time. Heritage implies continuity and a link with the past, while festival implies breaking the continuity of time and celebrating the present as if it were eternal. Heritage is about continuity and order while festival is about transgression and mocking in public the temporal authority of tradition. These conceptions of time are coupled with perceptions of space. For the archaeologist it is ancient, sedimented in the past, a static space to be meticulously picked over, catalogued and mapped in order that we might come to know more about a dead time. For the heritage tourist, the meaning of this space is also dead but this time as a dead space in living time (memory being the recreation of meaningful time); tourists can only visit spaces, but the nostalgia and the attempt to possess something different from the present leads to the re-temporalizing of heritage spaces. Stonehenge is what survives from another time, it resonates with pastness, but this is a past that can only be recaptured in memory. As such it is also for the tourist, like the archaeologist, and an institution like the National Trust, a space that is to be preserved rather than used, a space to be gazed upon (Urry, 1990) but not changed, used or touched.

For the New Age travellers Stonehenge represents not the archaeological sediment of historical memory but a renewal of the present in a world in which the continuity of time is disrupted. These visitors worship in effect the aura of the present, of what they see as the living ambience created by the stones. It is fitting that a prominent feature of their lifestyle should be a transient life on the roads. Shunning a sedentary way of life, these 'nomads of the present' (Melucci, 1989) live a different time, one that has seasonal continuity, but exists disjunctively with everyone else. Their calendar is a regulated one suited to stopping in winter and moving in summer. The travel from festival to festival, which often take place at ancient pagan sites such as stone circles, of which Stonehenge is only the most famous, forms a significant feature of their life on the road.

In order to interpret the significance of the competing meanings and identities attached to Stonehenge, I shall start by claiming that the contestation of the meaning of a site such as Stonehenge derives from the modern dislocation or 'disembedding' of our everyday lives in time and space (Giddens, 1990) and the sub-sequent attempt to resolve resulting uncertainties through the creation of 'place myths' that are one of the results of this process. Stonehenge as a contemporary site is significant as both a heritage space and a festival space as both are defined in relation to the disintegration in everyday life of communally created meaningful spaces, which represent continuity in time, and of place as a collective basis for identity and culture, by the fleeting, disjunctive experience of time within a capitalist society always disrupting the spatial stability of everyday life (Simmel, 1990; Harvey, 1989; Giddens, 1990). Stonehenge, as a modern site, provides us with a good example of a topos of insecurity that symbolically articulates the consequences of conflicts surrounding the ambiguity of lifeworld experiences of place as detached from the *durée* of every-day life.

The fear of 'chaos', disordered practices that are out of place, and its production by processes of modernization in which the temporal aspects of human relationships are both reified in particu-lar practices and uncoupled from the spatially proximate aspects of those relationships, serve to make spatial rather than temporal relationships the basis of giving order to everyday life. But modern disembedded spaces remain aporial and a source of ontological insecurity. All forms of feeling, emotion and affective sociality can only be allowed to exist in public if those spaces are clearly defined and regulated, as in the sporting arena. But this sociality is a persistent part of the underlying basis to everyday life, normally repressed and confined to the private lives of individuals; however, it continually emerges from that realm as the basis for new life-styles offering a challenge to the mundane and routine that have become the common experience in the private lives of many. Public space becomes for some the space in which to transgress the routinized and emotionless character of public life and to create new meaningful identities and lifestyles out of a disordered exist-ence.

We also witness the counter-measures to this process. Any space where the appropriate activity for the setting is in any doubt is subjected to policing and surveillance. As a consequence Stonehenge, as a mysterious space, becomes the site of conflict between modern and counter-modern perspectives. Not only does it offer the possibility through the various interpretations of heritage of a sense of continuity and order, it also offers the possibility of mystery and disordered uses expunged from the modern consciousness. Pagan, expressive, emotive, magical, carnival, ritualized and full of uncertainty, the un-appropriated uses of Stonehenge threaten to spill out into the outside world. The source of anxiety and the strength of the reaction by the 'locals' is due not to any physical danger (although it may be articulated as such), but is related to uncertainties surrounding new visible lifestyles which are associated by default as the source of the modern characteristic to disrupt the indexicality of place.

Subsequently those who celebrate festival at this space are treated as *Other* because they adopt a lifestyle that, given its self-produced form, represents the chaotic, disorganized and transient features of modern life that transgress the routines and familiarities of everyday life. Collectively, they constitute and identify with the stranger that inhabits the modern world who, in Simmel's words, 'comes today and stays tomorrow – the potential wanderer so to speak, who, although he has gone no further, has not quite got over the freedom of coming and going' (Simmel, 1971: 143).

Just as has been the case with Jews and gypsies down the centuries, the 'New Age travellers' are hated not because they are always on the move but because they might stay and 'contaminate' through their ambivalence and bring down all manner of horrors upon the 'locals' (Bauman, 1990). They are out of place not because they belong somewhere else, as in the case of an enemy, but because they belong nowhere and are thus not simply unplaceable, but in their celebration of festival and mobility are outside of time itself; they inhabit the disjuncture between experiences of time and place in human relationships; 'unclean', 'slimey' (Douglas, 1984), their status is as uncertain as their origins. Above all as strangers who are harbingers of uncertainty and discontinuity, their lifestyle is associated with sources of *risk*. It is notable that 'the horrified', when commenting on the travellers, saw them not only as dirty, scrounging thieves and peddlers in drugs, but also as a source of pollution (Rojek, 1988).

While these anxieties may be clothed in expressions of horror in relation to dirt, disease and drug-taking, an attempt is made to make visible unseen anxieties, by defining those with a visibly different lifestyle in terms of the source of risk. It is something of

91

an irony, not to say a self-fulfilling prophecy, that those who construct their lifestyles differently should do so latterly around the very risks that they have become associated with. They end up putting themselves in danger from the things others fear so much: transientness, eviction, ostracism, placeless identities, poverty, harassment and uncertainty in one's life.

It is not surprising therefore that those who deliberately assume 'risk identities', who celebrate chaotic and expressive lifestyles, should adopt a 'timeless' space like Stonehenge as their spiritual 'home'. This lifestyle strikes directly at the opposing world-view that is associated with heritage. Those attending the festival would see this as an outlook running counter to the original sacred significance of the stones, yet while their festival is meant to be an enactment of renewal it is also a deliberate political challenge to those they know will be offended by their activities.

The festivals of the past were intimately related to the continuity of the calendar in a world where the succession of time was ordered in terms of seasons and the *durée* of human life and therefore had a natural meaning. In the past natural disasters and disruptions were hazards expected with fatalism and celebrated through the carnivalesque practices of grotesque imagery and of death (Bakhtin, 1984). The contemporary festival lifestyle reintroduces this into the modern life-world, with all its disorder, drug-taking and the fact of uncertainty in our lives through processes of consumption. Through their hedonistic, anti-authoritarian stance, their dress, drugs, visible expressions of release from imposed social constraints, the festival-goers mock, through carnival, all those who hold ideals of progress and satisfaction through effort.

CONSUMPTION AND SOCIALITY

To bring all these elements together – time-space relations, festival, risk and consumption – what is required is a theory of sociality and sociation, that is, an understanding of the social preconditions, the emotional bases to the collective experience of the activities involved and the forms this takes as distinct lifestyles (Maffesoli, 1989; Amirou, 1989; Hetherington, 1990; Shields, 1991b). In order to understand the significance of the combination of features that I have suggested are associated with Stonehenge, one needs to consider two processes that are involved, the deregulation through modernization and individualization of the modern forms of solidarity and identity based on class occupation, locality and gender (Beck, 1992) and the recomposition into 'tribal' identities and forms of sociation (Maffesoli, 1988). Such processes that stem from changes within capitalist economies produce a heightened, more reflexive form of individualism, which is no longer able to base itself in class cultures, regional identities or established gender roles, leading to a process of de-individualization as people seek to recombine in new forms of sociation based on political, cultural, sexual, religious and therapeutic identities. These non-ascriptive 'neo-Tribes' as Maffesoli calls them, are inherently unstable and not fixed by any of the established parameters of modern society; instead they are maintained through shared beliefs, styles of life, an expressive body-centredness, new moral beliefs and senses of injustice, and significantly through consumption practices. The participants are drawn primarily from the disaffected and disempowered, notably young middle-class people, whose former cultural identity was neither bourgeois nor proletarian, but centred around a culture of displacement so to speak, based on social, educational and spatial mobility, and on gender role and occupational displacement (Beck, 1992). All of which undermines a shared and meaningful social existence.

It would be wrong to see these 'tribes' as the creators of a new sense of *community*. As Schmalenbach argued over sixty years ago, drawing on not that dissimilar observations of the German Youth Movement in the early part of this century, the concept *Bund* or *communion* better captures the reality of these unstable affectual forms of sociation than that of community (*Gemeinschaft*) (Schmalenbach, 1977). A *Bund* is an intense form of affectual solidarity, that is inherently unstable and liable to break down very rapidly unless it is consciously maintained through the symbolically mediated interactions of its members.[2]

As well as being small-scale, achieved rather than ascribed, unstable and affectual forms of sociation (Schmalenbach, 1977), *Bünde* are also maintained symbolically and through active, reflexive monitoring of group solidarity by those involved, in other words they are highly self-referential and involve creating a medium of symbolic practices through which a particular lifestyle emerges. The social bonding involved is very weak, requiring considerable effort in maintenance (Gurvitch, 1941). As marginalized risk identities are involved, these *Bünde* are self-enclosed and very tribal or autotelic – that is, as social forms they rapidly become their own goal; styles of dress, political or religious beliefs, adherence to musical styles or modes of living are often deliberately accentuated and defended. Associated with sites of transition or liminality (Turner, 1969), these *Bünde* are innovative, transgressive and often involve a re-skilling or empowering of the life-worlds of their 'members'. They are a sociation that combines aesthetic, ethical and expressive styles of life into impassioned group identities often centred around charismatic leaders or strongly held beliefs. As forms of sociation they most clearly encapsulate the seemingly contradictory modern processes of individualization and de-individualization. They are places where individuals, burdened with their sense of displaced individuality, go to lose themselves, only to rediscover the fact that strong group identities of this sort require personal skills and a reflexive sense of self. The intensity of interpersonal relations, and of a re-emergent individualism can only lead to the fragmentation of a *Bund* and its re-combination and transition into more stable forms of sociation. This is a form of sociation whose sociality is at once intense and fragile, strongly empowering but the source of possible bitter recrimination.

Amongst the travellers, we find many *Bünde*; some have names (both real and imagined): the Tibetan Ukrainian Mountain Troupe, the Rainbow Warriors, the Rainbow People, the Brew Crew and before them the Yellow Tipi as well as a whole host whose names are lost or unknown! Many of the named groups could be divided into sub-groups often hostile to one another, and 'membership' need not be exclusive to one group. However, it is consumption, notably at festivals, that plays a strong part in holding this lifestyle together. They often have a rugged, dirty appearance, some with bright clothes, others in dark greens. Ethnic jewellery, multicoloured blankets, lovingly cared-for tools and hand-made objects of various sorts all provide some of the symbolic cement that goes into holding together an otherwise fragile form of sociation. Drugs of course are important, significantly cannabis and acid, although speed and heroin are not unheard of (cocaine though tends to be too expensive). Alcohol is also significant, notably Special Brew. The type of vehicle often provides status; they have tended to get bigger over the years, and double-decker buses are now favoured, especially ones with diesel engines (some even have microwaves and cell phones), although horse-drawn caravans and canal boats look set to become significant.

Travellers have a variety of sources of income, festivals and fairs being the most significant but also seasonal work, selling bits of scrap, car-boot sales, selling the products of learned craft skills, entertainment, music, drug-dealing and social-security payments. This is one of the reasons why the festivals are so important; they are the place to make lots of money, to get one's vehicle roadworthy, to buy furniture and clothing. Skills and resources are shared amongst travellers (the festival at Stonehenge was perhaps the finest example of intricate networks of relationships that go to make up the black economy). But also these consumption practices play a significant part in maintaining a lifestyle derived from a *Bund*. Partly this is symbolic, but significantly it is social, ties of reciprocity, gift (in Mauss's sense of honour, status and debt) (Mauss, 1969). The festival also acts as a social gathering and meeting place at which to make collective decisions just as at the markets of old.

Areas of the festival field 'spontaneously' found themselves organized into pitches from which 'tribes' sold their goods, sometimes through the money economy, sometimes through barter, sometimes through gift-exchange. The whole ethos of gift underlay these *free* festivals, yet at the same time some real cut-throat business was conducted with consequences for anyone who didn't follow the rules! The symbolic relations of gift with their association with honour and debt are well suited to the *Bund* form that requires, self-conscious, ritualized and symbolic practices of group maintenance that counterpose with more contractual relationships.

As well as being invested with the symbolism of gift, these *Bünde* are also the sites of re-skilling, what Giddens, in another context called the 're-skilling of everyday life' (Giddens, 1990). While the activities, notably the commercial activities of these *Bünde*, may appear disorganized, ill-conceived, they have spawned both directly and indirectly a whole host of subsequent commercial practices. Magazines, pamphlets, craft skills, musical and other entertainment skills, skills derived from living on the road – vehicle maintenance, skills in seasonal labour. Although not directly related to the travellers, holistic medicine, therapies, New Age and occult shops it can be argued are all in some way related to such one-time counter-cultural, *Bund*-like activities, of which the travellers are just one of the more visible examples.

CONCLUSION

It has been argued here that the ambivalent *Bund*-like sociations produce, in the case of the travellers, a lifestyle and associated set of consumption practices that centre around risk identities; lifestyles that are feared and demonized as Other. Stonehenge represents a symbolic space over which the conflict surrounding this lifestyle is performed. Mediated through the social spatializations of heritage and festival, the symbolic representations become a source of real conflict. I have intended to show how this conflict surrounding Stonehenge can be seen as a symbol of the anxieties associated with modern life, in particular that the creation through processes of consumption of new lifestyles is often highly contested and not always the happy, ludic 'postmodern' game that is sometimes supposed. As a site of mystery its ambiguity attracts all sorts, modern pilgrims, so to speak, all searching for a single truth, and finding sometimes to their horror a heteroglossian babble, a plurivocal noise of assertion and counter-assertion.

But Stonehenge also represents the desires of those who would reject the idea that people should be free to follow their feelings and express themselves through newly created styles of living. It represents the ideal of heritage, of continuity, of a more certain yet threatened singular style of life through a counter-assertion of the power and often naked force of those attached to the belief in the unambiguous bourgeois persona. Heritage represents the desire to control through enclosure, as if by surrounding the stones in razor wire one could impose a single truth upon them, preserve them against the possibility that energy in the form of alternative truths might emanate from them. What is revealed by the events at Stonehenge over the past few years is that conflict has an inherently spatial dimension; use of space is fundamentally a conflict between control through surveillance and the establishment of new lifestyles in the *public* view. In this case the conflict is between heritage as enclosure and festival as opening, between hiding away the expressive and non-rational and celebrating them in public.

In the middle of all this are the travellers and their fellow festival-goers. The ritualized, symbolically mediated, nature of their *Bund*-like sociation finds in practices of consumption (but also art, politics, sexuality and religion) an ideal vehicle and a mode of symbolic expression. It is unwittingly the transitory, creative and yet destructive potential of consumption that so suits the *Bund*. Lifestyles deriving from this form of sociation are short-lived; they provide, as they are transformed, the potential for an intense form of commodification (look at punks for example), while also leaving so much waste behind, a host of discarded lifestyles, fads and fashions. The waste creates horror but the processes involved are transformed. Lifestyles adapt, they become more stable; gift becomes commerce, new skills are produced. Children are now being born into this lifestyle knowing no other. Consumption in this case is more than just shopping, it is a significant feature that helps to provide the stability while a new lifestyle is being created.

NOTES

1 There are a number of pamphlets that provide accounts of events at Stonehenge and the festival. I would like to thank Bruce Garrard of Unique Publications for supplying me with most these. I would also like to thank Alex Rosenberger, Vicki Stangroome, Penny Mellor, Sid Rawle and Alan Lodge for speaking to me about their experiences of the events I have described. They bear no responsibility for any factual errors or misinterpretations that I may have made.
2 As well as Schmalenbach's concept *Bund*, which was developed in response to the group surrounding Stefan Georg and also the German Youth Movement, Gurvitch (1941) and Turner (1969) have also developed similar concepts of 'Communion'. I intend here to produce a synthesis of the three.

REFERENCES

Amirou, R. (1989) 'Sociability/"Sociality" ', *Current Sociology* 37 (1): 115–20.
Bahktin, M. (1984) *Rabelais and His World*, Bloomington: Indiana University Press.
Bauman, Z. (1990) *Modernity and Ambivalence*, Cambridge: Polity Press.
Beck, U. (1992) *Risk Society: On the Way to an Another Modernity*, London: Sage.
Chippindale, C. (1983) *Stonehenge Complete*, London: Thames & Hudson.
Chippindale, C. et al. (1990) *Who Owns Stonehenge?*, London: Batsford.
Clarke, M. (1982) *The Politics of Pop Festivals*, London: Junction Books.
Douglas, M. (1984) *Purity and Danger: an Analysis of the Concepts of Pollution and Taboo*, London: Ark.
Giddens, A. (1990) *The Consequences of Modernity*, Cambridge: Polity Press.
Gurvitch, G. (1941) 'Mass Community and Communion', *Journal of Philosophy* 28: 485–96.

Harvey, D. (1989) *The Condition of Postmodernity*, Oxford: Basil Blackwell.

Hetherington, K. (1990) *On the Homecoming of the Stranger: New Social Movements or New Sociations*, Lancaster Regionalism Group Working Paper 39, Lancaster: University of Lancaster.

Maffesoli, M. (1988) *Les Temps des Tribus*, Paris: Meridians Klincksieck.

Maffesoli, M. (1989) 'The Sociology of Everyday Life (Episemological Elements)', *Current Sociology* 37 (1): 1–16.

Mauss, M. (1969) *The Gift*, London: Cohen & West.

Melucci, A. (1989) *Nomads of the Present*, London: Radius.

Piggott, S. (1985) *The Druids*, London: Thames & Hudson.

Rojek. C. (1988) 'The Convoy of Pollution', *Leisure Studies* 7: 21–31.

Schmalenbach, H. (1977) 'Communion – a Sociological Category', *Herman Schmalenbach: On Society and Experience*, Chicago: University of Chicago Press.

Shields, R. (1991a) *Places on the Margin: Alternative Geographies of Modernity*, London: Routledge.

Shields, R. (1991b) 'The Individual, Consumption Cultures and the Fate of Community', *BSA 1991 Conference Paper. Consumption and the Politics of Identity Stream.*

Simmel, G. (1971) *The Stranger'*, in Simmel, G. *On Individuality and Social Forms*, Chicago: University of Chicago Press.

Simmel, G. (1990) *The Philosophy of Money*, (Second Edition), London: Routledge.

Turner, V. (1969) *The Ritual Process: Structure and AntiStructure*, London: Routledge & Kegan Paul.

Urry, J. (1990) *The Tourist Gaze*, London: Sage.

5

THE INDIVIDUAL, CONSUMPTION CULTURES AND THE FATE OF COMMUNITY

Rob Shields

The changing status of individual identity in the context of consumption cultures and sites such as market squares and the mall environments of shopping centres is explored in this paper based on the experience of a comparative research project.[1] Amidst the slippage of traditional sociological identities and theoretical structures, it is possible to find the less-recognized interstitial persistence of affective communities, based on a basic 'sociability' which Simmel (1950) theorized as *sociality*. This *Einfühlung*, the 'affect' of the sociological categories, persists beyond the usefulness of these concepts and provides an unassuming but powerful basis for *continuing* cultural arrangements despite the rapid change in old identities which has been described as 'postmodernism'. The speculative nature of these comments must be underscored right here at the beginning.

My focus in this paper will be consumption as a form of social exchange through which community, influence and micro-powers (in the Foucauldian sense) are actualized. To the extent that consumption takes on a symbolic role, and to the degree to which commodities become valued for their 'aura' of symbolic meanings and values rather than their use or exchange value, we may speak of a qualitative change in the nature of commodity consumption. Commodities have become 're-enchanted'. In contradiction to Benjamin's thesis (1968), mass-produced commodities have re-acquired an aura of symbolic values. At the same time some of the illusions stressed as essential to the commodity form by Marxist theory, namely the illusory nature of exchange value as 'real value', appear to have dissipated. Many consumers are now ironic, knowing shoppers, conscious of the inequalities of exchange and the arbitrary nature of exchange value. As social actors, they attempt to consume the symbolic values of objects and the mall environment while avoiding the inequalities of exchange. They resort to browsing through stores as a leisure practice, shoplifting, the purchase of cheaper imitations and look-alikes, and by reclaiming the sites of consumption through a crowd practice which returns these (usually private) spaces to the public sphere of market square and street behaviour.

POSTMODERN REGIMES OF VALUE

The contemporary, 'postmodern' moment may be discussed as what I will be calling a new 'regime of value'. As a research hypothesis, postmodernity first evacuates and may eventually replace specific modernist universals of time (cf. Bergson) and space (cf. Mackinder; Harvey, 1987) which were in their time strategic responses but which became reified as universal forms (Shields, 1990; Giddens, 1984). Needless to say, this is not an 'all or nothing' transformation, but has an uneven geography (see Chua, Ch. 6; Clammer, Ch. 10), a disordered history and a fragmented sociology. In the words of Raymond Williams,

> The formulation of the modernist universals is in every case a productive but imperfect and in the end fallacious response to particular conditions of closure, breakdown, failure and frustration . . . from the stimulating strangeness of new and (as it seemed) unbonded social form . . . the supposed universals belong to a phase of history which was both creatively preceded and creatively succeeded . . . it is a characteristic of any major cultural phase that it takes its local and traceable positions as universal. This, which Modernism saw so clearly in the past which it was rejecting, remains true for itself.
>
> (Williams, 1985: 24)

The architectural historian Kenneth Frampton has referred to this same process as 'critical regionalism' (1983). As the universal categories of modernism have run aground on the rocks of difference and localism – which we might define as the move away from transcendental categories and 'grand theory' towards more relative, provisional and strictly bounded theory – there has been a gradual exposure of modernist illusions of presence and absence (see Shields, 1992) and of illusions surrounding language (cf. Saussure), money (cf. Simmel), the commodity form (cf. Marx) and the subject (cf. Freud). We do not have time to delve as deeply as the specificity of each of these forms deserves, but broadly speaking, these institutionalized forms represented the scaffolding of modern political economies,[2] which together formed a peculiarly modern regime of value and practices of valuation. Crucial to this was an emphasis on a logic of *identities* in philosophy, psychology, history and sociology which manifested itself in a stress on periodicization, functional models and analysis, formal logic, and authenticity (Maffesoli, 1990; Prigogine and Stengers, 1988).

Harvey (1987) links postmodernism with the changing social and spatial structures of capitalism, notably the development of global networks of production and new relations of consumption in urban public spaces which double as 'consumption spaces': the market, street vendors, and shopping centres.[3] These emerge as key sites of symbolic consumption as well as of new social movements and groupings whose mixing appears to defy the accepted logic of social classes based on relations to the means of production. These spaces are often privately owned and therefore public only in appearance and in surface texture (Shields, 1989). But this contradiction does not necessarily preclude the operation of private property places as public space. Some private places, such as the mall environments of shopping centres, successfully operate as public spaces and are appropriated by a community as 'theirs' (Brown, Sijpkes and Maclean, 1986; Ploegaerts and Momer, 1989) despite the most draconian regimes of private security. Gottdiener (1986), for example, has demonstrated that mall environments are merely a candy-sweet veil of masking instrumental and exploitative exchange relationships. But this condemnation of the semiotics of decor rests on a dubious dualism which sets up (false) appearances against a hidden, authentic reality rather than examining the seamless interconnection and depthless mutuality of images and social action.

COMMODITY CONSUMPTION AND SOCIAL EXCHANGE

Retail capital has always had a heavy burden of 'latent social functions' (Fowler, 1988) which envelope the exchange of commodities in social practices and rituals of commensality for both vendor and buyer. Yet, there is little *critical* sociological work on retail which takes this into consideration. Even when not character-ized by personal relationships of patronage of a store over long periods of time by customers, shopping for goods remains a social activity built around social exchange as well as simple commodity exchange. Consider the impersonal setting of a shopping mall where one usually deals not with owners but with clerks who are strangers and will remain so and will probably never be encount-ered again. Even here a purchase involves a codified social exchange with persons who are both temporary assistants and more long-term representatives of a store and its owner (see Chua, Ch. 6). There are pro-forma greetings and salutations, a banal, Goffmanesque (1963; 1973) interaction between scripted roles of shop assistant and the shopper – a shopper who may or may not become a purchaser.

The ambivalence of the shopper role is telling. Being a shopper is usually assumed to be synonymous with being a purchaser. Yet, often shopping does not involve purchase, which is merely one event which may or may not culminate the shopping process. For example, one may simply look or browse; goods on display invite the touch. Shopping, in this second usage, refers to a process, a social practice of exploration and sightseeing akin to tourism.[4] This process may take the form of an extended period of browsing, perhaps in more than a dozen stores, legitimized by an insignifi-cant purchase, or even that faintly frustrated feeling of unfulfilled desire. This activity takes on leisure forms as window-shopping and browsing. In this 'just looking' type of shopping, sampling, non-rational spontaneous purchases and the crowd practice of these 'public' spaces are the most important elements. On the other hand, to purchase too speedily is to relinquish a certain freedom of choice in the arena of consumer choices, possibly regret-ting a hasty decision later. Purchase also moves one to the extinc-tion of one's relationship with shop assistants as these servants become agents of an Other, the owner or store chain, or as a persona of eager expertise is dropped in favour of a hard-nosed concentration on verifying one's payment.

The broader, latent, social function of retail returns us to the historic importance of the market-place as a meeting-place, a site of communication and social exchange which often transcends the limits of propinquitous community. 'Market days', for example, have long been social occasions. The same has been true of stores. In nineteenth-century Canada, the rural post office usually took the form of a general store where both food and dry goods of all kinds were sold. These stores, complete with their benches and pot-belly stove, were the locus of weekday community interaction of residents of the surrounding region, complemented by the church and the male preserve of the barber's shop.

In the current-day context, this 'latent social function' continues to exist in the most commercially rationalized shopping centre homogenized by the dominance of chain-stores headquartered elsewhere. The chance meeting of an acquaintance, the tactile but not too physical interaction with a crowd, the sense of presence and social centrality – of something happening beyond the close world of oneself, motivates many who are marginal, alone or simply idle to visit shopping centres as passive observers. Lefebvre (1975), calls this the sense of *social centrality* which characterizes those good public spaces William Whyte calls 'shmoozing' spaces (1980). Lefebvre appropriates Heidegger's metaphor of the bridge or river ford to describe the 'gathering-together-ness' of the act of dwelling in the face of the diffuseness of the world (1981). Public spaces, and ultimately the urban as a whole is defined by this sense of social centrality: a wilful concentration which creates a node in a wider landscape of continual dispersion. Our experience of mall environments or of market squares as sites of social centrality is generally not coded into a phenomenological language, yet the observation holds true. For example, men claim to be 'checking out the crowds,' and women, 'seeing what's "in" style'.[5] It is the character and 'texture' of the gathering that fascinates people.

The 'crowd practice' of social centrality is supported by two factors. First, it is engaged in by all present whether willingly or unwillingly. Even if anonymously, one is present as part of a crowd, present for others and thus an object of their surveillance, scorn, commentary, cooperation, prejudice and so on. The public nature of a site crowded with other people is inescapable and undeniable. Such is its pervasiveness, immigrants, visible minorities, women or others who lack influence or are objects of vilification or prejudice may avoid all public sites (Gardner, 1982; Walby 1990). Second, the crowd practice of social centrality crosses social divisions. Even in conflict pushed to the extreme of a riotous confrontation of two mobs the sense of both publicness and centrality remains. In such a space, one can intuitively affirm 'this is where it's at', where conflicting views and practices are brought together, centralized in confrontation.

This is not the 'lonely crowd' of Reisman's analysis (1950). Such sites are marked by a performative orientation towards the other reminiscent of Bakhtin's dialogism (1984), but not necessarily including Bakhtin's presumed dialogical ethics which he left implicit in his work on the carnivalesque. After Gurevitch (1990), the interaction in public spaces is actually the product of three interlinked ethical relationships between persons and between groups: ethics of commodities, gifts and dialogues. First, the highly emphasized ethic of commodities focuses on exchange. The other person is an object to interact with. Second, the ethic of the gift highlights two dialectics of freedom and obligation, generosity and self-interest. The 'Real gift is the giving. One gives one's self, that is, gives the *giving* of the thing and not the thing. The thing merely serves as a concretization and a measure of the giving. The dynamic of debt and indebtedness created is a dynamic of giving' (Gurevitch, 1990: 185). The gift is imbued with social and religious elements which highlight social ties, committing a receiver to participate in the connection. A social bond thus becomes the main theme of the social act of gift-giving rather than the interdependent concern with commodities which links sellers and buyers. Third, dialogue also stresses making a social connection for its own dialogic sake. Dialogue has elements of commodity exchange but its ethics resemble the gift: not distributive justice or equity but acknowledgement of the Other as a self with whom a connection is to be initiated and sustained (Gurevitch, 1990: 184) – with whom a conversation is to be kept going or an encounter sustained.

INTO THE HEART OF URBANITY: SOCIAL CENTRALITY

The enclosed mall environment of shopping centres attempts to reproduce the vicarious pleasures of the market square or hall, presenting itself as the continuation of the tradition of such public spaces. This is more than a simulated sense of social centrality – of being the 'heart of urbanity'. These people, so-called 'shoppers' but in reality a heterogeneous crowd with diverse purposes, are not actors paid to simulate the interaction of a public space. They cannot be denigrated by ascetic sociologists as pseudo-actors. While an urban built-environment can be simulated in plaster board and plastic, social centrality only occurs if a space is appropriated as public by people.

104

A shopping centre is 'analysable', then, according to its purely political-economic function of the property circuits of capital intersecting with global commodity-exchange relations (Gottdiener, 1986). However, a less Cartesian approach reveals that the factor which accounts for the success of shopping centres is their development as sites of social centrality. A less fragmented approach to the subject reveals that commodity exchange is more thoroughly than ever interlaced with symbolic and dialogical elements. Shopping and other consumption activities were considered under categories of convenience, proximity and rational economic choice especially from the 1950s through the 1970s. Such analyses lead to the construction of suburban 'strip malls' oriented to automobile-born shoppers desiring choice amongst a range of shops but easy and convenient access with the rapid completion of their shopping task the goal. But, as in Benjamin's portrait of the nineteenth-century arcades (1989), commodity exchange and its sites are again at the heart of what we have called social centrality, above. Shopping centres have mutated away from the heyday of convenience shopping. This change is an important development in regimes of value as private property adopts the guise of public space and then takes over its social roles.

So essential is social centrality to commercial success that social centrality is cultivated by shopping centres. This suggests that rather than being a latent function of retail, retail is one form of exchange among several. Perhaps exchange and consumption are latent functions of social centrality. Thus shopping centres attempt to capture community events (sponsoring jazz festivals, charity fund-raising events, community bake sales) and to insert themselves into the cyclical time of the calendar of seasons (e.g. fall sales, 'Winter Madness') and feast days (children's Santa Claus at Christmas, Mother's Day, Valentine's). The commercialization of these events and periods proceeds hand in hand with the attempt of shopping centres to gain an identity on the basis of locality. They are often named after the place – 'Such-and-such Town Centre – encouraging locals to identify with and patronize 'their' mall. In recently constructed North American suburbs, malls which foster community events actively build this sense of locality, bringing, in the words of one developer's handbook, a 'sense of place to a placeless environment' (Dawson and Lord, 1983).

AND THE HEART OF COMMUNITY: FORMS OF SOCIALITY

While 'social centrality' describes the site, the basic experience which is amplified and concentrated in such spaces is more sociologically described by Georg Simmel and Max Scheler (Scheler, 1960: 464–72, cited in Amirou, 1988: 115) as 'sociality', the *glutinum mundi* and connecting tissues of everyday interaction and cooperation. Sociality is as old as people living together but is not simply Tönnies' *Gemeinschaft*, which is one organization of sociability and social communion which sociality may take (Tönnies, 1957). Neither is this merely 'friendship' – a type of social communion which forms unstable groups, or '*Bünde*' – a category which Schmalenbach pointed out is neglected in Tönnies' dualist typology of *Gemeinschaft and Gesellschaft* (Schmalenbach, 1977). Under modernity, all forms of sociality were disciplined under a regime of rationality and utility. Sociality was banished into the realm of private life (in the form of privatized leisure and sociability), the domestic (part of 'family life'), or as women's activity in public (as gossip, window shopping). The public sphere was purified as a new '*res publicans*' – the space of the *pubes*, of men and above all rational men who constructed in their image the notion of the 'reasonable man' of civic law and practice (Landes, 1988; see Walby, 1990).

Sociality accounts for the maintenance of an atmosphere of 'normality', even in the midst of personal antagonism or tensely obvious structural divisions along lines of gender, race, class or even style. Thus it is that one might interact politely (but coldly) with a rude stranger while suppressing the desire to hit him or her. Sociality is the duplicitous foundation for our self-inscription into disadvantaged positions and groups. It is the ironic, complicitous silence of the oppressed. But sociality also refers us back to the power of the collective, the sense of being together, the urge to 'get by' and the injunction 'to get along together'. Durkheim builds his notion of a 'conscience collective' or collective soul on this basic sociality. Despite the institutional structures and power of 'society', there remains a basic 'sociality', an affirmative power that restates the never-ending game of sociability, of solidarity and of reciprocity, and which anchors a sociology of everyday life (Maffesoli, 1988). By contrast with the legalism of society depending on clients, blood and family ties, sociality represents a primordial social effervescence which is unifying, anonymous and incorruptible (Maffesoli, 1978a, in Amirou, 1988:116).

Sociability is often defined as a group 'ethos', a community's manner of relating to the wider whole, and by this whole, of locating itself in time and space. In this 'ethos' (Maffesoli, 1988) the polyvocality and heteroglossia of individual opinions are wilfully suppressed or tempered by individuals anxious to belong above all else; to 'fit in' rather than to stand out as opinionated or idiosyncratic (this complex point is argued in Shields, 1990: 230).

THE SUBJECTS OF SOCIALITY:
FROM INDIVIDUAL TO PERSONA

One tends to forget that the modern individuality so beloved of intellectuals from the Enlightenment onwards is a one-sided ideal type. In its place, sociality exposes plural subjects who duplicitously drop their individuality to adopt a *persona* which allows convivial interaction with a given group at a given time and place. This is more than a 'façade', it is a mask (*persona*), and like all masks has transformative possibilities for the subject, allowing them to 'become', in this case not someone else, but themselves. The strategy of the engaged, continuously re-created and situationally rooted persona allows one to play one's role in a given group. However, one's persona is not freely created but more often imposed by a group. While persona has irresistible strategic possibilities for the individual in this situation, there is a two-way street of tactics and stereotyping which forces identification on to a person. Foucault identified this as the operation of micro-power which charges everyday life (1980). Power creates a nearly magnetic field of legitimated influence and allegiance, hierarchical order, poles and attractions out of the limitless possibilities and the fluid *Gestalt* of sociality. As one often says without too much thought, we 'wear many hats'. As this idiom implies, we change amongst a veritable *dramatis personae* of masks. Each momentary identification corresponds to a role in a given social 'scene' – a scene dominated by a group and the group ethos.

As part of a more general process characteristic of the 'postmodern condition', an epistemological order of identities, of the *individuum*, is replaced by a superficial, tactile *logic of identification*, of the *persona* (Maffesoli, 1990). Baudrillard (1983) and some other theorists such as Kroker and Cook (1988) have argued that all that remains is 'bodies', fractal entities, which are only 'tattooed' with a fictive individuality, defying entropy in a dis-ordered cultural space (Serres, 1982). But this highly abstract notion of the subject can never be more than transitory. Rather than the bedrock of subjectivity, the body, itself unqualified, is unstable and never left exposed and without an identity. The body in Baudrillard's theoretical speculations represents only the unmasked *persona*, stripped of powers and disempowered: artificially frozen in the interstitial moment between identifications.

TRIBES IN MALLS: THE FORM OF COMMUNITY

We might expand our argument with Maffesoli's further hypothesis that, in such (consumption) spaces of social centrality, the proliferating contacts of sociality do not simply produce a homogeneous mass. While the status of the individual is eroded in favour of the group, beyond the Reismanian vision of a faceless mob of anonymous strangers, the participants are granted their own unique identifications in lieu of individualistic identities. Personas are 'unfurled' and mutually adjusted. The performative orientation toward the Other in these sites of social centrality and sociality draws people together one by one. Tribe-like but temporary groups and circles condense out of the homogeneity of the mass (Maffesoli, 1988; 1990). Schmalenbach (1977) is the seminal theorist of these '*Bünde*', an unstable middle form between *Gemeinschaft* and *Gesellschaft* which, in the 1920s, he predicted would characterize the period of the decline of postmodernist universals (Hetherington, 1990). Sociality, grounded in the sociability of everyday life, becomes the basis on which new affectual communities constitute themselves. The impulse of sociality founds class coalitions at the local, neighbourhood scale, affectual cliques and clubs: a chain-reaction of neighbourhoods, counterspaces, heteronymies, local 'tribes' (Maffesoli, 1988) and transient subcultures which transgress the grid and group divisions of society. The metaphor of the tribe is used here because these groups appear to be marked by their orientation around rituals of inclusion and exclusion, membership and rites of passage rather than legalistic codes of conduct and membership. These affectual cliques are distinguished as much by their transient membership as by their refusal of the 'grand narratives' of hegemonic ideologies and their embrace of the 'local authority' of what is 'close to home', based on local territoriality; dependable and micro-social (Shields, 1992). It has been proposed that such group-ings anchor the so-called 'new' social movements (Melucci, 1988) which often attempt to occupy precisely these urban consumption spaces (for example, attempting to picket in shopping malls with resulting conflicts over their status as private property).

LIFE AFTER POSTMODERNITY: THE FATE OF COMMUNITY AND OF FRIENDSHIP

However, according to one group of postmodern theorists, under such conditions of erosion of individual identities, community identity or the closure of insiders against outsiders become difficult: if the self is an empty sign, then companionship as reciprocity is cancelled out by the radical isolation of these depthless souls (Kroker and Cook, 1988). How can there be 'friendship' as we know it, between anything but discrete individuals? Further, can there be 'community' without the modernist universals underlying the old divisions between insiders and outsiders – divisions which turned on 'bindings of space and time' such as class structures? It thus becomes important to account for and explain why people bother to continue congregating in public spaces, shopping centres, or market squares. Is the entire postmodern thesis wrong or merely parts of it? Also, the remaining popular ideologies of individualism and privatism become very problematic for any serious 'postmod-ern sociology'.

The answer may turn on the repressed nature of social central-ity, of sociality and its spaces, such that they were not recognized under modernity. Such sites have *always* been important, despite the sociospatial process known as *modernization*, which recoded space as property – a part of the capitalist system of exchange values which inhibited the growth of attachment and community sentiment which might have formed an alternative system of social-ity or emotional community (Weber's *Gemeinde*) outside of the system of structured and policed grid-group relations of society (Lefebvre, 1972; 1981). Yet the banishment of sociality to the private and domestic, was never complete. It continued to thrive in the interstitial, unrationalized spaces such as the old market-places and, in North America, fairgrounds, which, although obedi-ent to the rule of commodification, retained elements of an older freedom in their disorderly bustle. Hence the association of market-places and carnivalesque inversions of social norms, and the persistence of 'free speech', which Bakhtin terms 'billingsgate' after the old London market (1984; Stallybrass and White, 1986). As opposed to something new, *post*-modern, sociality and public spaces have thus survived repression under modernity from earlier periods when they were the heart of community life as market and town squares, sites of carnival and of everyday life. Although their specific mode has changed, they have retained a recognizable cultural form. In this sense, the spaces of community, of sociality are *trans*-modern, having existed before, during, and after modernity.

In the current context, shopping is more clearly than ever far more than commodity exchange. The latent social functions of retail capital and retail institutions such as the shopping-centre move to the foreground, overwhelming the rational pursuit of commodities. Once one is in the shopping scene, usually for initial 'rational' reasons, non-rational (but not irrational) browsing, touching, lingering, impulse buying and detours to look at the latest fashion on display are the rule. The proof of this lies in the fact that shopping malls have become *de facto* community centres and that markets have become tourist sites – not just for sightseeing but for the taste of exotic food, their odours, cries and shouts and tactile experiences of crowds of not only buyers and sellers but of other tourists who attempt to lose their outsider status by entering into the economic exchange process, even if just to buy whimsical souvenirs. Thus, for example, one of the most important tourist activities is shopping. Consumption as commodity exchange hasn't disappeared but it is now less significant in determining the whole 'play' of the scene. This 'tactility' of crowd practice as sociality draws attention to the untheorized aspect of the 'contact' community of the metropolis, of crowds at sporting events, and of the collective euphoria of concerts and popular celebrations, as opposed to the 'contract' community which characterized modern life according to Tönnies (1957). It is necessary to recognize that consumption itself is partly determined by the non-rational, cultural, element of sociality. Shopping is not just a functional activity. Consumption has become a communal activity, even a form of solidarity. Thus there is frustration with shopping centres and department stores and reactions to their failure to deliver on promises of an experience of social centrality.

In this paper I have used a speculative approach to outline a possible re-theorization of the decline of modernist universals as a new regime of value in which mass-produced commodities are re-enchanted with an 'aura' of social symbolism. Consumption, an ambivalent and multi-faceted activity, takes on more and more social functions as a form of sociality. This serves in the reconstruction and realignment community around the tactility of the crowd practices and 'tribal' ethos of the new urban spaces of consumption. *Persona*, a new cultural form of the subject in the postmodern public sphere, names the changeable nature of personal identity which defies formal rationalism and describes the decline of the modernist individual. Nonetheless, it cannot be concluded that we are witnessing or should fear the death of reciprocity, friendship or community. Instead it is only the pain of discarding a modernist regime of value and a logic of identity already laid aside by those who frequent the spaces of sociality.

NOTES

1 This research was made possible by the generous funding of the Social Sciences and Humanities Council of Canada over two years, 1989–91. The further assistance of Lancaster University in the form of a travel grant and hospitality along with the welcome given to me at the Centre d'Etudes sur l'Actuel et le Quotidien, Université de Paris V – La Sorbonne, are also gratefully acknowledged.

2 Often centred on the conquest of the state for one reason or another (see Wallerstein, 1990). From this viewpoint, liberal, conservative and socialist ideologies and agendas may be seen to share in common the conquest of the state power by select groups pressing their interests.

3 For example, in the UK, the MetroCentre, Tyneside, or indeed any one of the multitude of towns and cities vying for the status of sub-regional shopping centres, such as Lancaster and Preston.

4 On the gaze and tourism, see Urry, 1990. On looking and consumption in the context of mens' clothing retail in the UK see Nixon, Ch. 8. See also Finkelstein, 1989.

5 Interview data, gathered in the course of a postdoctoral research fellowship to compare shopping centres and other 'consumption spaces' as sites of cultural change.

REFERENCES

Amirou, R. (1988) 'Sociability/sociality', *Current Sociology*, 36: 115–20.

Anand, R. (1987) *Task Force on the Law Concerning Trespass to Publicly-Used Property as it affects Youth and Minorities*, Toronto: Ministry of the Attorney-General's Office.

Bakhtin, M. M. (1984) *Rabelais and his World*, London: Midland.

Baudrillard, J. (1983) *The Precession of Simulacra*, New York: Semiotexte.

111

Benjamin, W. (1968) 'The work of art in the age of its mechanical reproduction', *Illuminations*, New York: Harcourt.

Benjamin, W. (1989) *Paris, Capitale du XIXᵉ siècle. Le Livre des passages* (tr. J. Lacoste), Paris: Editions du CERF.

Bourdieu, P. (1984) *Distinction: A Social Critique of the Judgement of Taste*, London: Routledge & Kegan Paul.

Brown, D. and Sijpkes, P. (1983) 'The behaviour of elderly people in Montreal's indoor city', *Plan Canada* 23 (1) (June): 14–22.

Brown, D., Sijpkes, P. and Maclean, M. (1983) 'Hanging around the mall. Informal leisure activities of the elderly in the city', *Recreation Canada*, Parks and Recreation Association of Canada: 44–6.

Brown, D., Sijpkes, P. and Maclean, M. (1986) 'The community role of public indoor space', *Journal of Architecture and Planning Research* 3: 161–72.

Carrithers, M., Collins, S. and Lukes, S. (eds) (1985) *The Category of the Person*, Cambridge: Cambridge University Press.

Dawson, J. and Lord, J. D. (1983) *Shopping Centre Development*, New York: Longman.

Finkelstein, J. (1991) *The Fashioned Self*, Cambridge: Polity Press.

Foucault, M. (1979) *Discipline and Punish*, New York: Vintage.

Foucault, M. (1980) *Power/Knowledge*, New York: Pantheon.

Fowler, D. (1988) ' "Centerites", making public use of private property: the case of urban shopping centres', MA thesis, McGill University, Montreal.

Frampton, K. (1983) 'Critical regionalism: towards an architecture of resistance; in H. Forster (ed.) *The Anti-Aesthetic: Essays on Postmodern Culture*, Port Townsend, WA: Bay Press.

Freud, S. (1976) *The Interpretation of Dreams* (ed. A. Richards), Harmondsworth: Penguin.

Gardner, C. B. (1982) 'Analyzing Gender in Public Places', *American Sociologist* 20: 42–56.

Giddens, A. (1984) *The Constitution of Society*, Cambridge: Polity.

Goffman, E. (1963) *Behaviour in Public Places*, Glencoe: Free Press.

Goffman, E. (1973) *The Presentation of Self in Everyday Life*, Woodstock: Overlook Press.

Gottdiener, M. (1986) 'Recapturing the center: a semiotic analysis of shopping malls', in M. Gottdiener and A. P. Lagopolous (eds) *The City and the Sign*, New York: Columbia University Press, 288–302.

Gurevitch, Z. D. (1990) 'The dialogic connection and the ethics of dialogue', *British Journal of Sociology* 41 (2) (June): 181–96.

Harvey, D. (1987) 'Flexible accumulation through urbanization. Reflections on "post-modernism" in the American city', paper presented at an urban and regional studies seminar, University of Sussex, May, mimeo.

Heidegger, M. (1968) 'Building dwelling thinking', in A. Hofstadter (trs.) *Basic Writings of Martin Heidegger*, New York: Academic, 323–39.

Hetherington, K. (1990) 'On the Homecoming of the Stranger. New Social Movements or New Sociations?', Lancaster Regionalism Working Paper 39, Lancaster: University of Lancaster.

King, A. (1990) *Global Cities*, London: Routledge.

Kroker, A. and Cook, D. (1988) *The Postmodern Scene. Excremental Culture and Hyper-Aesthetics*, Toronto: New World Perspectives and Macmillan.

Landes, J. (1988) *Women and the Public Sphere*, Ithaca: Cornell.

Lefebvre, H. (1972) *La Pensée marxiste et la ville*, Paris: Casterman.

Lefebvre, H. (1975) *Le Droit à la ville*, Paris: Editions Anthropos.

Lefebvre, H. (1981) *La Production de l'espace* (2nd edn; originally published 1974), Paris: Editions Anthropos.

Maffesoli, M. (1988) *Le Temps des tribus*, Paris: Méridiens Klincksieck (forthcoming in translation, Sage).

Maffesoli, M. (1990) *Au Creux des apparences*, Paris: Plon.

Mauss, M. (1938) 'Une Catégorie de l'esprit humain: la notion de personne, celle de "Moi" ', in *Journal of the Royal Anthropological Institute* 68.

Melucci, A. (1989) *Nomads of the Present*, in J. Kean and P. Mier (eds), London: Hutchinson Radius.

Ploegaerts, L. and Momer, B. (1989) 'L'Appropriation des espaces commerciaux par les personnes agées', *Metropolis* 87: 31–42.

Prigogine, I. and Stengers, I. (1988) *Entre le temps et l'éternité*, Paris: Fayard.

Reisman, D. (1950) *The Lonely Crowd: A Study of the Changing American Character*, New Haven: Yale University Press.

Schmalenbach, H. (1977) *Herman Schmalenbach on Society and Experience*, (ed. and tr. G. Lüschen and G. P. Stone), Chicago: University of Chigaco Press.

Serres, M. (1982) *Hermes: Literature, Sciences, Philosophy*, Baltimore: Johns Hopkins University Press.

Shields, R. (1989) 'Social spatialisation and the built environment', *Environment and Planning D: Society and Space* 7(2): 147–64.

Shields, R. (1990) *Places on the Margin. Alternative Geographies of Modernity*, London: Routledge.

Shields, R. (1992) 'A Truant Proximity. Presence and absence in the space of modernity', forthcoming in *Environment and Planning D: Society and Space* 10:1.

Simmel, G. (1950) *The Sociology of Georg Simmel*, K. Wolf (ed.). New York: Tree Press.

Stallybrass, P. and White, A. (1986) *The Politics and Poetics of Transgression*, London: Methuen.

Tönnies, F. (1957) *Community and Society. Gemeinschaft und Gesellschaft*, London: Harper.

Urry, J. (1990) *The Tourist Gaze*, London: Sage.

Walby, S. (1990) *Theorizing Patriarchy*, London: Routledge.

Wallerstein, I. (1990) 'Three statist ideologies', unpublished seminar paper presented in the series 'Ideology and the State' organized by E. Balibar and I. Wallerstein at Maison des Sciences de l'Homme, Paris, Jan.

Whyte, W. (1980) *Social Life of Small Urban Spaces*, Washington: Conservation Foundation.

Williams, R. (1985) 'The metropolis and modernism', in E. Timms and D. Kelley, *Unreal City. Urban Experience in Modern European Literature and Art*, Manchester: Manchester University Press, 13–24.

6

SHOPPING FOR WOMEN'S FASHION IN SINGAPORE

Beng Huat Chua

> The surface of the body seems everywhere to be treated, not
> only as the boundary of the individual as a biological and
> psychological entity but as the frontier of the social self as
> well . . . The surface of the body becomes the symbolic state
> upon which the drama of socialization is enacted, and bodily
> adornment becomes the language through which it is
> expressed.
>
> (Turner, 1980: 112)

The convergence of the social and the individual in bodily adornment is conceptualized sociologically in the seminal but somewhat
neglected essay, 'Appearance and the self', by Gregory Stone
(1962). Stone points out that the social self is situationally sustained by the workings of two basic elements, namely, appearance
and discourse. He argues that the best 'guarantee' for meaningful
social interaction is through the situated actors' 'identification of'
and 'identification with' each other in sequential order, for if one
cannot make out the other's identity claim, there can be no identification with the other's identity. The 'identifications of one
another are ordinarily facilitated by appearance and are often
accomplished silently or non-verbally' (Stone, 1962: 90). There is,
therefore, a primacy of appearance over discourse: appearance 'sets
the stage for, permits, sustains, and delimits the possibilities of
discourse by underwriting the possibilities of meaningful discussion' (Stone, 1962: 90).

Appearance is a composite concept that includes all the physical
attributes and movements of the person, namely, (i) the body and
its gestures, and (ii) the transformation of this given physical body
by adornments such as clothes, accessories, and cosmetics. Of the

114

two, the latter may be subjected to a greater degree and ease of manipulation at will. The body itself, of course, has its own qualities of colour, texture, shape and dimension, each with socially acquired meanings. However, the ways in which a given body may be wrapped by different bodily adornments could significantly change the situational assessment of a person's physical attributes by others. Indeed, conceptually one may argue that, once the adornments are identified, the physical body may recede into the background and lose much of its relevance in the ensuing interaction. For example, a person in police uniform is immediately responded to as the embodiment of public authority symbolized by the uniform, rather than the bodily attributes clothed in it.

Uniforms may be extreme in their suppression of the personal attributes of the wearers; a uniform emphasizes the regulatory discipline imposed by uniformity, itself symbolized by the uniform. Usually, the physical attributes of the individual are worked into his or her clothes, using the latter to bring certain features into focus while downplaying or even hiding others, simultaneously (it is in this hiding and showing that clothing fascinates). Hence, within the composite concept of appearance, the easily manipulatable elements have primacy of attention for the individual, and within the manipulatable set, clothes have the central place in contemporary societies.

PROGRAMMING APPEARANCE

The process of putting together the components of appearance is conceptualized succinctly by Stone as 'programming'; one programmes one's appearance according to the identity one desires to project. The programmed appearance is a person's claim to identity, value, mood and attitude; correspondingly, others can dovetail their revue by placing those aspects announced by the former (1962: 92). Stone neglected to mention that this programming is, necessarily, a backstage activity (Goffman, 1959). This point is particularly significant when one considers the intrinsic features of clothing as a means of encoding and communicating information of the self.

First, clothes are presented visually, directly to a potentially infinite audience. Second, this audience is situationally reduced, by an individual, to an anticipated audience for a particular event in which he or she is to present himself or herself. The anticipated

115

audience acts as the significant others to which the individual is oriented; they and the normative nature of the event jointly specify the boundaries of 'appropriateness' for the individual's adornment. The anticipated audience and the event itself help the individual to pre-figure what to wear. Third, the pre-figuring is temporally separate and discrete from the actual display and presentation of the configuration to the actual audience. Fourth, the identity information that is encoded in the configuration is sustained for the entire duration of the event; this is in contrast to discursive information which fades immediately after it is broadcast. Finally, once the programmed configuration is presented, it can be subjected to only very limited modifications, if any. This is, again, in contrast to discursive information which may be subjected to a complex set of corrective procedures.[1]

The above intrinsic characteristics of clothes as a medium of signification and communication make the programming of clothes a risky business. Since the programming time and presentation time are separate and discrete, one must depend entirely on the accuracy of one's anticipation of the audience. Given that the presented configuration can only be subjected to very minor modifications and the non-fading of its message throughout the duration of the event, a mismatch of the anticipated and the actual audience will produce a situation of sustained embarrassment (Silver *et al.*, 1987) for the wearer of 'inappropriate' clothes, the intensity being dependent largely on the seriousness of community sanctions imposed by the clothing code. To avoid embarrassment, individuals programme their clothing configurations daily.

As this pre-figuring is a backstage activity, we are not privileged to making direct observations of the entire process. Discussions in sociology of fashion tend to assume it, and seek confirmation through analysing the already presented adornment or from interviews regarding attitudes toward clothes (Koester and May, 1985; Kroeber, 1957). There is, therefore, a need to devise an unobtrusive observation of this programming process in order better to understand it.

The situation to be observed must possess the situational features of an individual donning clothes to test his or her image against an audience without presentation to the actual audience of a specific event. That is, the audience against whom an individual tests the clothes is different from that which will see the clothes presented. The donning of clothes would, therefore, be

116

purely part of the programming process without courting possible embarrassment because subsequent presentation is forestalled. The one situation that possesses these necessary features which permit observation is when a person is trying on clothes in a shop!

SHOPS AS EXPERIMENTAL STAGES

The shop is a place in which one gets in and out of clothes without incurring any embarrassment. In the shop, clothing is tried on and assessed in terms of its 'fit' with one's self-image and of its 'appropriateness' for situations in which possible purchases may be used as part of a configuration. Just like the dressing-room in the privacy of one's own home, the shop is an experimental stage in which clothing configurations are tried out and changes made. The clothing shop is a 'neutral' space in terms of interactional relevancies. The shopping situation thus provides us with opportunities to observe the programming process, at least partially, because one is not privileged to observe the programming of other accessories of self-adornment.

To study this partial programming process, four weeks of field observation of shopping activities was conducted in four designer-clothes boutiques. The typical characteristics of these premises, as described below, render them a conducive milieu to make close observations. Given the limited floor areas in the shops and the clients' propensity to step out of the fitting room and discuss the outfits with their shopping companions and sales people, the attention of the clients towards the clothes can be observed and their remarks recorded. Before reporting on the observations a methodological note is necessary.

METHODOLOGICAL NOTE

Certain conditions were imposed by the proprietors, lest the research disturb the normal flow of business: no interviews or conversations were to be conducted with the clients, unless the latter inquired directly about my presence; conversations with the sales staff were to focus on clarifications of their job activities and not labour relations, and there was to be no attempt to discover the profitability of the trade. With these constraints, the researcher's role was essentially a passive one; it remained entirely at the observational level and never developed into one of participant. The observational focus was primarily on the actual activities of the sales staff and the customers.

Abstention from conversational engagement with the clients served to reduce my already too intrusive male presence in the small spaces of these premises. This was unavoidable because, given the high rent for these premises, there were no spare spaces in which I could place myself without being seen. Furthermore, the process of shopping for clothes is a rather private affair. Thus any attempt to hide my presence might in fact give rise to more discomforting conjectures than being out where everyone could see. Nevertheless, the observable presence of a male in the shop, scribbling into a notebook, was readily noted by many of the clients and caused sufficient discomfort that they would not step out of the fitting rooms when trying on clothes. Fortunately, all the fitting rooms had mirrors round the four walls and were large enough to accommodate both the client and a salesperson comfortably.

Finally, the wisdom of disallowing conversations with clients was born out in fieldwork, when I inadvertently made a comment which caused a client who was enamoured by an outfit to abandon her desire. Still, absence of interviews with the clients was regrettable. It prevented the discovery of the motivational aspect of their clothing-consumption behaviour.

SETTING AND ROUTINES AT DESIGNER FASHION SHOPS

With mass production, what was once the concern of the privileged is now consumed by everyone. However, the ubiquity of fashion consciousness does not eliminate its class dimension, which lies in the 'differences between the hand-sewn originals and the cavalry of often shoddy copies that followed with varying degrees of loyalty' (Ewen and Ewen, 1982: 181). With the emergence of the middle class in industrialized societies, a new line of clothes has been inserted between the hand-sewn original and the poor imitations, namely, the designer-label ready-to-wear clothes. These are machine-sewn limited editions of original designs produced under the auspices of the design houses. In price they are not exorbitant 'one-of-a-kinds' but, since relative exclusivity within each city is protected by franchise arrangements, they are certainly up-market commodities.

This internationalization of designer clothes is made possible by the low production costs of manufacturing quality garments in newly industrialized countries, particularly Asia (Morawetz, 1981). Their relative affordability, along with international advertising efforts, have made French, Italian, Japanese and American designers' labels, often unpronounceable to the locals of the consuming nations, household names in the entire spectrum of the middle-class, worldwide. Indeed, the names have even penetrated the consumption horizon of the working class, as there are plenty of fakes that bring the 'names' to within their reach, even if they cannot afford 'the real thing'.

Setting

In Singapore, where this research was conducted, the best clothes are often marketed through small shops run by individual entrepreneurs. Such shops are furnished to make shopping comfortable and leisurely. Fashion magazines abound; always the latest editions, and pages where the represented designers' clothes are featured or advertised are tagged to draw the readers' attention. The shops are generally small enough for one to visually take them all in without much effort, even from the outside where all window shoppers are confined.

Indeed, to maintain exclusivity, the shops are 'hermetically' sealed with plate-glass windows and doors. The doors are barriers of intimidation to browsers who cannot afford the high-priced designer items. The setting is intimidating in its emptiness; the emptiness being itself a measure of exclusivity. As soon as one passes the glass doors, one is immediately the centre of attention of the salespeople, for there are generally more staff than clients in the shop and anyone not used to such attention can only respond with nervousness. Occasionally, an inadvertent browser may break the seal and wander into the shop, only to be shocked by the price tags on the display items and beat a hasty retreat out of the shop without uttering a word (Chua, 1990).

The setting is in sharp contrast with the completely permeable wide-open store fronts of self-serve mass marketing – settings in which most people, in Singapore as elsewhere, do their shopping, whether it be fresh produce or clothing. In the latter, browsers and buyers enter and exit at will, pick up, try on and carelessly leaving the items as they please, all without any serious attention from the salespeople who are stationed either at the cash registers or at the front of the rows of fitting rooms, policing against shop-lifting.

Routines

The designer shops are highly staffed and aim to provide indi-vidualized service to every customer. Usually, two salespersons serve one customer: one directly helps the customer with her fit-tings, while the other puts aside the items selected, removes the items found unsuitable, and brings fresh outfits for more fittings. A tailor is at hand when substantial alterations are needed; minor alterations are noted by the salespeople themselves.

The overwhelming majority of the customers are established clients.[2] The regularity with which they come to the shops will astonish anyone unfamiliar with the trade. So regular are their visits that salespeople claim that some come every day; even if this were apocryphal, it nevertheless emphasizes the frequency! So familiar are the clients with the salespeople that the shops are used as meeting places by clients who travel in the same social circles.

Two features of designer-clothes shopping contribute to this high frequency. First is the very nature of fashion itself as a social phenomenon. Fashion in clothes is characterized by constant and rapid changes. To be 'in fashion' requires one to keep pace with these changes ceaselessly; one must vigilantly watch for the latest, make the purchases and wear the clothes before others. All this keeps one returning to the shops.

Second is the set of activities that cumulatively constitute a completed purchase. The activities, of course, start with trying on the clothes. If a suitable item is found, minor alterations are generally necessary, thus another trip to the store is required. If the client has taken her purchase without alteration but changed her mind within days, she might return for an exchange, though refunds are not permissible. If she cannot find suitable items to exchange, a credit will be established for subsequent trips. If she found an item that required alterations, a third trip will then be required, and so on, until suitable clothes are selected and pur-chased. As a result of these purchasing trips which are made in rapid succession and the 'just browsing' trips, one is likely to see the same set of women in the shop with stunning frequency! The frequency also reflects the clients' determination to stay in fashion, which in turn reflects the seriousness with which they treat their appearances.

The bulk of the business is conducted between half-past two and half-past five in the afternoon, a three-hour period between a leisurely lunch and before dinner. Even during these hours, the number of customers is never large. In a shop of four sales-staff, three customers at a time appears to be the limit of service. In a regular work day, more than ten customers will constitute a hectic day for the staff of four because of the extensive time each customer takes to deliberate and make selections.

The time of business and the frequency of trips to the shops also disclose the social status of the clients. According to one proprietor, the clients are 'either self-employed professionals' or 'unemployed', i.e. those who are either born or married rich, or otherwise associated with wealth. The overwhelming majority of the clients observed were non-working wives, with professionals in the distinct minority. This accounted for the activity pattern in the shops: the three-hour period in the afternoon in which the need to engage in housekeeping activities is at the lowest.

Now, to the observations.

THE IMAGINED STAGE

Appearance is always appearance on stage. The shop, as suggested, is suitable as an experimental stage to don and doff different configurations. For it to be so used successfully, one must be able to conjure up the plausible occasions in which a particular configuration could be outstandingly, or at least appropriately, presented. Details of each imagined stage vary; if one were shopping for an outfit for a specific event, then the details could be quite particular. For example, a casino evening on a holiday cruise will have its established conventions of glitter and slinky glamour.

However, more often than not, a client shops without a particular occasion in mind. The imagined stages are thus left in very general outlines, especially when shopping for the less formal outfits. Components of these generalized stages are reflected in the limited vocabulary of the shoppers and the salespeople to categorize the clothes. This consists of two variables, namely, (i) degree of formality of the possible events, and (ii) the time of the day during which these possible events are likely to take place. The

Formality

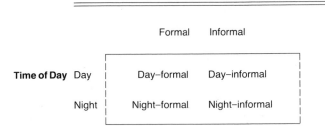

Figure 6.1 Components of the categorization of clothes

time of year, i.e. the fashion season, is taken for granted because these clients shop only 'in season'.[3] These two variables can be represented diagrammatically as shown in Figure 6.1.

The resulting four combinations not only serve to categorize the clothes but also describe the occasions, or stages, in which the clothes can be deemed appropriate. For example, a night-formal dress is for a night-formal event. The restricted vocabulary is thus functional in that it provides for generalized and simplified, imaginable stages that can accommodate many unspecified actual occasions.

Substantively, day-formal and night-informal wear overlap; hence office clothes can slide into after-work dinner engagements. As the following generic statement from a fashion magazine suggests:

> The day is not always predictable and you can never say at the beginning of it what surprises could be in store. Hopefully they are pleasant surprises, such as an invitation for a night on the town. Today's dressing allows you to set out for the office in the morning wearing an outfit that, come evening, is glamorous enough to take you on into the night.

On the other hand, day-informal and night-formal are diametrically at opposite ends in cut, material and detailing.

Such a simplified frame for the classification of clothes and their appropriateness on plausible occasions is a reflection of the relative openness of the dress code in contemporary society where sumptuary laws have all but disappeared. Ours is a situation in which ranks and stations are no longer built into the clothes one wears

(Wilson, 1985) with the exception of military and paramilitary uniforms. Thus, while clothes can still be used to carry signs and expressions of purchasing power of the wearer, no established sumptuary authority is in the position to dictate what another may wear, such is the nature of fashion democracy. In terms of social norms, our dress codes are characterized largely by 'may' rules rather than 'must' or 'shall' rules (see Enninger, 1985: 95).

This absence of strict clothing regulations is both the result and, in turn, the reinforcement of two developments in the social conventions of fashion. First, fashion in contemporary society is no longer simply dictated by the fashion tastes of the elite as in the seventeenth, eighteenth and nineteenth century.[4] This challenges the traditional sociological theory of fashion (Simmel, 1904) which argues that the elite's styles automatically acquire prestige in the eyes of the lower class, who in turn seek to emulate the former, thus forcing the elite to devise yet new ways to distinguish themselves and resulting 'in an incessant and recurrent process of innovation and emulation' (Blumer, 1969: 278).

From empirical observation of the fashion trade in Paris, Blumer suggests that the elite themselves are immersed in fashion and are thus responding to its direction in contemporary society. Furthermore, the early 1960s saw 'probably the first time in the history of fashion that the expensive clothes have been influenced by the cheap' (Amies, 1964: 351).[5] The elite have been replaced by the buyers for retailers who, as Blumer points out, are 'the unwitting surrogates of the fashion public' (1969: 278). This observation is supported by that of the British couturier, Hardy Amies:

> I must also emphasize here the all-important influence of the buyer, for she usually is the filter through which fashion passes. She must buy what she thinks she can sell rather than what she personally likes or what she personally believes in.
>
> (1964: 349)

This development reflects the importance of the consumers' preferences.

Fashion freedom is carried further by a second development. Since perhaps the 1950s, intentional breaking of the already loosely maintained dress code is often practised by individuals or identifiable groups as a fashion statement. If the vocabulary of such anti-fashion statements caught on, then it might produce its own

123

conventions. Anti-fashion thus cannot escape the processes of fashion itself (Wolfe, 1973; Konig, 1973: 198–208). Thus, situationally 'inappropriate' clothes may be at least tolerated if a deliberate intent can be ascribed to the wearer. It is, however, difficult to distinguish inappropriate configuration from intentional code-breaking. It is, therefore, possible for an individual to 'pass off' an inappropriate configuration for an intentional statement and sustain a personal-identity claim as one who desires to maintain a distance from the audience and a critic of the conforming tendencies of the others.

In general, the expressive element of clothes in a personal-identity claim must deviate from the socially, situationally appropriate clothes in either of two ways. First, the clothing items may be marked deviations from the socially established patterns of clothing repertoire, as in outrageous anti-fashion. As Enninger points out, 'Unlike ill-formed sentences which lose part or all of their meaning, ill-formed clothing configurations are interpretable as lexical individualizers' (1985: 92). Second, the clothing items may be individualizers who nevertheless stay within the limits of conventional clothing behaviour. An example would be the way a tie serves as an individualizing marker in the uniform garbs or executives (Gross and Stone, 1964: 4). Most individuals tend to stay within the loosely formulated dress code and distinguish themselves with individualizing items. Thus the increasing consciousness of accessories in a complete image.

The loose formulation of the dress code and the possibility of passing off everything that one wears as individualizers combine to enable the drastic simplification of imagined occasions into the above four plausible situations, when trying on clothes in a shop.

THE AUDIENCE

If the stages are wholly imaginary, not all the possible audiences are absent; some of them are present in the shop, namely, the client herself as an audience, her shopping companions and the salesperson. However, these individuals do not exhaust the list of audiences that a clothes-buyer responds to. In addition to them are the socially relevant others who, although situationally absent from the shop, are nevertheless taken into consideration by those who are present. The absent others include both concrete individuals in the client's daily life and, at a more abstract level, the significant others who may be co-present when a configuration of purchased items is actually presented. As will be shown, these significant others are expressed through a concern with the norms of propriety with regard to the clothing configurations in question.

The audience can, therefore, be divided into two groups, namely, those co-present with the client and those who are absent from the shop. The interactional relevance of the two groups is different. As the following field observation will demonstrate, the former group may be said to play essentially an evaluative/supportive role to the client's decision about the suitability of a particular configuration, whereas the latter play an evaluative/inhibitive role.

THE AUDIENCE AT HAND

Self as audience

The absence of a stringent dress code reinforces the donning of clothes as an act of self-expression, including the choice to suppress overt individuality and express group solidarity in one's attire. 'What should I wear this morning?' is always the first existential question one must face daily, so long as there is more than one possible configuration of clothes in the closet. As a medium of self-expression, the clothes one purchases and wears must, above all other considerations, 'fit' one's own self-image. This self-image is, of course, the result of looking at oneself as the other, materially reflected in the ubiquitous mirrors at the shop. The self is, therefore always the first audience that must be satisfied. This self-referencing is captured in the psychoanalytic understanding of fashion consciousness as a symptom of narcissism – 'the tendency to admire one's own body and display it to others, so that these others can share in the admiration' (Flugel 1950: 86).

At the shop floor, this 'self as audience' is observable in two ways. First, it is the absolute conviction of salespeople that each client has her own 'style and taste'. They are convinced that 'once you know a client's taste, selling clothes is very easy'. The mark of a good salesperson is thus the ability to read a client's style and make the appropriate suggestions. That salespeople do read their clients' styles with some accuracy is reflected in their work. One of the salesperson's responsibilities to a client is to inform and to hold in reserve new arrivals that are within the latter's style. This gives the client a first chance to try out the clothes, if she declines to buy, the new clothes are then placed on general display. Should the salesperson fail in helping the client to stay ahead in the competition – an essential feature of fashion – she is liable to be subjected to the client's displeasure and complaint. This reflects the social inequality between salesperson and client – the responsibility of one is the privilege of the other.

Second, no matter how 'new' is the style or how interesting the detailing, a client will not make a purchase unless the item fits their self-image. For example, many Singaporean men past their mid-30s, especially those who are less western-educated, have a definable shirt vocabulary: tight-fitting, very lightweight, even see-through fabric although the middle-age thickening of the waist may have set in. Accustomed to such a sartorial idiom, many are unable to 'see' themselves in loosely cut, heavier-weight designer shirts of cotton or linen. During one fieldwork occasion, a woman client had bought a shirt for her male friend whose clothing sense fitted the above description. The couple returned to the shop for an exchange because the shirt was 'too big'. He went through the entire range of men's shirt selection in the shop with consistently the same 'too big' complaint. He was deaf to the girlfriend's and the salesperson's encouragements and compliments and their insistence that loose cut is the 'look' and essence of designer shirts. The occasion was particularly telling in that the cost element was already eliminated because the shirt was a gift, and the 'in-fashion' feature of the shirts was guaranteed. The securing of these two elements served to emphasize the primacy of self-image over economic and design considerations.

Salesperson as audience

The salespeople have an important institutionalized place in the social organization of fashion. 'Their job is to interpret the couturier's idea, as demonstrated in the Collection and to supervise the fittings of the customer' (Amies, 1964: 346). In the ready-to-wear trade the salesperson's position is not as weighty as in *haute couture*, although her role of interpreting or instructing the client on the proper way of wearing an outfit remains as part of her relation to the client.

As mentioned earlier, the salespeople believe that understanding clients' style is essential to selling clothes. This is a distilled understanding which enables a salesperson to recognize when a new configuration is 'within the style' of a particular client, even before the latter has seen the clothes. She is, therefore, not only an audience *in situ* at the shop but also a 'gate-keeper' of the client's clothes closet, so to speak.

The salespeople have yet another obligation. They must gain knowledge of the social circle that a client might travel in, amongst those who shop at the shop. It is their responsibility to inform the client when a member of the social circle has bought similar outfits so as to prevent two clients from turning up at the same occasion in the same clothes, an unacceptable and most embarrassing fashion happening, in which difference is the norm. Any embarrassment caused would be blamed on the salesperson. This particular responsibility of the salesperson may be in part a result of the smallness of the client base of the high-fashion boutiques; consequently, it is possible for the salesperson to keep track of purchases made by different individuals in the fixed stable of clients (Chua, 1990). However, if a client insists on making a purchase after having been duly informed, the salesperson is then absolved of future blame. Presumably, the clients will coordinate their dressing so as to avoid possible embarrassment.

Obviously, given the pecuniary interest of the salesperson, since her income is dependent on sales commissions, she would certainly play the role of supportive audience to the client. Nevertheless, the salesperson would not support every enthusiastic choice of a client. She will have reservations about certain selections precisely because of her own financial interest. Hers is a long-term interest that benefits from a client's sustained and repeat purchases. For this relationship to last, the client must be able to count on the salesperson's presumed professional judgements. An inappropriate selection could be blamed on the salesperson, terminating future transactions and bringing the latter's professionalism into doubt, and, along with it, shaking the salesperson's self-esteem in her job. This is a significant difference from the mass-marketing context in which every sale is a one-off exchange with no considerations for future purchases.

'Hard sell' is, therefore, not permitted in the designer-clothes shop. Consequently, new sales-staff are repeatedly reminded to tone down their sales enthusiasm. Reservations, i.e. negative assessments, must be made. In order not to offend the client's self-esteem by casting aspersions on her choices, the interactional strategy most used by salespersons as a gloss over their reservations is to express preferences for a configuration over the ones in question. There is, therefore, an evaluative role for the salesperson and its efficacy should not be overlooked.

Shopping companion as audience

As mentioned earlier, clients are often accompanied by others. While the salesperson has to dress up her negative comments, the companions tend to offer their comments more freely. The significance attached by the client to these comments depends entirely on the social relationship she has with the companion, i.e. a reflection of the companion's status as an audience to the client's self-image. Three categories of companions have been observed at the shop.

First, it sometimes happens that the person(s) with whom a client arrives at the shop is not her shopping companion. Rather, for some other reason, they happen to be together when the client decides to drop into the shop. Such 'incidental companions' are immediately identifiable by the sartorial difference between them and the client. Understandably, such companions' comments are completely irrelevant, if offered at all, because she is 'not in the know' about fashion. This is often disclosed by the companion herself through aghast expressions when informed of the prices in the shop. One illustrative observed instance involved a client in her mid-20s with a middle-aged lady. The latter was so stunned by the US$250 price tag on a white shirt that she could not suppress her remarks, 'You've got to be out of your tree. Who would know where you buy your clothes from?!'

Second, the proper shopping companion of a client is readily identifiable by the compatible attire between them. In such instances, the latter's opinions are treated as informed opinions. This can be quickly confirmed. Her comments are not restricted to the 'fit' of the configurations tried on by the client but include other relevant immanent features such as form, texture and detailing and, furthermore, an ability to make comparative references to other pieces of clothes either of the same designers, or other designers, or which the client has in her possession. Such companions have intertextual knowledge with reference to clothes and their critical comments are often heeded.

Significantly, in the shopping instance, the commonly repeated sentiment that competition is the essence of fashion is not mani-

festly observable. Instead, the shoppers are mutually very supportive and the companions readily turn clients themselves. It is
common for all the women shopping together to be trying on
clothes and making their purchases in the same shop.

The incidental and the explicit companions tend to be women.
The third category of companion is the male friend or husband of
the client who either abstains from or partakes actively in the
selection of clothes. In either case, his comments are always
sought, whether he is knowledgeable about fashion or not. He
tends to provide minimalist comments of either agreement or dis-
agreement with 'the look' of the configuration on the client. These
comments almost always amount to the decision to make or decline
to purchase. One may say he has a veto power over the client's
decisions. The weightiness of the minimalist comment is due in
part to the fact that it is often he who pays the relatively hefty
bill. For the concerns of this essay, what is more significant is that
he is most likely the one to be seen next to the client when the
latter presents her purchased configuration in an event with audience. During such occasions, it is thus as much the presentation
of himself as that of the client. In this light, his sanctions might
be seen as more collaborative than judgemental, or worse, a mere
power play. However, that there is an element of power in the
purse strings cannot be denied as we shall see when we consider
the abstract audience, i.e. those not present at the shop but whose
opinions must be considered.

THE AUDIENCE IN ABSENTIA

Arbiter as audience

One common practice in the boutiques is that clients sometimes
make purchases on 'approval' basis. As the name implies, approval
is being sought from someone not present and the latter's decision
is final. Although no specific person may be named in such
instances, there is no doubt that he or she is the one who holds
the purse strings. The latter's status as the significant audience
means that his or her absence must be ratified by the private
showing. Since the overwhelming majority of the clients are housewives, it is generally assumed that the husband's approval is the
final arbiter. Evidence supporting this assumption is available on
the shop floor, where it is common to hear clients hankering after

certain outfits but lamenting that unfortunately their husbands did not like them. Furthermore, as observed above, whenever a woman is shopping with her husband, his approval is invariably sought and his decision is final, unless he leaves the room for the woman to exercise her choice.

Since the process of seeking approval is done in the privacy of the client's home, the actual interactional exchanges that lead to a decision are not observable. We may, nevertheless, identify the different rational basis that each party may assume for this unseen interaction. On the client's part, the husband's approval is sought as the final decision to ratify her own choice in deference either to his position as the financial provider who pays for the clothes, as most of the clients are not employed wives, or to his 'taste' because he is the one most likely to be seen with her when the outfit in question is donned. On his part, however, the decision is not necessarily based on financial considerations for it is assumed that he can afford the prices. Thus, one may suggest that his decision would rather be based in part on whether he likes 'the look' of the outfit on his wife. As such, he is then the *arbiter elegant* – a judge of elegance and matters of taste – with particular reference to his wife's appearance. In this subjective judgement, he may or may not be technically knowledgeable about fashion but, as the saying goes, 'he knows what he likes'.

In addition, as suggested earlier, the wife's self-presentation is as much the husband's own self-presentation, and vice versa; on the occasions when they are seen together, he may also consider the appropriateness of the outfit for the society in which they are expected to circulate. This may be the reason why the wife seeks his agreement in the first place. If so, the approval process is, again, more a conscious effort to be collaborative as a husband-wife team than one of a subordinate seeking dispensation from the dominant partner, although the latter consideration cannot be entirely absent if the wife is financially wholly dependent.

Whatever the basis of his judgement, and of the judgement itself, conceptually the husband's approval plays an evaluative/inhibitive role in the purchasing decision. It is inhibitive because the client, having already decided that she likes the clothes, is necessarily oriented towards the possibility of his disapproval, although a positive judgement remains possible. Indeed, one may suggest that she would have sensed that disapproval was a distinct possibility in the first instance; otherwise, she could have acted on her own and trusted that the husband would accept her choice.

Propriety as audience

If the private negotiations between a client and her husband as audience cannot be observed directly, the evaluative sanctions of the society can be readily discerned in the attention to 'social propriety' in the discussions and decisions to purchase. This attention is oriented to a sense of the 'generalized others' as audience. Rather than a concern with only the evaluations of the audience present at a specific occasion, this is a concern with the infinity of possible audiences who may perchance see the client in the clothing configuration in question.

As social propriety is culture-bound, it is shaped by the general norms of its society. The Asian cultures that constitute multi-ethnic Singapore have strong normative sanctions against overt exposure of the body. For example, Malay women will swim in the sea fully clothed, and the two-piece swimsuit is still uncommon on Singapore's beaches, although increasingly used among those below thirty years of age. Clothes that even suggest exposure will therefore generally be avoided. Consequently, clothes that must be worn bra-less, although ubiquitous in contemporary designs, are generally shunned. For example, in a line of design that is popular with the clients, every variation of the line will be sold quickly except the one that has a deep cut in the back so that no bra can be worn. This avoidance is even more intensely observed when it comes to skirts. For example, many clients tried and were enamoured by an evening dress with an unlined bronze-coloured organza skirt that was cleverly folded with only hints at exposure, but none would buy it. As a norm, avoidance of exposure operates across all age groups. It plays a significant part in determining the fashion items that are available in the shops, which in turn reinforces the norm itself. Thus, teenagers and mid-20s women will more often than not wear tube-tops with bras. Halter-tops are all but non-existent as a clothing item on this tropical island. A woman in her mid-40s, when shown a bra-less evening dress in a shop, exclaimed, 'I am a mother of four children, not me!' A boutique owner who experimented with bringing in bra-less dresses has decided that the experiments will stop. A buyer for a very successful departmental store says that her first request to any suppliers is, 'No plunging necklines, please!', in spite of the fact that she wears so-called 'daringly cut' dresses herself. Apparently, she accepts that her customers prefer covered-up styles. Yet another salesperson is convinced that Japanese fashions sell well in Singapore because they are generally 'not body-conscious', i.e. they do not show off the curves of the body.

In addition to this anti-exposure norm, the established wisdom regarding fashion adoption, i.e. 'one wants to keep in step with the fashion without being ahead of it' (Konig, 1973: 180), continues to operate as a check on the purchases. Salespeople complain that a new item will sit in the shop until 'it is established' and that the more 'fashion-conscious' pieces are difficult to sell. Such a generalized cautious attitude arises from a concern that the boundaries of good manners in adornment are not transgressed. The avant-garde of fashion pay a price of being 'strange' or 'weird' in the eyes of the majority.

It should be apparent that generalized norms of social propriety have an essentially inhibitive role that significantly checks an individual's clothing adornment. Significantly, although sumptuary authority no longer exists in contemporary society, and fashion freedom appears to be the norm, dress codes have not altogether disappeared. The restrictive function of the dress code has been absorbed by abstract norms of social propriety. However, it should be recognized that by their abstract and generalized quality, these norms inevitably provide for a greater degree of freedom and self-expression in bodily adornment through the use of 'individualizing' items and accessories.

The norms of propriety which serve as the symbolic manifestations of the generalized others complete the list of audiences to which a female fashion shopper will orientate herself in her deliberations when making purchases.

CONCLUSION

Clothes have always been conceived as part of an individual's identity claims. Individuals, therefore, take pains to programme their clothes as part of their appearance. The analytic focus is generally on the clothing configurations that are actually worn by individuals. Direct investigation of the programming activities is made difficult by the fact that it is essentially a backstage activity conducted in the privacy of one's dressing space. It is argued in this essay that a direct access to this programming activity can be gained by analytically treating the fashion shop as a surrogate for the private dressing-room. Conceptually and substantively, trying on clothes in a shop is necessarily part of the programming activity as the decision to purchase is based on the imagined stages and audiences that an individual might have to respond to when a selection of the purchased items are presented as a programme configuration on actual occasions.

Several substantive findings can be drawn from the field observations. First, given the loosely formulated dress codes of contemporary society, the occasions on which clothing configurations can adorn can be generalized into four or even three categories, namely, day/informal, night/formal, day/formal and night/informal events, with the last two being interchangeable. The possible exceptions to this set may be ritual occasions on which a strict dress code may be prescribed. Second, the absence of a strict dress code does not mean the complete absence of inhibition or restrictions of choice of adornment. The inhibitive element is now cast in terms of general norms of social propriety or 'good manners'. Third, within the permissible horizon of propriety, an individual is oriented to a series of audiences, each with a different evaluative status. The first of these audiences is the self. The rest can be broadly grouped into supportive or inhibitive audiences with the spouse of the individual as the primary figure in the latter category. With the assistance of the evaluation assessments of these audiences and the attention to social propriety generally, the chances of an individual appearing inappropriately attired at a specific event are greatly reduced, if not completely eliminated.

To the extent that the prevailing ideology of fashion emphasizes individuality, it may be argued that the above discussions overly privilege the social constraints of fashion choice. A number of points can be raised against the argument: first, the overwhelming majority of the population tends to keep within the loosely defined clothing codes and relies on individualizing items to exercise their fashion freedom and expressions. Second, and more significantly, even those who may be said to have exercised complete freedom in clothes, namely those who use anti-fashion as a fashion statement, must nevertheless be aware of the existing norms of social propriety if only to break them. Between individualizing items and anti-fashion is a wide space for mixing and matching with good manners.

NOTES

1 An extensive list of the semiotic character of clothes is provided by Enninger (1985). Strategies for correcting discursive information is the research terrain discovered by the conversation analysts, whose works are now legend.

2 For a discussion of the processes of becoming a regular client, see Chua (1990).

3 There is a reduced opportunity for observing the influence of seasons in the·imagined stage in the present study because Singapore, where the fieldwork is conducted, is in the tropics and hence not subjected to seasonal changes. However, clients in the shops studied do buy winter clothes for their travels abroad.

4 The decline in the position of the elite was noted by the 1920s by the famous American fashion economist Paul Nystrom. He pointed out in 1928 'What notables wear apparently means less and less to the masses of intelligent fashion-conscious women, unless these same notables are themselves apparelled in the current fashions of the day' (quoted by Brenninkmeyer, 1973: 275).

5 The elite 'trickling down' theory is also challenged by quantitative investigations that show that early adoption of a new style is not limited to the wealthy (see King, 1963 (1973)).

REFERENCES

Amies, H. (1964) 'What makes fashion?', in G. Willis and D. Midgley (eds) *Fashion Marketing*, London: Allen & Unwin (1973), 341–56.

Blumer, H. (1969) 'Fashion: from class differentiation to collective selection', *Sociological Quarterly* 10 (3): 275–91.

Brenninkmeyer, I. (1973) 'The diffusion of fashion' in G. Willis and D. Midgley (eds) *Fashion Marketing*, London: Allen & Unwin (1973), 259–302.

Chua, B. H. (1990) 'Steps to becoming a fashion consumer in Singapore', *Asia Pacific Journal of Management* 7: 31–48.

Enninger, W. (1985) 'The design features of clothing codes – The functions of clothing displays in interaction', *Kodikas/Code* 8: 81–109.

Ewen, S. and Ewen, E. (1982) *Channels of Desire: Mass Image and the Shaping of American Consciousness*, New York: McGraw-Hill.

Flugel, J. C. (1950) *The Psychology of Clothes*, London: Hogarth Press and the Institute of Psychoanalysis.

Goffman, E. (1959) *The Presentation of Self in Everyday Life*, New York: Doubleday Anchor.

Gross, E. and Stone, G. P. (1964) 'Embarrassment and the analysis of role requirements', *American Journal of Sociology* 70: 1–15.

King, C. W. (1963) 'A rebuttal to the "trickle down" theory', in G. Willis and D. Midgley (eds) *Fashion Marketing*, London: Allen & Unwin (1973), 215–27.

Koester, A. W. and May, J. K. (1985) 'Profiles of adolescents' clothing practices: purchase, daily selection, and care', *Adolescence* 20: 97–113.

Konig, R. (1973) *The Restless Image*, London: Allen & Unwin.

Kroeber, A. L. (1957) *Style and Civilizations*, Berkeley: University of California Press.

Morawetz, D. (1981) *Why the Emperor's New Clothes Are Not Made in Columbia*, New York: Oxford University Press.

Silver, M., Sabini, J. and Parrott W. G. (1987) 'Embarrassment: a dramaturgic account', *Journal for the Theory of Social Behaviour* 17: 47–61.

Simmel, G. (1904) 'Fashion', in G. Willis and D. Midgley (eds) *Fashion Marketing*, London: Allen & Unwin (1973), 171–92.

Stone, G. (1962) 'Appearance and the self' in A. Rose (ed.) *Human Behaviour and Social Process*, London: Routledge & Kegan Paul, 86–118.

Turner, T. S. (1980) 'The social skin', in J. Cherfas and R. Lewin (eds) *Not Work Alone*, London: Temple Smith, 112–13.

Wilson, E. (1985) *Adorned in Dreams*, Berkeley: University of California Press.

Wolfe, T. (1973) 'Introduction', in R. Konig, *The Restless Image*, London: Allen & Unwin (1973), 15–28.

7

RITUAL SPACE IN THE CANADIAN MUSEUM OF CIVILIZATION

Consuming Canadian identity

Jill Delaney

INTRODUCTION

The new Canadian Museum of Civilization (CMC) in Hull, Quebec, has been both positively and negatively compared to the Disney World (EPCOT) theme park. With its new emphasis on becoming a popular national attraction of 'infotainment', the CMC has moved the traditional concept of museum more fully into the realm of a place of consumption. This represents a controversial shift in thinking on the role of the (national) museum. The museum represents a new cross-breed in cultural institutions with its attempt at combining entertainment and consumption methods with those more traditionally used in popular museums. This essay will concentrate on the permanent exhibit known as the History Hall, as a means to understanding this new role of the national museum, specifically as a site of consumption of a prescribed national identity.

As a space of consumption, the History Hall also shares programme philosophy with the museum's gift shops, which can only be briefly noted here (see Blundell, 1989; 1991). In these areas of the museum, divided between a typical souvenir shop and a higher-end craft, artifact and reproduction shop, the visitor is able to practise consumption through the actual purchase of items relating to the various exhibits of the CMC. For the museum, these shops act as a key tool in the dispersion of cultural knowledge and identity. The shops allow both Canadian and foreign visitors to take home an artifact (whether genuine or reproduction) which is a 'totem' symbolic of their initiation into Canadian culture.[1]

The spatiality of the History Hall should be read at a variety of levels in order to understand how the exhibit was designed to function as a space for the leisurely consumption of Canadian history and culture. One of the most promising definitions of space in this regard is provided by Rob Shields in his article on West Edmonton Mall, in which he states that

> spatial practices are concretized in the built environment and sedimented in the landscape. Such practices 'articulate' the multitudinous possibilities of sites. They are part of the constitution of the qualitative reality of sites as places where certain events and actions are known and expected to take place.

(Shields, 1989: 147–64)

Space as we understand it is not an ontological entity, but something that is formed largely through social action. But Shields also alludes to that other, conceptually opposing characteristic of space, namely that spaces can in some sense control the actions which take place within them.

At a broader level of understanding, Henri Lefebvre has pointed out the relativity of spaces to their own epochs.[2] The uniqueness of created spaces within the historical framework thus becomes an important problem in relation to the attempt to recreate these spaces within the homogeneous environment of a single structure. This seems doubly so in the Canadian context where the additional problem of regionality must be considered. Analytical problems arise because the History Hall's maze of interiors, façades and courtyards presents a succession of simulations of architectural and urban spaces originally constructed by our cultures. This creates a distanciation, both physically (as the spaces are removed from their original settings) and intellectually (as the spaces are interpretive recreations of original creations). The History Hall cannot therefore be understood simply as a space created through historically located social action, but as a specifically ideological recreation and interpretation of the original spaces, for a purpose that is also different from the original. Their role in the exhibit is their archetypal, mythological and sentimental character symbolic of the progressive development of Canada as a multicultural and regionally diverse nation.

Also of relevance to our analysis is Soja's spatial concept of territoriality, as it relates to the creation of the nation-state. Certainly the depiction of Canadian history and identity through the recreation of various built environments from across the nation reinforces the modern concept of a nation-state as territorially defined. Within the peculiar Canadian search for a national identity, this spatio-physical definition may be seen by the state as a means of reaffirming that there is a unique and identifiable state in existence. The connection between this political agenda and director George MacDonald's museological agenda becomes clear in the latter's writings, which will be subsequently examined. The concept of a spatially defined nation-state is particularly relevant in relation to MacDonald's constant return to the concepts of the 'global village', of Canada as a 'world-class' nation and the broader debates around the globalization of capital and culture which appears in everyday life as mass consumption.

THE EXHIBIT

The History Hall is configured as an integral part of a larger exhibition programme of the museum as a highly organized series of spaces. At least some of this can be understood as post-rationalization by the museum staff of architect Douglas Cardinal's expressionistically 'natural' building design. However, the exhibits have been arranged within the structure of the building in order to produce a 'temporal progression from distant past to recent past' (Alsford and MacDonald, 1989: 69). The History Hall is meant to tell the 'story of French and English settlement and the relationship between the European newcomers and the established natives as well as the role of other immigrant groups in the development of the country' (Alsford and MacDonald, 1989: 72).

The spaces of the History Hall occur in chronological sequence allowing one to walk through the following themes:

- Early explorations by the Norse and later by the Basque whaling ships.
- Early settlement by the Acadians.
- The wilderness of the fur traders existence in the early nineteenth century.
- Frontier development by the British.
- The beginnings of urbanization and the rise of the Anglo middle class as seen in a southwestern Ontario townscape, ship construction and a train station.
- The opening up of the Prairies as represented by a prairie

railroad station, a grain elevator, the interior of a western farm and farm machinery of the period.[3]

- The development of the industrial city as seen through a garment factory, commercial businesses, a house, a union temple and a Ukrainian church.

- Finally, an exhibit about modern Canada, from 1940 on, depicts the Canadian home war experiences, the joining of Newfoundland to the Confederation, representations of British Columbia, the Yukon and the far north as the last frontier (MacDonald and Alsford, 1989: 98).

The History Hall thus seeks to exhibit many of the key themes of Canadian history, although in a largely symbolic or gestural sense. There is a concentration of what are generally understood to be the positive developments in Canadian history, especially as they relate to economic and political growth, and an eschewing of negative events. This character is a key component in the development of ritual space as a purveyor of the correct Canadian history.

RITUAL SPACE

The concept of ritual space can be seen as an essential motivating idea in the design of the History Hall and the CMC. While the concept derives largely from the anthropological bent of George MacDonald's philosophy and training, it also fits neatly with some of the more 'practical' and politically formulated programmatic requirements set for the museum (such as cultural tourism):

> As a temple of culture, CMC is very much a ritual space. This fact has been a key to the types of experiences it has sought to programme into its new facilities.

> The product is a microcosmic reflection of the global village and, at the same time, its spiritual counterpart the universal church, celebrating the cultural achievement of humanity (especially Canadians) from the Ice Age Shaman who painted the caverns as Lascaux to the Space Age wizards who plot spiritual pathways in fibre-optic cables.
>
> (Alsford and MacDonald, 1989: 3–4)

MacDonald begins this mystification of the museum by likening a visit to the CMC to an 'initiation into the national identity', and later in the book offers this interpretive guidance:

One way in which CMC makes itself meaningful is that, as a shrine containing national treasures it can be seen by Canadians as an appropriate *pilgrimage destination where their experience of natural culture/identity will help transform them into 'good citizens'*. All Canadians should feel a certain obligation to visit their national capital and to visit the CMC as an integral part of that pilgrimage.

(Alsford and MacDonald, 1989: 59, emphasis added)

Thus MacDonald conceives of the CMC and the History Hall as an essential part of the process of the development of 'good' Canadian citizens, a virtual rite of initiation into Canadianism. A visit to the museum will allow the purchase of this essential commodity of Canadian knowledge and identity, and allow it in a single, easy stop. The links between the exhibits and the concept of ritual space thus affect the very roots of the programming of the exhibits. Ritual space implies a place set aside, or better still specially created, by the knowledge-possessing members of a society in which the initiation process of the neophytes will take place. One must enter this special place, gain the required knowledge through certain rites, and pass out the 'other side' in order to become a fully fledged member of that group. While it would not be wise to carry this metaphor too far, there are certain characteristics which bear examining.

The creation of a special and specific place for the gaining of at least the knowledge half of this object is more problematic, and involves the whole issue of inclusion/exclusion. By its programmatic character, ritual space must create a sense of otherness with its surroundings. It must help to make the initiate unaware of other surroundings, and the space becomes autonomous, seemingly complete on its own. It must also achieve a sense of timelessness, or perhaps time*ful*ness in which all sense of time is collapsed into this particular space-frame. Foucault calls such spaces heterotopias:

There also exist, and this is probably true for all cultures and all civilizations, real and effective spaces which are outlined in the very institution of society, but which constitute a sort of counter-arrangement of effectively realized utopia, in which all the real arrangements, all the other arrangements that can be found within society are at one and the same time represented, challenged and overturned: a sort of place that lies outside all places and yet is actually localizable.

(Foucault, 1986: 15)

Foucault places contemporary museums in the tradition of nineteenth-century western culture, where there is an attempt to collect and enclose all times and all their products within one place, as one type of heterotopia (Foucault, 1986: 15). 'Heterotopias always presuppose a system of opening and closing that isolates them and makes them penetrable at one and the same time . . . One can only enter by special permission and after one has completed a certain number of gestures' (Foucault, 1986: 16). And although Foucault recognizes this process as 'heterochronism' he also acknowledges the coinciding characteristic of the 'abolishment' of time. He uses the example of the typical 'get-away-from-it-all vacations', in which the visitor is able to enter another and usually more 'primitive' culture temporarily. With the ability of members of modern western society to experience these 'past' societies in their totality through current forms of consumption Foucault asks, 'is not time abolished at the very moment in which it is found again?' (Foucault, 1986: 16).

Within this problematic there is the implication, in the creation of the ritual space of the CMC, of the total involvement of the visitor, and thus their subjectivity. The process of initiation involves this submission of the senses and the spirit to the perceived surroundings and actions, in order to create a link with the greater forces at play. Not only must the visitor engage with the exhibit intellectually, but physically as well. Thus there is a lack of distance between the visitor and the information being imparted by the environment. In a sense, the visitor is 'consumed' by the museum. The conception of 'psychical distance' as forwarded by Bertolt Brecht in relation to the theatre holds particular import here. Brecht recognized the danger of a lack of distance between the viewer and the play, in that the viewer would not be able to interpret what they were seeing, and thus learn from that experience.[4]

THE CONTRADICTION OF THE HISTORY HALL

But what does all of this mystification have to do with an exhibit that purports to represent 'a temporal progression from distant past to recent past' of Canadian existence? There is a basic contradiction between the concept of 'ritual space' and the linearity of the 'temporal progression' of history as supposedly concretized in the exhibit. Instead of an exhibit which explores the complex history and histories of Canadians, the Hall becomes a static series of seamless but arbitrarily linked spaces which first neutralize and then sentimentalize even the most recent characteristics and objects of our collective past. The compact and nostalgic character of the exhibit is essential to the packaging of Canadian history for easy (and unquestioning) consumption by the general public.

The three main characteristics of ritual space which aid in this presentation can be found in the History Hall exhibit: power/ knowledge relations, the inclusion/exclusion dichotomy, and compensatory illusion. Power/knowledge relations are inherent in the creation of a special place of learning/initiation. In his response to George MacDonald's presentation of the CMC in 1989, Tony Bennett confronted this problem of the patriarchal impartment of knowledge in the museum exhibits. Bennett pointed to two major problems in MacDonald's presentation of the CMC as a democratic institution; the naive use of technology as the medium that would break down the barriers between exhibit and viewer, and the desire/need for museums to become 'market oriented' (Bennett, 1989).

The most basic form of this power/knowledge system according to Bennett is in the 'control and governance' in the planning of the museum itself. The visitors become 'clientele', 'passive consumers of knowledge and experience' (Bennett, 1989). In 'The Exhibitionary Complex', Bennett identifies this as one of the main historically grounded characteristics of the institution of the museum.

> The exhibitionary complex . . . sought not to map the social body in order to know the populace by rendering it visible to power. Instead, through the provision of object lessons in power – the power to command and arrange things and bodies for public display – they sought to allow people, and *en masse* rather than individually, to know rather than be known, to become the subjects rather than the objects of knowledge. Yet ideally, they sought also to allow the people to know and thence to regulate themselves.
>
> (Bennett, 1988b)

Consumption of knowledge/experience/identity in the History Hall becomes a ritual, a 'rite of passage'. MacDonald believes that by 'engulfing' the visitor in the exhibits and technological wizardry of the museum, a truly interactive process will take place. But as Bennett has shown, the action is still really only taking place in one direction. The exhibit acts to imprint a national identity on to the visitor by enclosing the body in its presence, by removing the opportunity for intellectual distance. The viewer remains a passive consumer, rather than the creator of her own history or identity.

This passivity is embedded in the conceptualization of the History Hall as a ritual space, a space complete in itself that allows for no real alternative creations or definitions beyond what physically engulfs the visitor. What is of particular interest in this programme, however, is the convenient manner in which it serves the state. Much of the jargon and conceptual framework that appear in MacDonald's rather mystical writings about the CMC also appear in an earlier document, the *(Draft) Tourism Master Plan* (Kelly, 1987). This document explicitly confronts the harsh new reality of cultural management in Canada – economic justification. Museums in Canada are under increasing pressure from the federal government to show themselves to be worthy of their tax-based funding, especially through programming which can be marketed to and easily consumed by a very broadly based, general audience. The CMC must present itself as the sole possessor of the knowledge and power required to transform its visitors into true Canadian citizens, in order for it to attract enough visitors to become economically justifiable. Tourism and cultural tourism reach new metaphysical heights in this plan, which recognizes, 'the need [of cultural tourists] to become transformed through having visited a symbolically significant destination' (Moore, 1980, cited in Kelly, 1987: 10). Terms such as 'sacred space', 'obligations as a citizen' and 'ritual' are used repeatedly. But it is perhaps the following statement which sums up the views held by management and consultants about the CMC and its users.

> Museums are the settings for rites of passage that make us more worthy members of our own culture; the places where people who occupy a certain position in a society must have been.
>
> (Kelly, 1987: 22)

Thus one can achieve not only the knowledge offered by the CMC through a visit, but also perhaps move into a subject position where one can share in the power and 'cultural capital' of the elites who are the normal patrons of such an institution.

This development of the CMC as the appropriate place for a 'rite of passage' into Canadian citizenry helps to set the stage for the actual viewing and 'experiencing' of Canadian history as configured in the spaces of the History Hall. This leads to the next difficulty of this exhibit, its inevitable problem of inclusion/exclusion. The Hall's programme seems to be very much informed by the state-approved understanding of Canada as a multicultural nation, and this in itself should not be criticized. However, there is a distinct privileging of multiculturalism (especially biculturalism), in favour of other representations of the diversity of Canadians, thus creating some large silences. The represented spaces of Canadian history relate almost exclusively to the pioneering efforts of those immigrant groups who slowly populated the geographic space from East to West.[5]

Ritual space does not allow for the exploration of these themes in Canadian history, or more problematically, in the present. Historical space is reduced to a single ideological point in the nation's progress, and excludes the involvement of various other groups, both positive and negative, in the building of their own lives, and their additions to the present experiences of being Canadians. But it also negates the presence of events in the Canadian past, events as basic as Confederation, the Riel rebellions, or the Winnipeg general strike, events that could presumably help us identify more clearly with the relationship between past and present.

Instead, what we are left with is the passive consumption of the experience of visiting the History Hall, and a vicarious sense of belonging. In this space one can be 'at one' with the history of the nation, and experience the totality of 'Canadianism'. The time and space of the nation have been collapsed into a passage through the single space of the History Hall. This vision is legitimated by the 'engulfing' of the visitor by the exhibit spaces. It is generally only possible to view the spaces of the History Hall while in the exhibit, thus creating that sense of completeness and self-referentiality necessary to a ritual space. The space becomes a simulacrum, defined by Baudrillard as a system which is composed solely and completely through signification of itself. Nostalgia becomes paramount, through 'a proliferation of myths of origin and signs of reality', creating a 'resurrection of the figurative where the object and substance have disappeared' (Baudrillard, 1988: 170).

It is ironic that Baudrillard sees Disneyland as the perfect model of such simulacrum, considering George MacDonald's troubling embrace of the Disney World model as a possible type of the future for museums:

> I can only say that my very best slides of the Temple of Heaven were taken under sunny Florida skies, and I show them in preference to those I took of the real thing later in Beijing under leaden skies and years of neglect during the cultural revolution. My Epcot slides portray the Temple of Heaven as Emperors would have dreamed it.
>
> (MacDonald, 1988: 27)

This position has caused much distress and anger in the Canadian historical and museum community, as it poses a serious ideological and political threat to their constitution as public institutions of serious academic research and presentation.

Baudrillard's simulacrum is analogous to Foucault's final characteristic of heterotopia, 'creating a space of illusion that reveals how all real space is more illusory' (Foucault, 1986: 17). But these spaces are also necessarily real spaces, so highly manipulated as to be perfect in comparison with the chaos of the other reality (Foucault, 1986). Most importantly, Foucault sees these as heterotopias of *compensation*, rather than illusion, in the same manner that Baudrillard's simulacrum creates nostalgia. The concept of compensation is particularly relevant to the CMC and the History Hall, if we think back to MacDonald's vision of the museum as *the* place to experience and consume the history of Canada, and of being Canadian. Surely this is an experience of compensation, offered to those who have been convinced that history or identity cannot be found or experienced in the realm of everyday life.

The most disturbing aspect of this reading of the museum is that it reveals the existence of a neo-conservative state agenda that can be found throughout the Canadian federal apparatus. As a space of compensation, the History Hall (and by extension the entire CMC) re-creates and re-presents Canadian history in a manner which will allow a particular understanding of the nation to be transmitted to and consumed by the general public. This is an understanding promoted by conservative, pro-restructuring government interests, of Canada as a 'world-class nation', as an active participant and perhaps even leader in the new global village, a village that seems to be largely characterized by the globalization of capital, industry, and increasingly, culture. Under the auspices of such a conception, it is possible to both increase patriotism and globalization. This is because the new patriotism is characterized by a view of Canada as a nation that is able to compete with all others on the world stage. Nationalism is no longer contingent on being different, but rather on being the same.[6]

CONCLUSION

However, it is interesting to note that a space such as the History Hall can and is being subverted by at least some visitors to the CMC. These are the visitors who will treat the History Hall and Epcot Centre in much the same way – as places of entertainment, where one is entertained by the technological abilities of the creators as much as by the intended programme. If spaces are created through social action, then the action of the visitors must be taken into consideration, and not all of these can be expected to behave in the intended fashion. The intended programme cannot entirely eliminate different types of appropriation by a wide variety of users, or prevent resistance to its single historical narrative, or to an exhibit format which seeks primarily to control. In informal conversations with a number of visitors to the museum, the tangential experience of the History Hall as an interesting technical and construction exercise but a failure in intellectual engagement, would appear to be one of the primary reactions to the exhibit. The overdetermined sense of path and progress in the space propels the visitors through the exhibit in a manner that seems to make the thoughtful contemplation of the reconstructions and artifacts uncomfortable. Children use the space as a maze, rather than an 'interactive' display of interesting information and artifacts. Ironically then, it is the exhibit that aids in this subversion, in essence subverting itself. In attempting to create a hegemonic discourse of national identity, the CMC did not account for the possibility of a variety of consumption activities and consumers.

It must be acknowledged however, that for a large portion of the general public, the institution of the museum is an awesome and intimidating place, even when cloaked in the guise of a populist consumption-experience. The museum is a place in which one seeks the knowledge and status held by expert- and elite-Others. The best resistance would be in a general rejection of this type of national museum, and the development of locally and regionally generated and focused cultural institutions and exhibits, in which the people can take an active part in the production of their collective histories.

NOTES

1 George MacDonald, 'The Canadian Museum of Civilization', presentation to the Conference on Communication and Cultural Studies, Carleton University, 8 April 1989.
2 'An Interview with Henri Lefebvre', *Environment and Planning D: Society and Space*, 5 (1): 27–38.
3 The exhibition was only partially completed at the time of writing (1990). The following spaces had not been constructed.
4 Robert Scott Stewart, 'Bertolt Brecht, Edward Bullough and Psychical Distance', unpublished paper, 1986. Tony Bennett has also recognized the value of Brecht's thinking in regard to the museum in one of his lectures at the Conference on Communication and Cultural Studies, Carleton University, 5–8 April 1989.
5 This is particularly noticeable in the separation of exhibits representing native peoples and that of 'Canadian history'. It is as if there was no historical time before the arrival of the first Europeans, who brought with them the civilizing notions of time (history) and space (geography).
6 See Anthony D. King, *Global Cities. Post-Imperialism and the Internationalisation of London* (1990a) and *Urbanism, Colonialism and the World-Economy* (1990b) for an analysis of globalism, the city and the state.

REFERENCES

Alsford, S. and MacDonald, G. (1989) *Museum for the Global Village*, Hull, Canada: Canadian Museum of Civilization.
Baudrillard, J. (1988) 'Simulacra and Simulations', in M. Poster (ed.) *Jean Baudrillard: Selected Writings*, Stanford, Stanford University Press.
Bennett, T. (1988a) 'Museums and "the people" ', in R. Lumley (ed.) *The Museum Time Machine*, London: Routledge, 63–86.
Bennett, T. (1988b) 'The Exhibitionary Complex', *New Formations* 4 (Spring): 73–102.
Bennett, T. (1989) 'Response to Dr George MacDonald's presentation in the Canadian Museum of Civilization', presentation to the Conference on Communication and Cultural Studies, Ottawa: Centre for Research on Culture and Society, Carleton University, 8 April.
Blundell, V. (1989) ' "Take home Canada" representations of aboriginal peoples as tourist souvenirs', presentation to the Conference on Communication and Cultural Studies, Ottawa: Centre for Research on Cul-

ture and Society, Carleton University, 8 April; forthcoming in S. Riggins (ed.) *Material Culture*, Hawthorne, NY: Walter de Gruyter.

Blundell, V. (1991) 'Mass produced souvenirs and issues of "cultural appropriation" ', paper presented to CASCA 1991; copies available from the Centre for Research on Culture and Society, Carleton University, Ottawa.

Burgel, G., Burgel, G. and Dezes, M. G. (1986) 'Interview with Henri Lefebvre' (tr. E. Kofman), *Society and Space* 5(1): 27–38; originally published in *Villes en Parallèle* 7, special issue on 'Marxisme et Géographie Urbaine' (1983).

Foucault, M. (1986) 'Other spaces: the principles of heterotopia', *Lotus International* 48/49: 9–17.

Kelly, R. (1987) *Draft Tourism Master Plan*, for the Canadian Museum of Civilization (Kelly Consultants Ltd), Hull, Canada: Canadian Museum of Civilization.

King, A. D. (1990a) *Global Cities. Post-Imperialism and the Internationalisation of London*, London: Routledge.

King, A. D. (1990b) *Urbanism Colonialism and the World-Economy*, London: Routledge.

MacDonald, G. (1987) 'Crossroads of culture: the new Canadian Museum of Civilization', unpublished paper, October; copies available from Canadian Museum of Civilization, Hull, Quebec.

MacDonald, G. (1988) 'Epcot Centre in museological perspective', *Muse* (Spring): 27–9.

MacDonald, G. (1989) 'The Canadian Museum of Civilization', presentation to the Conference on Communication and Cultural Studes, Ottawa: Centre for Research on Culture and Society, Carleton University, 8 April.

Shields, R. (1989) 'Social spatialization and the built environment: the West Edmonton Mall', *Environment and Planning D: Society and Space* 7 (2): 147–64.

Soja, E. (1971) *The Political Organization of Space*, Association of American Geographers, resource paper 8.

Stewart, R. S. (1986) 'Bertolt Brecht, Edward Bullough and psychical distance', unpublished paper, Waterloo, Canada: University of Waterloo.

8

HAVE YOU GOT THE LOOK?

Masculinities and shopping spectacle

Sean Nixon

Passive manipulation or active appropriation, escapist delusion or Utopian fantasy, consumerism can be all or none of these. The first step in its analysis is rapprochement . . . a recognition and reformulation of demands (our own included) for the pleasures which consumerism offers.

(Carter, 1984)[1]

Recent explorations of popular consumption – and I'm thinking in particular of studies developed from work in the early 1970s on youth cultures[2] – have attempted the kind of rapprochement with consumption urged by Erica Carter, above. An interest in what patterns of consumption can reveal about popular experiences, pleasures and desires has come out of a more nuanced theorizing of the popular market-place, in which the languages of consumerism – as well as regulating and shaping – are seen to have to produce some resonance with popular aspirations and desires.[3] Informed by developments in theories of subjectivity, discourse and ideology, these recent writings have also considered popular consumption as a crucial set of sites and practices through which identities are produced, circulated and contested. Ros Coward's *Female Desire*,[4] to take one example, follows such a course in tracing the incitement and organization, together with some of the contradictions, of femininity and female desire. A reassessment of pleasure and a concern with the body also comes out of these writings; and one could map a number of injunctions which underpin the move towards a proper engagement in the networks of popular pleasures: strands within feminism, gay politics, and the writings of Barthes, Deleuze and Guattari, and Foucault come to mind.[5] Such interventions represent an attempt to go beyond

149

moralistic dismissals of the 'degraded pleasures and commodified desires'[6] of a left cultural pessimism.[7] In a British left context this has meant challenging the moral languages established at the turn of the century between evangelical religion and the labour movement.[8]

These writings also emerge at a moment of increasingly rapid changes in the structures of contemporary capitalism. Whether conceptualized as part of the logic of late capitalism, postmodernism, or 'post-Fordism', or, at a lower level of abstraction assigned to significant shifts in advertising, marketing and retailing strategy, the domain of popular consumption and leisure is seen to be on the cusp of some potentially deep structural shifts. It is within this dramatic conjuncture and the recent explorations of popular consumption that I want to locate this paper. What particularly interests me are the processes of looking and the 'visual pleasures' which are immanent within contemporary practices of consumption.

The 'spectacular' qualities of consumerism have figured large in its impact on the textures of everyday life from the earliest moments of consumer culture. Rachel Bowlby reads the signs of this new consumer culture – from deluxe goods to gaslit shops – in the works of Zola, Gissing and Dreiser, and quotes the writer Hippolyte Taine's perception that 'Europe was now on the move to look at merchandise' (Bowlby, 1985:1).[9] Walter Benjamin, in his extensive study of Baudelaire and nineteenth-century Paris, similarly makes clear this new staging of the commodity in the arcades, and later in the department store (Benjamin, 1973). Amongst the exemplary figures that populate Benjamin's 'prehistory' of Parisian Modernity[10] – the prostitute, the thief, the ragpicker – it is the *flâneur*, the male stroller in the modern city, who best symbolizes this new spectacle of consumption in 'modern life'. In the post-war period, with the coming of mass consumption, Guy Debord further highlighted the visual allures of consumerism, in what he termed the 'society of the spectacle' (Debord, 1969).

The very spectacle of consumption – the windows filled with goods, the lighting, the displays, the other shoppers, the places to meet – has also historically been signalled as a feminine domain, and associated with femininity. From the department stores at the turn of the century with their clientele of middle-class ladies,[11] to the 'consuming housewife' of 1950s advertising, the dominant imagined addressee of the languages of consumerism has been unmistakably feminine. Consumption associated with the body, beautification and adornment in particular, has historically spoken to a feminine consumer, producing her as an 'active' consumer but also as 'spectacle' herself – to be looked at, subject to a predominantly masculine gaze. As an illustration from *La Vie de Londres* (1890) titled '*Shopping dans Regent Street*' put it, 'Shopping is checking out the stores – for ladies; for gentlemen, it's checking out the lady shoppers! Shop *qui peut!*' (quoted in Bowlby, 1985: 80–1). My concern in this piece is specifically contemporary. Taking some recent shifts within popular consumerism – specifically in retailing – I want to consider the way *men* are addressed and positioned within contemporary shopping 'spectacles', and ask what's at stake in these new visual addresses to men within the practices of shopping.

A consideration of the layout and design of menswear stores provides a way into this consideration. By exploring shop design, we can get a preliminary sense of how looking is organized within shopping. The design and layout of shops inform and incites acts of looking and some of the visual pleasures on offer. More markedly in recent years the design also attempts to effect specific (segmented) addresses to men as consumers.

How are we to think of the incitement and exchange of looks – what can be thought of as a language of looks – that make up a large and often neglected part (within critical commentaries) of the experience of shopping. How, centrally, are we to conceptualize looking? An approach which I've found fruitful in tackling this question is to draw from some psychoanalytical (psy) readings of the gaze and the look. From Freud's writings on scopophilia to Lacan's work on the 'mirror phase' and the gaze, psychoanalysis has interrogated the field of vision.[12] Stressing the visuality of structures of identification, and their unconscious organization and splitting through narcissism, fetishism and fantasy (which includes their chanelling along the unstable polarities of masculine and feminine), psychoanalysis endows looking with a formidable grammar. In exposing some of the workings of visual pleasures, the psy tradition has importantly informed, in what is now almost an orthodoxy, the analysis of filmic pleasures. Developments within film theory have further extended the parameters within a psy-informed reading for thinking about looking and visual pleasures. We can note here the important stress placed on the gendering of access to forms of looking, as was clearly set out in Laura Mulvey's seminal essay 'Visual pleasure and narrative cinema'.[13]

Of course the psy-informed route is only one way of conceptualizing the look and one has to take along some very contestable theoretical baggage. From a very different tradition Walter Benjamin's use of allegory through the figure of the *flâneur*, in his analysis of the nineteenth-century Parisian arcades, suggests an alternative way of reading the visual pleasures of shopping. Although I want to explore the usefulness of the psy agenda, Benjamin's stress on the necessarily historical specificity of particular languages of looking is a concern that I want to hold on to.

What, then, have I found useful from the psy debates. What can they offer to the specific questions I want to address? That is, how can we conceptualize how men look at themselves within the addresses from the commodities within the shop and shop window; how might men visualize their bodies through the assemblage of clothes in particular styles; how might men look at other men; how might masculine identities be staked out within the repertoire of looks in play within the practices of shopping; how are all these looks organized within the language of looks incited and regulated by shopping spaces? From surveying the psy debates I found most suggestive the place given to narcissism within theories of looking and identification.

NARCISSISM, IDENTIFICATION AND HISTORICIZING THE LOOK

Freud suggested that from the earliest moments a 'pleasure in looking' or 'the fascination to see' (scopophilia), was a component of human sexuality. This pleasure in looking could be channelled along different routes, one of which, for Freud, was a narcissistic fascination with the human form. This narcissism, which could permeate acts of looking, provided Freud – and later, within a more rigorous framework, Lacan – with the mechanics for theorizing the dynamics of identification, the pathways which form the basis of the identities lived by individuals.[14] Identification, then, involves an act of self-recognition in an image, a representation, a form of address. From this we can suggest that narcissistic identification is about the establishment of a monitoring relationship in the interplay of 'self' and 'other' (images, other people, etc.). There is a constant movement, if you like, in our own self-visualizations: a playing-off between a visualized sense of ourselves and those other (self-) 'imaginings' in images, other people, and so on. Within the context of shopping, this sense of the monitoring aspect of the look's narcissistic register has suggestive purchase. The pay-off from such a conception is particularly marked in considering acts of looking which involve mirrors, and the shop window and its displays – looks which hook into, often literally, mirror images and position the shopper within shopping space. What I'm suggesting, then, is that the narcissistic components of looking can be read as a form of self-surveillance, a self-visualiz-ation within the modes of address at play within the processes of looking and buying. The concept of the monitoring register to narcissism also grounds the ambivalent connotations of 'look': that is, a look being about (as I'm insisting) (social) ways of seeing, but also connoting physical appearance – the assemblage of clothes, haircut, stance, 'attitude' ('look').

Narcissism can also come into play within visual languages in another, related, sense. Through the signification of the body within representational repertoires – which might include photo-graphic displays within the shop or other representations in circu-lation – narcissistic pleasures may be connoted around that body. Narcissism in this sense is displayed. This might involve the high-lighting of the tactile pleasure of clothes being worn, indicating their texture and feel next to the body. Such representations then might invite both identification with the image shown and visual pleasure in looking at that image.

Thinking about the language of looks themselves within shop-ping needs some conception of the inscription or installation of these looks, precisely as a particular, historically specific language or languages. Within film theory this has taken the form of seeing the pleasure in looking as a fixed gaze, organized within the spec-tatorship of the cinema. Here I want to emphasize the *scanning* quality of the look and its more disrupted forms: the way modes of looking are interrupted, broken, caught in a network of glances.

Two crucial points arise from this. I only want to note the first point here. It relates, in a way, as a backdrop to some of what is being said. I'm drawing on the insistence that it is within the context of *modernity*, with the thorough commodification of everyday life and the production of new modes of perception, that we see a transformation of 'the relationship between the human body and the object world which surrounds it' (Huyssen, 1986) and which begins to produce what I want to call the *spectatorial* positions of the consumer. Benjamin's figure of the *flâneur* – the male stroller in the arcades of nineteenth-century Paris – is an allegorical condensation of just such a position, and casts suggestive light on how we might think of contemporary forms of subjectivity within the language of looks incited and organized by shopping spaces.[15] The production of particular spectatorial positions for men as consumers is the big concern of this paper that I want to underline. Linking with discussion of narcissism above, we can suggest that shopping space is important both for the production of spectatorial positions and frames forms of address that mobilize the narcissistic register of the look. In other words the spectatorial position of the consumer is also the site for (potential) narcissistic elements in *that* look.

Second, and relatedly, we need to suggest that an analysis of the forms of looking within the 'spectacle' of shopping can only go so far by concentrating solely on the specific sites in question (i.e. the shops) and the forms of looking produced at those sites. The looking invited and staged within shopping spaces is deeply informed, I would argue, by the staging of the look at other sites and in other 'texts'. In the case of menswear retail I want to focus on the place of popular style magazines within the structuring of a language of looks. Through their fashion spreads and their 'directory' quality the magazines frame a repertoire of looks which inform a wider repertoire of looking.

We come now to a final point I want to make in this conceptualization of forms of looking within the practices of shopping. It concerns the sense – exemplarily put by Mulvey, Irigaray, and Coward, for example[16] – that the visual field is shot through with gendered power relations. Mulvey puts this clearly with her strongly negative conception of the cinematic gaze and its organization in the policing of femininity and the production of femininity under a patriarchal gaze. Behind this contention is the implication that the feminine is coded as visual spectacle, with the masculine positioned as the bearer of the look; Coward extends this in her work to make clear that filmic texts are only one set of a plurality of discursive practices which sustain this split in the organization of looking.

Can we say any more though about the inscription of masculinities within the organization of looking? Are ways of looking always organized around this split, as Coward suggests? Our focus here on the narcissistic aspects of the look to some extent circumvents the immediacy of such comments, but we do need to comment on the gendering of the look as it is inscribed within discursive practices. I would want to argue that the positioning of the masculine as bearer of the look (across a range of social practices) is deeply predicated on, and in part sustained by, the possibility of discursive positions through which the masculine can escape scrutiny and definition in terms of passivity and sexualization. Specific representational regimes do break with this hegemonic coding – for example, within the iconography of gay representation, certain codings of black masculinities and some framings of working-class masculinities.[17] Turning to the popular style magazines, and taking stock of the representations of masculinities they've carried in recent years, we see a limited but significant shift in the visual languages of maleness. As Frank Mort has suggested, passive pleasures are now offered around the male body in some of these representations, often sexualizing the bodies or connoting the display of narcissism.[18] It is important to note the differences within these magazine representations. It is also important, I would suggest, to note the context of many of these representations within the post-punk take-up of the commodity. I will come back to this dimension later. Importantly however, I suggest these texts frame forms of masculine-masculine looking,[19] playing up narcissism, of distinctive pleasures around the body.

How do these different dimensions of the look enable us to address the language of looks in play within shopping space? At the concrete level of the shop, we can begin to ground this exploration of masculinity and shopping spectacle. It takes us to our focus on retail design and some of the shifts that have occurred in retailing in recent years and which have reworked the terms within which men are inscribed as consumers.

DESIGN AND RETAIL SEGMENTATION: NEXT, DAVIES AND TOP MAN

The inputs from the design industries, particularly retail and graphic design, have been central to the experience of shopping in the 1980s. In the UK, design businesses like Fitch–RS, David Davies Associates, Din Associates and Michael Peters Group which have offered specialized retail design services have boomed through the past decade, fully asserting their dominance in the domain of shop design and layout previously dominated by shop-fitting firms and architects. The effect has been, during a period of booming retail sales, to produce a quicker turnover in the lifespan of shop interiors and, more importantly, a greater stress on visual pleasure and style.[20] Despite sometimes having the appearance of a management fad, and being weighted with almost mystical and wholly novel powers,[21] design has significantly reshaped the appearance of the High Street and other sites of popular consumption, such as the new city-centre shopping centres and out-of-town retailing parks. Listening to what the professionals themselves have to say about design provides a way into considering the application and impact of retail design in recent years. For James Woudhuyssen and Rodney Fitch of Fitch–RS, a large design consultancy with groups like Burton's on its client list, retail design can be deployed strategically in a number of areas. They cite four ways of using design 'strategically': the focusing of retailing or segmentation; differentiation; repositioning; and the production of stores as brands.[22] They further stress the use of design to help retailers create 'a powerful interface between shopping and leisure', and enthusiastically emphasize the 'emotional' importance of design: design is about 'capturing the consumer's imagination' . . . 'design is about needs and desires' . . . 'touching people in their hearts as well as their pockets' (McFayden, 1988). They also stress the conception of a good designer as one who 'conducts a continuous enquiry into the consumer's visual, tactile and spacial consciousness' (McFayden, ibid.). Such comments, despite their lyricism, do suggest important terms that are articulated within contemporary retail design and retailing strategy. Fitch's own redesign of Debenhams, in Oxford Street, London, is a spectacular example of the application of these 'new' design/retailing principles. Undertaken over a twelve-month period, the redesign aimed to 'reposition' the store; to shift, as Carl Gardner puts it, its 'dull and worthy image' (Gardner, 1987), and counter falling sales and ageing customer profile. The overall effect of the work is to produce a glitzy, brightly lit store – 'Busby Berkeley meets Norman Foster at the disco', to quote Carl Gardner's apt, if somewhat awestruck, description (ibid.). A sort of 1980s rehash of the department store in its heyday; shopping here defined as overblown spectacle, playing off all the right cues about luxury, glamour and status.

The Debenhams refit is, then, one type of design 'solution'. What particularly interests me here, however, is the application of design to mark out more carefully targeted retailing strategies; those aimed at specific consumer segments. Talk of consumer segments and of a more segmented market-place has become increasingly operative within retailing and marketing discourse over the last ten to fifteen years, and is contiguous with similar rethinks within advertising.[23] Informed by the expanded and revitalized use of psychographics – a psychological and motivational clustering of consumer types – and 'lifestyle' profiling of consumers within marketing strategies – addressing consumers through their 'values and lifestyles' rather than strictly by socio-economic class (the familiar A, B, C1, C2, D, and E) – one effect has been to produce a more differentiated, though often overlapping, range of modes of address to consumers. As each of us is addressed within a range of more tightly defined consumer discourses, so more bits of our identities are inscribed within retailing or advertising addresses that more deliberately foreground the indices of social/ cultural distinction. As Frank Mort has succinctly put it, what's on offer then is a proliferation of individualities, of the number of '*you's*' (Mort, 1989: 168). The effect has been, then, to focus greater attention, within for example ad campaigns, on getting the tone and atmosphere of the address right for the target segment or *lifestyle* group. In relation to masculinity there have been attempts to open up male markets. The advertising agency McCann-Erickson's 'Man Study', for example, sliced up male consumers into the following categories: avant-gardians, pontificators, self-admirers, self-exploiters, chameleons, token triers, sleepwalkers and passive endurers (IPA, 1989). The emphasis has been, then, on the increased segmentalizing of identities on offer to men within the market-place.[24] With the explosion of menswear in the 1980s, came the possibility of 'buying into' a diverse range of imagined 'you's': Next's new service-class professional, Edwardian foppery, Armani's cool Italian macho, the urban cowboy, retro rockabilly, or Hard Times distressed denim . . . Within retailing, then, design has occupied an important role within part of this process at the level of marking out the retail address to the aimed-for consumer segment.

The development of Next, the former Hepworths offshoot launched in 1982,[25] condenses very clearly this strategy of 'pick-your-segment-and-run' retailing, and has been important in establishing a distinctive (and perhaps increasingly overworn) design vocabulary within forms of contemporary retailing. Targeting initially the woman of 25+ years and her working wardrobe, Next developed through a proliferation of its retailing forms – Next for Men, Next Too, Department X, Next Directory – providing what became through the 1980s an increasingly *de rigueur* look for those employed in parts of the expanding service industries, as well as making a bid for the look of your home and garden. The distinctive design of Next put into wider circulation an identifiable design vocabulary for addressing and marking out the early 20s to 45-year-olds market segment, who are, in the case of Next, in work and fashion-conscious but who find more avant-garde styles anathema. We can pursue this by considering the design and layout of Next for Men, trying to suggest the ways in which the shopping space is coded and organized. I want to then follow that with a similar consideration of two other menswear shops, Davies and Top Man.

Next for Men

Central to the Next design is its use of space and materials. The frontage gives the first indication of this: a large window set in a dark matt grey frame beneath the trademark signage – *next* in lower-case lettering. The window displays, within the framing of the frontage, also exhibit a definite economy. Taking an example from August 1989, we see the clothes displayed on two abstract mannequins, backed by jumbo boards giving a description of this new range – 'Navajo', American-Indian influences. The boards themselves – featuring details of the clothes being worn and with clear copy dramatizing the clothes – echo or link through their layout and lettering with themes (of space, colour, line) within the store. In themselves the boards clearly serve as an introduction to the store, indicating some of what you will find inside; and signalling the combination of clothes put together in a particular style. Inside, the lighting, colourings and organization of space are distinctive. Here we see features which form a now familiar design vocabulary: bleached wooden floors; a mix of matt metal fittings and dark wooden pigeon-holes and dresser units; the downlighting spotlights. In many of the stores the staircase is a big feature, gently spiralled with a matt black banister. The overall 'feel' of the shop is laconic, bringing together a restrained, clean-lined, metallic edge with references to traditional gentlemen's outfitters; an effective mix of cruise-liner aesthetics, echoes of Eva Jiricna's understated design style,[26] and the warmer 'English' colourings of dark wood.[27] The display of the clothes re-emphasizes this 'less is more' design: a feature consisting of a few folded jumpers; hangers with three jackets; socks folded in pigeon-holes, or shoes displayed individually on bleached wooden units. The downlighters focus attention on the thematic display features, perhaps picking out a jacket combined with a shirt. We are beginning here to get a sense of the design articulating the shopping space. A central unit, standing on a classic woven carpet, provides a centripetal counterpoint to the displays set against the walls, encouraging a circulation around the shop as you move through it. The design thus sets up a particular feel for the shop, a set of connotations concerning style and sensibility, and sets up preferred pathways of moving and looking in that space. A narrativization of shopping space is produced from this: in the arrangement of jackets, jumpers, shirts, suits, ties. Within the display combination is furthermore a kind of story of what clothes might go together.

Davies

Davies is one of a pair of shops within central London started by *d.d.a.*, the design consultancy, selling a mixture of 'furniture and clothes for a temperate Isle'.[28] Like Next it incorporates some of the dominant themes of this type of design vocabulary. Davies, however, plays up a markedly retro feel through the careful placing of a range of distinctive props: old-fashioned cricket bats, an ancient-looking canoe; authentic cigarette cases and lighters in a dark wood-framed, glass cabinet; an antique dressing mirror. A huge canvas in the window depicting, in a 1930s pastelly wash, a men's tennis match with figures complete in classic baggy flannels, further adds to the effect. Add to this the gentle wafts of scent from the beeswax candles at the rear of the shop – and the connotations are distinctly reminiscent of the visual style and ambiance of Merchant and Ivory's film versions of E. M. Forster's novels.[29] Clothes and accessories for your 'room with a view'.

Top Man

Despite being a more exclusive store than a multiple like Next, Davies plays off a similar coding and organization of its shopping space. In comparison Burton's Top Man is orientated towards the younger end of the male markets and positioned more firmly within the broad centre of the popular market-place. We can focus on the most recent design incarnation of the shop being unfolded across the country. The new layout and lettering attempt to give Top Man a slightly older profile, deploying some of the design features we've considered already. Thus we see bleached wooden floors and display units, together with a shift in the lettering and frontage away from the Memphis-inspired exuberance (the 1970s bright plastic chunks) to a more restrained look. The layout inside also features some new display techniques for Top Man: for example, the slatted wooden units displaying a suit combined with a possible shirt, shoes and socks. The overall feel, however, continues to emphasize the brightly lit, crowded shop floor: lots of clothes bulging from hangers on cluster displays. The emphasis here is on quantity and diversity. It isn't easy to see all the clothes displayed, and in terms of their spatial organization, the preferred pathway invites a movement around each cluster and on to the next.

Bringing the shopper back in

What can we identify, then, from these examples, about the immediate framing of the look within shopping space? The first thing to say is that we are seeing within these examples design itself as spectacle. It isn't just the clothes that are to be looked at – you are invited to take pleasure in the shop itself. This very awareness of the shop produces, then, a more self-conscious experience of shopping. The space of the shop and the articulation of its elements sets the consumer in a particular relation to the shop around him. One effect, within the 'spaciousness' of Next for example, is that the consumer is put on display; this is further encouraged through the positioning of mirrors, in which you might catch a glimpse of yourself. We are beginning to see then a staging of self-monitoring looks. Similarly through the addresses from the displayed clothes – which includes their 'articulation' with that environment – the consumer is invited to invest narcissistic pleasure, to 'buy into' the connoted identities: Next's professional

with the integrated lifestyle, or Davies's 'temperate Isle' Englishness or Top Man's 'brash' leisure styles.

Is there anything new, however, about the framing of these
looks? There is certainly a good deal of continuity (in the general
terms of shopping spectacle) with the *spectatorial* consumer positions
which, we noted earlier, emerged at the turn of the century. But,
now, it is the specific connotations coming from the shop address
which are worth noting, and the greater stress on visual pleasure
(through the design input) to target that address from High Street
shops. Turning to men's inscription within consumption practices,
we similarly see strong continuities. Menswear shops and boutiques from the 1950s, and particularly the 1960s, with the rise of
Carnaby Street and its ilk, have explicitly offered men a range of
narcissistic investments as consumers of clothes.[30] Within current
retailing strategies a wider constituency of men is now addressed,
in different areas of the market through the segmentalized
addresses we've talked about. Current menswear retailing is also
embedded within wider consumption practices which are contigu-
ously encouraging men to take pleasure in consuming around their
bodies. The rise of magazines concerned with addressing men
through style, their bodies and consumption is indicative of such
a shift.

A reading such as this takes you only so far, as I suggested earlier.
The incitements of the narcissistic elements of the look within
shoppin 3 space are deeply informed by other texts which constitute
the language of looks in play within the practices of shopping.
And I suggested here the importance of the style mags, to which
we've referred. The codings of the male body in the repertoire of
representations the mags circulate play an important role in the
narcissistic work of consumption. Through the 1980s the style
mags exemplarily articulated the diversity and eclecticism of post-
punk youth cultures. Pasting together a multi-media collage of
influences, mags such as *The Face*, *I-D* and *Blitz* became influential
through the decade by offering a running commentary on the more
innovative edge of youth cultures. Within this post-subcultural
milieu, as a number of writers have argued, a greater emphasis
was placed on the mixing of meanings within styles. Representing
a break with some of the spectacular forms of subcultural style
pre-punk, such as the mods, which tended to produce a more fixed
and coherent identity against the classless addresses of the market-

place, 1980s styles played up the ambivalent possibilities of the signifiers of dress. The formalization, then, of styles such as those epitomized by Ray Petri in the pages of *The Face* and Iain Webb in *Blitz*, placed stress on the unfixed nature of identities: mixing different bits and pieces in the self-conscious assemblage of a look. The overall tone was that of irony, ambiguity and self-conscious play with identity. At its most interesting, what came out of these stylings was less of an assertion of an 'essential', true masculinity than acts of play with the signs of maleness. Now, the continuing importance of these mags, and their 'avant-garde' project which peaked in the mid–late 1980s, is open to question; particularly with a shift in the register and forms of youth cultural style post-Acid House to less 'body-conscious' styles. However, the visual language of *Arena*, older brother of *The Face*, launched in October 1986 and aimed at an exclusively male older reader, and *Sky*, launched in 1987 for a mixed readership and representing a mix between *Smash Hits* and *The Face*, testify to the influence of the stylistic movement of the mid–late 1980s. These magazines also remain important in their articulation of forms of popular knowledge concerning style, and definitions of taste and lifestyle.

As a way of getting some grasp on these visual languages, we can take a brief look at a couple of examples. If we take the fashion spread from *The Face* (Fig. 8.1), we can make some summary comments.[31] Three key dimensions of the representations are worth noting: questions around the choice of model; the styling; and posture and expression. In this spread the model is young, with hard, strong features. I want to suggest that this is a combination of boyishness with a 'tough', assertive masculinity. His body is foregrounded, emphasizing its physicality and muscularity. Framing this body, the styling of the clothes brings together a collision course of elements. Here motorcycle boots are worn with trunks or lacy boxers, topped off with tank-top and jacket; or else, Doc Marten boots mix with jumper and trunks replete with knuckleduster. The mixing-up of conventional signifiers of male dress is then dramatized by the posing and expressions. The conventions of posing are knowingly drawn upon, in the staging of the perfect pout and moody stares, while an aggressive masculine pose is parodied. A distinctive series of elements come together then in this spread. Putting it in short-hand, these are: boyishness/toughness; softness/hardness. The effect is of camped-up 'hard' boys. A couple of important points follow. First, there is a playing around in this spread with the conventional signifiers of male dress and masculine posture and expression, which produces a less fixed assertion of masculinity. In other words, there is a marked ambivalence set up around the signs of maleness. Second, a repertoire of looks is established which are about visually taking stock of the model's 'look': an incitement to look at the male body in a scrutinizing way, and to 'imagine' oneself in that 'look'/look.[32] Before we get too carried away with this reading, it is important to stress that we are talking here about the more avant-garde end of the spectrum of representations in the magazines. In a perhaps more immediate relation to the range of clothes offered by shops like Next and Davies are fashion spreads in men's magazines, such as *GQ*.[33] Again putting it very briefly, these play on and evoke what we can call an 'Edwardian Englishness'. Avowedly white models with 'foppish' haircuts,[34] plunder a casually formal wardrobe of wools, cottons and linens in 'country colours'. Set against the backdrop of cloud-blown, spring skies and flat, sand beaches, a 'temperate Isle' Englishness[35] is evoked around notions of the countryside and weather conditions. With a less marked staging of the ambivalent mix of softness and hardness that the spread from *The Face* displays, the 'foppishness' signified here produces a dramatized sense of maleness secured through a narrowly based version of Englishness.[36] In comparison to *The Face*'s 'street style', appeals to 'Edwardian Englishness' are less playful in their signification of maleness, but do invite this scrutinizing look at the models and clothes.

We would need to substantiate more carefully the distinctions, shifts and turns within these repertoires – and their links with particular communities of style, to develop this argument. As a general assertion however, we can suggest that the mags, through their fashion spreads, do offer imaginary identifications and pleasures in looking for men – (narcissistic) identifications with the pleasures displayed in the representations, and pleasures in looking at the representation. At the level of the image, within these exchanges of looks, masculinity is consciously put together through the assemblage of clothes and haircut; attention is focused on the production of a particular 'look'. Beyond this is the incitement to participate in rituals of adornment; the putting together of an 'appearance'.

Perhaps I can end with two notes. I have placed stress on the importance of the 'style mags' in locating some of the forms of

Figure 8.1 Fashion pages from *The Face*
Source: The Face magazine, 72, April 1986. Thanks to Jamie Morgan for permission
to reproduce these illustrations

looking in play within the visual repertoires of shopping. Looked at in a slightly different way, the mags also suggest the circulation of forms of popular knowledge open to men – knowledge concerning adornment and style. Such stylistic self-consciousness – which is what it amounts to – is clearly not new. It is emblematic of all the spectacular male working-class subcultures of the post-war period, as well as, through different inflections, being present in the discursive baggage of middle-class masculinities (I'm thinking here of notions of the 'gentleman's wardrobe'). These contemporary knowledges however do, at their most interesting, circulate more open significations of masculinities; less armour-plated masculinities. The question to ask then becomes – if we take the positive potential of these partial shifts – how generative are they? How do they 'sit' with other forms of knowledge, competencies and investments which organize the lived experience of masculinities? I would want to be cautious at reading too much off from changing visual texts.

The focus on shopping spaces suggests the importance of particular spaces and sites, with their repertoires of gestures and looks, within which consumers make specific investments (in this case, masculinities), and which provide some of the terms through which our identities are lived and remade. The 'visual revolution' on the High Street suggests the heightened importance of visual pleasures in the seductive appeal of shopping and consumerism.

The final question is, of course, have *you* got the *look*?

ACKNOWLEDGEMENT

Special thanks to Stuart Hall, with whom the early formulations of this paper were discussed. Thanks also to Angela McRobbie, Frank Mort and Robert Kincaid, and to Rob Shields for editorial comments.

NOTES AND REFERENCES

1 E. Carter, 'Alice in consumer Wonderland: West German case studies in gender and consumer culture', in A. McRobbie and M. Nava (eds) *Gender and Generation*, London: Macmillan, 1984.
2 For the seminal texts see S. Hall and T. Jefferson, (eds) *Resistance Through Rituals: Youth Sub-Cultures in Post-War Britain*, London: Hutchinson, 1976; D. Hebdige, *Subculture: The Meaning of Style*, London: Methuen, 1979. Of the developments see: A. McRobbie and M. Nava

(eds) *Gender and Generation*, op. cit.; A. McRobbie (ed.) *Zoot Suits and Second Hand Dresses – An Anthology of Fashion and Music*, London: Macmillan, 1989; I. Chambers, *Popular Culture – The Metropolitan Experience*, London: Methuen, 1986; D. Hebdige, *Cut and Mix* and *Hiding in the Light* London: Comedia, 1987 and 1988; S. Hall, 'The Culture Gap', *Marxism Today*, Jan. 1984; F. Mort and N. Green, 'You've never had it so good – again!', *Marxism Today*, May 1988.

3 The 'turn' to Gramsci is also significant here. See: The Open University's *Popular Culture Course U203*, Milton Keynes: The Open University Press, 1982; S. Hall, 'Notes on deconstructing the popular', in R. Samuel (ed.) *People's History and Socialist Theory*, London: Routledge & Kegan Paul, 1981.

4 R. Coward, *Female Desire – Women's Sexuality Today*, London: Paladin, 1984.

5 See, for example: J. Williamson, *Decoding Advertisements* and *Consuming Passions*, London: Marion Boyars, 1977 and 1986; E. Wilson, *Adorned in Dreams – Fashion and Modernity*, London: Virago, 1986; F. Mort, 'Sexuality – Regulation and Contestation', in Gay Left Collective, *Homosexuality: Power and Politics*, London: Alison and Busby, 1980; R. Barthes, *The Pleasure of the Text*, London: Cape, 1976; G. Deleuze and F. Guattari, 'Rhizome', in *I & Co* 8 (1981); M. Foucault, *Power/Knowledge* (ed. C. Gordon), Brighton: Harvester, 1980.

6 A phrase used by F. Jameson in 'Pleasure: a political issue', *Formations of Pleasure*, London: Routledge & Kegan Paul, 1983: 3.

7 For a further brief discussion of this, see my review 'Mix and match', in *New Formations* 11 (Summer 1990).

8 See: B. Taylor, *Eve and the New Jerusalem*, London: Virago, 1983; F. Mort, 'Boys Own? Masculinity, Style and Popular Culture', in R. Chapman and J. Rutherford (eds), *Male Order – Unwrapping Masculinity*, London: Lawrence & Wishart, 1988.

9 The quote is from Benjamin, referring to the Grandeville or world exhibitions: 'World exhibitions were places of pilgrimage to the fetish commodity. "All Europe has set off to view goods" ("L'Europe s'est déplace pour voir les marchandises"), said Taine in 1855'; in W. Benjamin, *Charles Baudelaire – A Lyric Poet in the Era of High Capitalism*, London: NLB, 1973, 165.

10 The phrase 'pre-history' of modernity is David Frisby's. See D. Frisby, *Fragments of Modernity*, London: Polity Press, 1985.

11 See, for example, E. Zola, *Au bonheur des dames*, Paris: Editions Galimard, 1980.

12 See: S. Freud, 'On narcissism' and 'Instincts and their vicissitudes', in vol. 11 *On Metapsychology*, and 'Three essays on the theory of sexuality' and 'Fetishism', in vol.7 *On Sexuality*, London: Pelican Freud Library, 1984; J. Lacan, 'The mirror phase as formative of the function of the "I" ', in *Ecrits: A Selection*, London: Tavistock 1977; J. Lacan, *The Four Fundamental Concepts of Psychoanalysis*, London: Peregrine, 1977.

13 L. Mulvey, in *Visual and Other Pleasures* London: Macmillan, 1989.

14 See J. Lacan, op. cit.

15 To give some flavour of the *flâneur*'s stance and ways of looking, listen to Baudelaire:

> For the perfect *flâneur*, for the passionate spectator, it is an immense joy to set up house in the heart of the multitude, amid the ebb and flow of movement, in the midst of the fugitive and the infinite. To be away from home and yet to feel oneself everywhere at home; to see the world, to be a centre of the world, and yet to remain hidden to the world. The spectator is a prince who everywhere rejoices in his incognito.
>
> (Frisby, op. cit.: 17)

Modern life here is seen as 'the transitory, fugitive elements, whose metamorphoses are so rapid' (ibid.: 18). This underscores my sense of scanning looks.

16 See: Mulvey, op. cit.; Coward, op. cit.; L. Irigaray, quoted in C. Owens, 'The discourse of the others – feminisms and postmodernism', in H. Foster, *Postmodern Culture*, London: Pluto Press, 1985.

17 See, for a good analysis of this, K. Mercer 'Imaging the black man's sex', in *Photography/Politics 2*, London: Comedia, 1987; and see C. Steadman, 'Class of heroes', *New Statesman and Society*, 14 April 1989, 26.

18 F. Mort, op. cit.

19 By this I mean the (preferred) gendered character of the look that the model invites. This is produced through an exchange of looks within the frame (e.g. two men looking at each other) or in the connotations of gesture, posture and expression, and the cropping of the photo.

20 Gardner and Sheppard quote figures showing a trebling of design business in the five years up to 1985 – a growth rate they calculate as 24.3 per cent a year; see C. Gardner and J. Sheppard, *Consuming Passion – The Rise of Retail Culture*, London: Unwin Hyman, 1989. From mid-1989 onwards the recession has signalled the end of these 'salad days'.

21 See Stephen Bayley, in *Design* 486 (June 1989).

22 For a fuller explanation, see McFayden (1988).

23 See *Campaign*, the weekly advertising magazine.

24 See, for example, the 'New fathers' of the VW Passat ad and Audi's 'Head and heart' ad, run on Independent Television 1989/90.

25 Hepworths was, to quote A. Rawsthorn, a 'dowdy menswear group that took over an equally dowdy womenswear group'. Next emerged out of that merger and experienced phenomenal growth through the 1980s: from £4 million pre-tax profits in 1982 to £92 million in 1987. Since 1988, however, the waters have got considerably choppier for Next. See the interview with Next's former chairman and chief executive, George Davies, with Rawsthorne in *Direction*, 23 Sept. 1988.

26 Eva Jiricna, a Czechoslovakian-born architect/designer, who produced influential work for Joseph shops in the 1980s. Her hallmarks are 'industrial' materials, and an assertive minimalism.

27 See the interview with David Davies on his work on Next's interiors, in *Design* 472: 38–9.
28 Drawn from the Davies catalogue (1989).
29 Notably the films *Maurice* (1988) and *A Room With a View* (1985).
30 See N. Cohn, *Today There Are No Gentlemen*, London: Weidenfeld & Nicolson, 1971.
31 The argument is only glossed here. For a more extensive discussion, see my 'From buffalo boys to Edwardian fops: imaging masculinity in contemporary men's magazines', paper presented at the British Sociological Association Annual Conference, Manchester, March 1991. My reading comes out of a critical dialogue with Frank Mort's suggestive comments in 'Boys Own? Masculinity, Style and Popular Culture', in Chapman and Rutherford, op. cit.
32 Again, see Mort, op. cit.
33 See, for example, *GQ* magazine, 'A Young Man's Fancy', 2 (1989), and 'Colony Club', 3 (1989).
34 By this I mean hair cropped at the sides and back, leaving the top long and with enough weight to be pushed back and lightly greased.
35 Taken from the Davies catalogue, op. cit.
36 See my 'From buffalo boys to Edwardian fops', for a fuller discussion of this, and also I. Chambers, *Border Dialogues*, London: Routledge, 1990, 14–51.

BIBLIOGRAPHY

Bowlby, R. (1985) *Just Looking – Consumer Culture in Dreiser, Gissing and Zola*, London: Methuen.
Deobard, G. (1970) *Society of the Spectacle*, Detroit: Black and Red.
Gardner, C. 'The new retail theatre', *Design* 460 (April 1987).
Huyssen, A. (1986) *After the Great Divide – Modernism, Mass Culture and Postmodernism*, London: Macmillan.
Institute of Practiners in Advertising (1989) *Lifestyles and Psychographics* London: IPA.
McFayden, E. (1988) *The Changing Face of British Retailing*, London: Newman.
Mort, F. (1989) 'The politics of consumption', in S. Hall and M. Jacques (eds) *New Times – The Changing Face of British Politics*, London: Lawrence & Wishart.

9

CHANGES IN THE ADAMLESS EDEN

The spatial and sexual transformation of a Brisbane department store 1930–90

Gail Reekie

A small leaflet announcing the opening of a 'festive market', McWhirters Marketplace, was placed in my letterbox towards the end of 1989. I was surprised and pleased to read that the developers planned to retain the façade of the old department store and incorporate much of its history into the festive market concept. I was also curious. Why a festive market-place, why here and why now? How did a festive market differ spatially from a department store, and how might those differences be interpreted? Recent studies of department stores and shopping centres (for example, Benson, 1986; Reekie, 1987a; Morris, 1988) have alerted us to some of the sexual meanings and processes of gender formation implicit in urban and public spaces, and to the strong association between consumption and the feminine. In McWhirters Market-place, however, the female character of consumption and retail space was less obvious.

The Marketplace was not an unambiguously feminine, or even a clearly sexed space. There was no identifiable demarcation between male and female territories, its clientele included men as well as women, and the goods sold were designed to appeal more or less equally to both sexes. A fundamental shift appears to have taken place in retailing, consumption and the sexual character of public space. The transformation of the department store into a festive market-place raises wider questions, therefore, about the relationship between changes in retail space and historical shifts in the meanings of masculinity and femininity.

This chapter traces the major spatial changes in the McWhirters department store building from its establishment in the 1890s, focusing particularly on the 1930s, to the Marketplace arrangement of 1989. In the absence of store records, I have drawn on the recollections of former McWhirters employees, and an interview with Dennis Lee, director and Group Manager Marketing of the McWhirters developers, Remm Pty Ltd in 1989.[1] Influenced by scholars such as Zukin (1988) and Morris (1988), who have argued for more historically and geographically sensitive readings of urban cultural sites, I have attempted to ground the general debate within cultural studies concerning the relationship between sites and subjectivities more firmly in a historic and site-specific analysis of cultural change. This case study of McWhirters indicates some broader transformations that have taken place in the fields of consumption and marketing in Australia since 1930, and the changing place of men and masculinity in consumer culture.

Many of the changes that took place in this period can be summarized as part of the shift from modernist to postmodernist forms of architecture. As Zukin (1988: 440) cautions, there are important continuities between postmodernist and modernist forms of retailing, and the 'marketing of design as both a spatial and a cultural commodity' within the department store dates to the 1920s, a period firmly located in modernism. Many of the features of the McWhirters Marketplace which appear to be distinctive to contemporary forms of marketing – festive lighting, organized entertainments, children's activities, displays with nationalist themes – may be found in the earlier period. These continuities signal, not merely the persistence, but the spectacular recapture of previously muted marketing strategies characteristic of the 'high' period of bureaucratic rational modernity. The changes that have taken place in the interior of the McWhirters building are indicative of significant cultural transformations in the period from 1930 to 1990. These developments are, as Jameson (1984) and Zukin (1988) suggest, clearly related to changes in technology, the internationalization of capital, investment and the production of urban space. This study, by contrast, examines sexual cultural factors; in particular, changes in demographic patterns, sexual politics, and the relationship between work and leisure.

THE HISTORY OF THE MCWHIRTERS
DEPARTMENT STORE

James McWhirter opened his 'cash drapers' in a small shop with a frontage of 33 feet and two storeys in Fortitude Valley, an inner suburb of Brisbane, in 1898.[2] Fortitude Valley at the turn of the century was a popular shopping area presenting 'a vivid scene of life and bustle' with customers reportedly standing five or six deep, waiting to be served at the counters of the large stores. These crowds of shoppers consisted almost entirely of women (*Tatler*, July 1905: 1).

The photograph taken in 1908 indicates that the store was known as a drapery (that is, dry goods) warehouse and direct importers, with its retailing focus on dress materials, haberdashery, millinery, manchester,[3] men's and women's clothing and fancy goods (see Fig. 9.1). A description of the goods sold by a rival store occupying the site immediately opposite McWhirters, T. C. Beirne and Co., gives some indication of the sexual differentiation of goods and departments characteristic of the Brisbane drapery store at the turn of the century. A wide assortment of furnishings, manchester goods, dress fabrics, trimmings, lace, gloves, hosiery, ladies' and children's underwear, millinery, and ladies' skirts and coats were presented 'to the eager gaze of the lady shopper', while the men's mercery department was designed to appeal to the 'male section of the general public'. The section devoted to men's goods in this report was noticeably smaller than those describing the women's departments. A new five-storey building was erected in 1912, a 'vast emporium' with

> a double row of island windows, divided by a stately vestibule covered with Mosaic tiling, while lead lights artistically introduced combine to make up a rich and striking effect, the like of which is not secured by any business establishment in any of the Southern capitals, and is said not to be surpassed even in the world's metropolis [sic]. When the whole of this frontage, which extends along two streets, is lighted up at night the effect obtained is one of great brilliance and splendour.
>
> (*Brisbane Courier*, 23 May 1913: 4)

Fittings throughout were made of silky oak, an Australian native tree with satiny timbers and oak-like grain, and goods were displayed in glass showcases and cabinets. In the first-floor showroom selling women's fashion goods, showcases were 'so arranged as to form little retreats or parlours, into which clients can retreat from the public gaze'. Mirrors, a 'costly carpet of special design', and a corset boudoir contributed to the discrete drawing-room atmos-

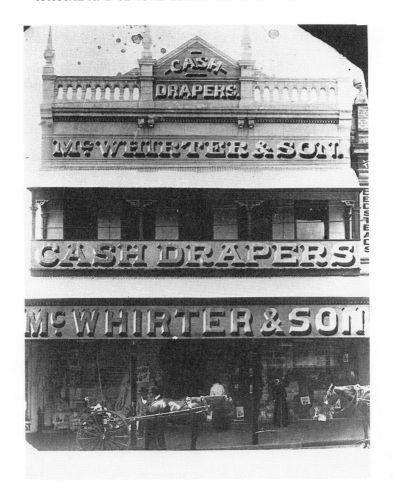

Figure 9.1 McWhirter and Son, Brisbane, 1908
Source: Courtesy of the John Oxley Library, Brisbane, Queensland, Australia

phere typical of the turn-of-the-century emporium showroom.
Space on the fourth floor was allocated to a tearoom where the
tired shopper could enjoy the cool sea breeze and 'a charming
view of river and suburbs'. The top floor was devoted to 'an
elaborate and ornate series of parlours' which constituted the
ladies' dressmaking and ladies' tailoring departments and the
workroom. Here the lady customer could mount a revolving ped-

estal in order to inspect the fit and hang of her hand-made garment. In addition, the store carried household requisites, musical instruments, perfumes, confectionery and patent medicines.

The store continued to expand in the 1920s and, with the final acquisition of the block on the corner of Brunswick and Wickham Streets, McWhirters increased its selling space to 5.5 acres in 1931.

The new premises were remarkable for the corner façade which exemplified what the *Architectural and Building Journal of Queensland* called a 'trend towards more colourful exteriors' in modern city architecture (see Fig. 9.2). The corner feature incorporated multi-coloured terracotta tiles 'finely modelled into a decorative feature, culminating in a pretty fernspray effect surmounted with the McWhirters monogram in a spray of lilies of the valley' (*ABJQ* Sept. 1931: 11). The lily-of-the-valley motif was the trademark attached to items such as mosquito nets manufactured by McWhirters at the time. Large, neon-lit, 'McWhirters' name signs, reportedly the first of their kind, ran vertically down each side of the corner façade (*Courier Mail*, 4 Aug. 1931: 26).

The opening of the new building in August 1931 (possibly to coincide with Exhibition week, an annual agricultural show) was marked by a number of promotional activities designed to encourage customers to come into the store. The nature of these promotions and store advertising in the weeks surrounding the opening suggest that McWhirters was perceived by its managers and marketing staff as a predominantly female space. The major attractions included daily mannequin parades attended by approximately 10,000 women over a four-day period. More than a fashion show, these three-hour entertainments included a dancing demonstration by Phyl and Ray, Australia's leading adagio dancers, and a live revue promoting Berlei corsets.[4] McWhirters secured the services of trained corsetière consultant Mrs Foster-Jones, who offered free advice on 'the art of correct corsetry and its relation to personal health, bodily comfort, individual charm and perfect frocking' to customers during the store's promotional week (*CM*, 28–9 July 1931). Other promotions included children's parties and pantomines, Max Factor make-up demonstrations, and a display of replicas of the English crown jewels (*CM*, 8 Aug. 1931: 1).

Shopping at McWhirters was presented as entertaining, educational, patriotic and pleasurable. The woman who shopped at this store could be assured that she was buying up-to-date, high-quality imported goods from a thoroughly modern retailer. The

Figure 9.2 McWhirters, Brisbane, 1938
Source: Courtesy of the John Oxley Library, Brisbane, Queensland, Australia

Berlei presentations clearly promoted the department store to women as a site of modern consumerism. An essential and very profitable drapery commodity since the early nineteenth century, by 1930 the corset was a high-fashion garment synonymous with

175

contemporary womanhood. At McWhirters any woman could purchase the persona of the desirable modern woman simply by buying a Berlei corset and the 'true-to-type figure beauty' it promised. A Berlei corset both literally and figuratively moulded her body into a standardized modern femininity.

This emphasis on the modern emerged clearly in a special *Courier Mail* feature published the day after the new building was opened. A brief history of the store stressed the expansion of the business, the gradual purchase of property and the 'creative destruction' of old buildings to make way for new premises (Harvey, 1989). As befitted a modern institution serving customers tied to the fast pace of urban life, the store was equipped with 'all the things that make shopping convenient, comfortable and speedy'. The store was reported to incorporate the latest developments in technology and engineering: fast pneumatic-tube cash systems, modern electric lighting, up-to-date plumbing, speedy elevators, a soda fountain that was the 'latest word' in convenience, speed and cleanliness, and 400 feet of neon tubing which presented 'a spectacle more beautiful than hitherto attainable by the more conventional methods'. The engineers erected the steelwork in 'record time'. The staff also performed with machine-like precision: the store operated according to a 'methodical system of division of labour', and the mail-order department processed orders with clockwork-like efficiency. The phrase 'the most modern' recurred repeatedly. The 1931 building surpassed even its ten-year-old predecessor in modernity (*CM*, 4 Aug. 1931: 26–7).

Inside, the four sales floors were covered in rubber matting of geometric design and sold goods displayed in large wood and glass casements and glass-topped counters and occasionally on open display tables. The store entrance, a popular meeting place, was dominated by a large, marble-panelled double staircase from which much of the store could be seen. By 1931, the 'Valley Corner' was a significant community nexus indistinguishable from, and defined by, McWhirters.

SPATIAL ARRANGEMENT, 1930

The internal arrangement of retail space in McWhirters in the 1930s conformed to the standard Australian department store layout of the inter-war years. The sexual organization of departments was one of the most important organizing principles and distinguishing features of the modern retail establishment. Men's and women's goods were located separately. The codes allocated to groups of departments suggests that store managers conceptualized department store retail space in sexed terms. The '6' group (women's and children's wear), for example, was distinct from the '5' group (men's wear). Table 9.1 shows the sexual arrangement of commodities on each floor of McWhirters in the early 1930s.

The basement and the first-floor showroom with its specially displayed quality garments were predominantly female spaces. The men's clothing, mercery and tobacco departments occupied less display area and were located in a peripheral position immediately inside the entrance from Brunswick Street. Drapery trade journals suggested that this arrangement allowed men, considered to be reluctant and self-conscious shoppers, to make a quick entrance and exit from the store on their way to or from work or shopping in their lunch hour (*Draper of Australasia*, April 1922: 183). Men's and women's goods were advertised on the front page of the *Courier Mail* on separate days.

Although men may have occasionally shopped at the men's clothing, hardware, or sports departments as independent consumers, and inspected the larger household items such as furniture with their wives, women continued to constitute the majority of customers, even on the more sexually ambiguous upper floors. Mercery, for example, was typically purchased by women for their menfolk. Informants agreed that 'mostly women' came to the store to shop. These impressions are corroborated by newspaper photographs and reports of mannequin parades which were watched by an exclusively female audience.

Despite changes in the size, nature and location of departments – a Youth Centre was added in the 1960s, for example – McWhirters retained the traditional department store sexual segregation of space and women probably continued to constitute the majority of consumers into the 1980s. McWhirters Ltd was purchased by the large Melbourne-based retail organization, Myer Emporium Ltd, in 1955, and ceased trading when developers Remm Property (Aust.) Pty Ltd completed the Myer Centre in the city centre in 1988. The refurbished building reopened in 1989 as McWhirters Marketplace.

Table 9.1 Organization of retail space in McWhirters department store, early 1930s

	Female	Female/Male	Male
3rd Floor	Crockery Cake shop Delicatessen Lending library	Furniture Electrical Hardware (including kitchenware) Café	
2nd Floor	Curtains & soft furnishings Linos & carpets Toys Grocery	Sporting goods Chiropodist Dentist	
1st Floor	Women's clothing Underwear & corsets Millinery Maid's wear Babywear Beachwear Hairdresser		Travel goods Men's & boys' clothing Mercery Hats Tobacco
Basement	Jewellery Stationery Hosiery Haberdashery Gloves Ribbons & laces Needlework Handbags Fancy Cosmetics Confectionery Toiletries Manchester Canvas goods Dress materials	Shoes (separate men's & women's sections)	

Sources: Interviews with Evelyn Glanford, Eileen Wooldridge and Walter Denning; *Courier Mail*, 3–8 Aug. 1931.
Note: Non-retail space, such as offices, cash desk, advertising and mail-order departments, patterns, dispatch, storerooms, not included.

MCWHIRTERS MARKETPLACE, 1989

The McWhirters Marketplace project was intimately connected to the desire of local residents, planners and politicians to revitalize

178

and restore prosperity to Fortitude Valley, in decline as a commercial district since the post-war period. The dilapidated state of the area's three main department store buildings – T. C. Beirnes, Overells and McWhirters – contributed to public perceptions that the area had lost its former grandeur (*Sunday Mail*, 9 April 1989: 8). Remm's plans, as the *Sunday Sun* noted in January 1989, dovetailed well with the recommendations made by an independent company employed by the Brisbane City Council to investigate the commercial potential of the Valley. Remm and the Council appear to have co-operated extensively on the McWhirters Marketplace development, particularly in the construction of a pedestrian mall, completed in December 1990, and the encouragement of sidewalk dining.[5]

Remm released its plans for the development of a \$70-million 'festive market' on the site of the old Myer store in March 1989. Remm vigorously promoted its McWhirters Marketplace project as 'a retailing innovation . . . set to transform Fortitude Valley' (Remm Pty Ltd, 1989a). The company was aware of the popularity in Brisbane of other forms of 'leisure retailing' such as inner-city Sunday trading (introduced in 1988), World Expo 1988 and the Sunday Riverside Markets featuring craft stalls, gifts, food and musical entertainment. The South Bank Corporation's plans, released shortly after Remm's proposals, to redevelop the old Expo site into a 'spectacular playground' were consistent with what it called a 'world wide trend towards urban leisure' (promotional brochure, 1989). People were, according to Dennis Lee, 'looking to be entertained, they were quite willing to spend a lot of time somewhere, enjoying being a participant'. Remm saw leisure retailing, in other words, as consumption promoted as a pleasurable and entertaining form of shopping interspersed with entertainment and the provision of food, normally at times when the buyer considered herself or himself to be 'at leisure' or a tourist.

THE FESTIVE MARKET AND COMMUNITY HISTORY

The 'festive market' concept is a more specific form of leisure retailing defined by the presence of a number of key features. First, a festive market is characterized by the redevelopment of a historically significant building situated in a depressed urban area. The history, heritage and sense of community characteristic of the Valley became important factors shaping the McWhirters project.

Remm consciously combined elements of the new and the old in refurbishing the McWhirters building, as Lee explained:

> I think the fundamental [feature] of the festive market concept is to take a historically significant building and refurbish it, but *not* to make it a museum, to contrast the refurbishment and retain the elements [of the old building] with bright contrast in terms of colour and material and life in terms of entertainment and retail. So you have this incredible contrast of the old with the vibrant.

Note the emphatic distinction drawn between the Marketplace and a museum, implying that the history represented in the festive market is perceived to be a dynamic, popular and living history of immediate relevance to the local population. The eclectic blending of the old with the new, with no attempt at presenting a chronologically unified statement, is characteristic of postmodern forms of architecture. Postmodernism conveys 'pastness' superficially and stylistically (Jameson, 1984: 67). Remm preserved the façade of the original building (which has a heritage listing) but added 'festive lighting' in the form of Harrods-style strings of light decorating the exterior. It also retained the high pressed-metal ceilings, original timbers and glass doors, while supplementing them with new, hand-painted, tiled columns and internal landscaping.

A key architectural feature of the new building was a 'magnificent, four-storey atrium space which will bathe each floor in natural light' (Remm Pty Ltd, 1989b). The incorporation of a high ceiling with natural lighting was also a feature of the company's Myer Centre development. Less disorienting than the 'hyperspaces' associated with the large postmodern hotels identified by Jameson, the McWhirters atrium is nevertheless unexpected. Australian department stores typically conformed to conventional floor arrangements and there is therefore a slightly disconcerting disjunction between interior space and external architecture.

As well as retaining and highlighting the 'historical' aspects of the building's architecture, Remm has consciously and actively sought to build in other aspects of the store's history. It decided to retain the store's original name and the logo devised by the first managing director of McWhirters, O. J. Landsdowne, probably in the 1920s or 1930s. The device assures customers of the longevity of the establishment and recalls the paternalism characteristic of the old store. Ex-employees of McWhirters such as Evelyn Glanford were appreciative of Remm's decision to name the market-barrow section the Landsdowne Markets. 'I was very pleased to see a barrow named Landsdowne. I was *really* pleased about that. Mr Landsdowne was a great old fellow, like a father to everybody. And I was pleased that they carried his name.'

Dennis Lee and his assistant sought out 260 photographs of the old store and the Valley shopping centre from the John Oxley Library, the local Retail Traders Association and from 'newspapers that were found under someone's linoleum' and placed them in a mural strip around the walls. Aesthetic principles rather than history governed the unchronological display of undated photos of the old McWhirters store and other Fortitude Valley shops, Brisbane street scenes, trams and trains, sporting and leisure activities, celebrations and parades, newspaper banners, McWhirters advertisements, pages from store catalogues, and family and employee portraits. Both men and women are represented.

Lee took particular pride in one photograph of the McWhirters staff taken about 1936, which was enlarged to 17 metres in length and placed along an entire wall of the Marketplace (see Fig. 9.3). He planned to place a small version of the photo on the viewing balustrade and encourage customers to fill in the names of people they recognized. He also wanted to set up a number of 'memorabilia cabinets' designed to display items from various eras of retailing history. The Marketplace management deliberately attempted, at least initially, to encourage customers to not only view but to participate in and literally recreate their own past.

The public interest in the staff photo and in the redevelopment generally suggests that festive markets, whether by their planners' intention or not, tend to serve as focal points for a collective memory, or community history of the local area. As Meaghan Morris argues, 'a unique sense of place' characterizes individual shopping centres that otherwise might be read as similar. Shopping-centre managements create distinctive myths of identity for their sites, identities that are firmly located within the character of their immediate surroundings. McWhirters has been marketed in ways which stress its connections with, perhaps commitment to, Fortitude Valley. One glossy brochure devotes a page to the history of the Valley:

Once one of Brisbane's most vibrant retail centres, 'The

Figure 9.3 McWhirters staff, Brisbane, *c.* 1936
Source: Courtesy of the John Oxley Library, Brisbane, Queensland, Australia

Valley' boasted a host of speciality retailers and three famous
department stores, Overells, T. C. Beirnes and McWhirters.
Trams would rattle up and down the streets, and the area
had its own unique charm and cosmopolitan hustle and
bustle.

(Remm Pty Ltd, 1989a)

Another points out that the development will create hundreds of
jobs and provide an 'economic boost' to Fortitude Valley and
Brisbane. Lee was enthusiastic about local people's attachment to
the store and the area:

> The Valley is pretty dear to most people. They seem to have
> amazing memories of . . . I mean part of the vernacular in
> those days was, you know, 'two to the Valley' when you
> caught a tram, two fares to the Valley. So many people
> remember the Christmas parades and Christmas windows
> that McWhirters used to do, and an incredible number of
> people remember Santa Claus getting positioned up on the
> awning on the corner of Wickham and Brunswick. So there
> are many memories that keep coming back for people . . .

Shop signs incorporate product-advertising images and 'old style'
lettering which suggests the Australianness of the goods on sale,
and would be familiar to many shoppers. Similarly, the company's
public identification with the revitalization of the Valley and its
role in helping establish a pedestrian mall welds transnational to
local politics. Remm promoted a public persona of saviour of the
Valley, which it envisioned as 'the Greenwich Village of Brisbane'
– a phrase subsequently incorporated into the rhetoric of state
politics (*Courier Mail*, 17 Aug. 1990). As well as close consultation
with the Brisbane City Council, Remm encouraged local business
people to lobby state and local governments to get more public-
sector buildings to move into the Valley. The Marketplace has, in
a number of ways, then, attempted to establish a strong local
identity based on and legitimated by its history in the Valley.

UNIQUE RETAIL

A second characteristic of a festive market is that it deals in what
its promoters call 'unique retail'. It is probably easiest to describe
unique retailing in terms of what it is *not*: that is, not the commodi-

ties or type of sales outlet characteristic of suburban shopping malls such as chain stores and supermarkets. Unique retail appears to refer not just to 'luxuries' (as opposed to 'necessary' items such as groceries and clothing), but any commodity that might be seen to be a little out of the ordinary such as unusual, hand-made, craft-type items or gifts. An advertising pamphlet describes the McWhirters' retail tenancies as specializing in 'one-off craft pieces, unusual but utilitarian objects, bric-à-brac and novelty leisure items'.

Retailers within the Marketplace included those selling craft items from non-Anglo cultures, jewellery, cushions, home-made fudge, posters and prints, soft animal toys, comics, wood and stone crafts, honey, perfumes, decorative items made out of shells and flowers, as well as more service-oriented outlets such as a news-agent, dry-cleaning, key-cutting and laminating services. Small, independent operators and tenants are preferred over chain oper-ators. Store names such as 'Just the Thing', 'All Things Different', 'The Irish Shop', 'The Lost Forests', 'Jungle Direct', 'Kultsutana's Exotic' and 'Everything Egyptian' suggest both the perceived pro-fitability of orientalism (Said, 1978), and the cultivation of a multi-cultural aesthetic. There are no high-fashion stores, the few cloth-ing outlets there are specializing in jeans, personalized T-shirts, 'gypsy' styles or clothing associated with ethnic cultures.

LEISURE RETAILING

This focus on the casual suggests a third theme in festive-market promotions: an emphasis on an informal, relaxed style of shopping, perhaps with an implied comparison with less pleasurable, utili-tarian forms of everyday or 'necessary' shopping. 'The predomi-nant feel of a Festive Market is one of relaxation. Visitors are made to feel at ease as they browse through each floor' (Remm Property, 1989a). Remm was apparently more concerned to cater to consumer desires than needs: the absence of groceries and basic clothing is impractical and frustrating for many shoppers. The relative informality of festive market shopping combines with the provision of various forms of entertainment and seven-day-a-week opening to create a venue which is designed to offer 'excitement and fun, with all the best elements of fairs and the public markets of bygone eras'.

On its grand opening weekend, Remm organized a range of

street and in-store entertainments including guest appearances by various prominent television personalities, comics and impersonators, a string quartet, jazz, rock, calypso and folk bands, buskers, street performers, a barbershop quartet and choirs, Chinese fan dancing, a conga line, juggling, stilt walking, sword swallowing, fireworks, and the release of hundreds of pigeons and balloons. The Marketplace's first major exhibition was a selection of museum artifacts and photos celebrating bush life from the Stockman's Hall of Fame in Longreach. Dennis Lee stated that his company had deliberately tried to differentiate its entertainment from that of suburban shopping centres: 'We're trying to do more spontaneous busking type entertainment, more reminiscent of the sidewalk entertainment of Expo without actually being there. So we want to create an atmosphere of, almost, a street happening every weekend, in the Valley mall.'

Lee hoped in 1989 that the mall would become a venue for market stalls, buskers, debates, poetry readings, and a 'speakers corner'. Lee's plans for sidewalk entertainment featuring walking statues was prefigured in the form of 'Mechanical Man' Monsieur de Patou, who attracted customers' attention in the 1930s by mimicking wax figures. The mall incorporated an entertainment stage and significantly enhanced the visual and architectural impact of McWhirters. It fixed the building within a more spacious, casual urban environment which helped disassociate shopping from work and reconnect it to leisure.

On none of the four levels of the McWhirters Marketplace is the sexual segmentation or the dominance of female space characteristic of the 1930s department store apparent (see Fig. 9.4).

The two main retail floors are supplemented by an Artspace on the fourth floor. The Artspace was, according to Lee, 'something that we genuinely wanted to do for art within this town'. The Artspace is a large, uncluttered and sunny space devoted to the work and products of local artists who rent studio space (cheaply, according to Lee) and paint, pot, make designer fashions or exclusive furniture while customers watch. This is a kind of art which is equivalent to the spectator sports patronized largely by men on weekends. Customers can purchase the goods they see being made at a co-operative artists' shop.

The significance of the festive market-place to postmodern forms of retailing lies in part in this physical proximity of artistic creation, design and consumption. As in the shops attached to

Figure 9.4 The non-gendered retail space in McWhirters Marketplace, 1989
Source: Courtesy of McWirters Marketplace, Brisbane, Queensland, Australia

most museums or heritage sites from which customers may purchase and therefore personally own a part of the past, the McWhirters Marketplace consumer has the opportunity to possess something that they have seen created. The Artspace and the retailing
spaces are linked by aesthetics: both appear to be ordered according to aesthetic principles and both display, for purchase, goods
whose most easily identifiable common characteristic is their artistic or craft quality. The spatial arrangement of the Marketplace
strongly suggests to the consumer that the creation of works of art
and the act of consumption are parallel, synonymous behaviours.

The spatial organization of the Marketplace suggests, therefore,
that a significant shift in the meanings of consumption has taken
place in the second half of the twentieth century. The female
department store shopper of the 1930s bought from the corset and
cosmetics counters an unambiguous feminine subjectivity whose
boundaries were set by a standard ideal of female beauty. The
masculine commodities she bought for her husband or sons, or
which they bought for themselves, were just as powerfully invested
with sexual meanings. The consumption activities promoted by
leisure retailing, on the other hand, constitute a form of creative
self-expression in which the self is defined by the purchase of a
variety of commodities, few of which are clearly sexed. The consumer of the 1990s, conceived of or promoted as genderless by the
managers of consumption, purchases for him or her self an identity
that can be assembled and reassembled from an apparently endless
repertoire of 'unique' or non-standard components. The sexual
organization characteristic of the modernist department store has
been disorganized – perhaps explicitly rejected – by a postmodern
retail institution in which sexual boundaries are more diffuse and
sexual meanings more ambiguous.[6]

This is not to say that consumption is not still a sexed activity
with sexed outcomes. Sexual identities remain firmly fixed within
contemporary culture, despite the efforts of the marketing industry
to encourage consumers to ignore the constraints of conventional
repertoires. The meanings, formulations and associations of masculinity and femininity are, however, subject historically to transformation, subversion, dis-connection and re-connection. The
sexual meanings associated with the clearly delineated spaces of
the department store have, in the festive market-place, become
disaggregated and dispersed. The sexual message that emerged so
clearly from the department store has become garbled. In place

of a limited range of male and female identities constituted by a given set of components, the festive market offers the consumer the opportunity to assemble and reassemble his or her sexed identity from a multiplicity of sexual references which have no identifiable spatial territory. Space and gender have been uncoupled.

MEN, MASCULINITY AND LEISURE RETAILING

How might these transformations of retail space be explained? Most obviously, significant changes in the characteristics of the shopping population and its habits have taken place in post-war Australia. Statistical indicators, such as the decline in the proportion of average income devoted to food and non-alcoholic beverages from 30 per cent in the early twentieth century to 15 per cent in 1975–6, suggest changing consumption habits (Shergold, 1987: 211). As a consequence of the combined effects of increased female workforce participation, demographic change, extended trading hours and the search for new markets (for example, children, teenagers and men), women no longer constitute the majority of shoppers in 'out of hours' shopping periods. The gradual shortening of the working week, the introduction of flexidays, the growing trend towards part-time work and job sharing (especially for women) and an ageing population have all contributed to an urban population with more leisure time to spend on consumer-related activities. Remm's plans for the McWhirters Marketplace were shaped by what Lee perceived to be the tendency for 'working couples to both participate in the retail venture'. Lee explicitly rejected the suggestion that the Marketplace was designed with one particular segment of the market in mind. The department store's carefully targeted female clientele has been replaced by a postmodernist emphasis on diversity and eclecticism.

The polarization of the leisure and work functions of shopping may also have influenced the perceived eclecticism of the clientele of McWhirters Marketplace. Where the department store was represented as a complex site of (white) female work and pleasure, the festive market is devoted to a more heterogeneous form of heterosexual leisure. Women's work associated with family shopping has been relegated to more mundane sites of consumption such as supermarkets, neighbourhood shops and suburban shopping centres. These functional shopping spaces, as Meaghan Morris indicates, involve 'practices regularly, if by no means

189

exclusively, carried out by women' (1988: 193). Sites of leisure retailing, on the other hand, are noticeably less feminine in character. By separating out the pleasure/leisure aspects of consumerism from its work-type functions, the festive market has allowed consumerist activity to become more permeable to masculine associations.

The close connection between leisure, creativity and consumption evident in McWhirters Marketplace is significant in this shift. Shopping is no longer seen, in this arena at least, as unskilled and demeaning work performed by women. In the Marketplace the consumer is encouraged to see shopping as creative, fun and skilled. Shopping appears to have undergone re-skilling, from a management task defined by the shopper's ability to select 'bargains' (or quality at low cost), to a creative task defined by the shopper's ability to locate unusual, unstandardized or personalized goods. Once certain kinds of shopping begin to lose their low-status denotations of feminine drudgery, consumption loses its unambiguously sexed associations.

The almost exclusively female territory of the department store has been transformed into a less clearly sexed but more explicitly sexualized public space. This transformation is consistent with a shift in the discourse of femininity within cultural institutions more generally, suggested by Walby (1990), away from a focus on private domesticity towards more public aspects of heterosexuality outside the family (as in pornography) as well as within. By manufacturing and promoting a consumer desire modelled on heterosexual desire, McWhirters Marketplace transforms consumption into a public and sexual event. 'Fall in love with McWhirters', urged an advertisement in February 1990: 'Valentines Day, a time to express love or longing to someone you admire, and McWhirters is just bursting at the seams with things you'll love to give'.

A controversial proposal to establish an adult entertainment zone or 'erotic leisure precinct' in Fortitude Valley (*CM*, 27 Dec. 1990) suggests an intriguing affinity between leisure retailing and the sex industry. Despite the illegal status of prostitution and what one television reporter called 'the recent campaign to tart the Valley up a bit', the area continues to occupy a distinctive place in the sexual geography of Brisbane. The Valley's well established reputation as a frequently violent site of male leisure, particularly in the area known as the 'sin triangle' remains intact. The new sex-leisure centre would, according to its promoter local peep-show entrepreneur Lindsay Johnston, include peep shows, body painting, kisses for sale, striptease shows, simulated sex acts on stage, and a 'love hotel'.

The promotional languages of local property developers and sex-industry promoters are remarkably similar. Both stress the commercial advantages of exotic or different commodities, the need to provide consumer choice, a culture of leisure, and the attraction of spectacular adult (that is, men's) playgrounds. The Brisbane City Council was ready to consider both the festive market and the adult entertainment zone in its attempts to bring people back to the Valley. As one local councillor opposed to the sex centre aptly put it, 'The Council doesn't recognize the difference between a sex shop and a fruit shop. We treat all businesses the same' (ABC TV, 1990).

In ironic contrast to Remm's avowed desire to clean up the Valley, there is a clear coincidence between the male leisure industry of the sin triangle and leisure retailing's embrace of the male consumer. Although men have tended to be marginalized or made invisible in the history of consumption, they have, at least since the rise of the department store, constituted a significant if troublesome target for retailers and marketing experts. Leisure retailing may represent only the latest in a long history of attempts to find new consumers among men. The distinctive achievement of the festive market is the apparently successful de-feminization of retail space. Men have moved into what was previously female territory.

The implications of this male encroachment into women's space and culture have yet to be determined but clearly deserve consideration. While feminism has itself had some impact historically on the de-feminization of retail spaces and the private assumptions which governed their arrangement, women may have something to lose in relinquishing what Susan Porter Benson (1986: 76) has called an 'Adamless Eden'. If department stores were dismissed as domestic female spaces, they were at least relatively safe from men and their often violent and sexually predatory behaviour on the streets and elsewhere. Women shoppers of the 1990s can no longer assume that shopping sites will offer sanctuary from male culture. Patriarchy, in its contemporary public form, is as evident in consumption as it is in production.

There is still much to be known about both the history of masculinity and the place of men in the history of consumerism. This study of McWhirters suggests that late twentieth-century

191

consumer culture has had a significant effect on the reformulation of both patriarchy and masculinity. In the 1930s it was unmanly to shop. In the 1990s, and clearly to the economic benefit of the marketing industry, it is possible for a man to simultaneously engage in consumer behaviour and maintain his masculine identity. The ideal of leisure, particularly men's leisure, and the shift towards more public forms of patriarchal regulation of heterosexuality have created some of the preconditions for these reformulations of consumerism and masculinity.

NOTES

1 I am grateful to Evelyn Glanford, Eileen Wooldridge, Walter Denning and Dennis Lee (previously of Remm Pty Ltd) for their help with this project. I was particularly fortunate late in 1989 in securing the co-operation of a representative from Remm who was both generous with his time and interested in the history of McWhirters.

2 Some sources give 1893, others 1898 and one gives 1899. It is possible that James McWhirter initially set up in business in South Brisbane in 1893 and transferred his business to the Valley five years later.

For brief details of the history of McWhirters, see *Courier Mail*, 27 Jan. 1989; *Telegraph*, 20 March 1965:6; *Queensland Society* magazine, April 1923; and an unmarked clipping dated 2 Oct. 1950, all in the McWhirters newspaper cutting file, John Oxley Library. See also 'McWhirters Limited', typescript, n.d.; and a photocopied unmarked article 'Honouring a "G. O. M." of retailing – O. J. Landsdowne' (1945), held by Remm Property Co. Ltd. The Myer Queensland Stores (Brookside) also hold a scrapbook marked 'State Administration Box 90' which contains a typescript 'The Myer organisation. Some brief notes of interest' (1966). The Coles Myer Archives, Melbourne, holds a few issues of *Myer News* (July 1962 and July 1957) which refer to McWhirters and the typescript 'brief histories' as above. Few of these accounts give little more than bare chronological outlines of the major building extensions and staff changes.

3 The term 'manchester', like others used in the Australian drapery trade, such as dresses (dress materials), mercery (men's shirts, collars, ties and underwear), haberdashery (sewing notions), mantles (cloaks or tailored outer garments) and costumes (matching skirts and jackets), derived from British rather than American conventions. The manchester department covered household linens such as sheets, pillow-slips, blankets, tablecloths, napkins and towels. At McWhirters, canvas goods and mosquito nets were sold in the manchester department.

4 Berlei had, since the late 1920s, promoted their products by highly successful theatrical performances in most of the large cities. In the week preceding the McWhirters opening, Berlei staged a presentation entitled 'Her Grace – the Lady of Line', in which the necessity of a

correctly fitted corset designed to banish figure faults and 'carelessness in figure culture' was promoted through a series of dramatized song-and-dance routines.

5 When (National Party) Premier Mike Ahern accused (Liberal) Lord Mayor Sally-Anne Atkinson of stalling over the proposals for the Valley, Atkinson retorted that Remm were 'very happy with the assistance they received from the Council's planning deparment' (*Sunday Sun*, 16 March 1989:16).

6 See Hassan's proposed opposition between genital/phallic and polymorphous/androgynous, included in his list of schematic differences between modernism and postmodernism, cited in David Harvey's *The Condition of Postmodernism*, 43.

REFERENCES

ABC TV (1990) *7.30 Report*, 11 December.

Architectural and Builders Journal of Queensland, Nov. 1930; Sept. 1931.

Benson, S. P. (1986) *Counter Cultures. Saleswomen, Managers and Customers in American Department Stores*, Urbana: University of Illinois Press.

Brisbane Courier, special edition, 23 May 1913.

Courier Mail, 28–9 July, 3–8 Aug. 1931; 17 Feb. 1967; 5 March 1988; 27 Jan. 1989; 19 May, 17 Aug., 27 Dec. 1990.

Denning, W. (1990) Interview conducted in Brisbane (tape and transcript in possession of author), 10 Feb.

Draper of Australasia, April 1922.

Glanford, E. and Wooldridge, E. (1990); interview conducted in Brisbane (tape and transcript in possession of author), 31 May.

Harvey, D. (1989) *The Condition of Postmodernity. An Enquiry into the Origins of Cultural Change*, Oxford: Blackwell.

Jameson F. (1984) 'Postmodernism, or the cultural logic of late capitalism', in *New Left Review* 146 (July/Aug.).

Lee. D. (1989); interview conducted in Brisbane (tape and transcript in possession of author), 27 Oct.

Morris, M. (1988) 'Things to do with shopping centres', in S. Sheridan (ed.) *Grafts. Feminist Cultural Criticism*, London: Verso 193–226.

Myer News, July 1957 (in Coles Myer Archives).

Queenslander, 28 July 1900.

Reekie, G. (1987a) 'Sydney's big stores 1880–1930: gender and mass marketing', Ph.D. thesis, University of Sydney.

Reekie, G. (1987b) ' "Humanising industry": paternalism, welfarism and labour control in Sydney's big stores 1890–1930', *Labour History* 53 (November): 1–19.

Reekie, G. (1988) 'The most beautiful store in the world', *Australian Left Review* (Feb./March): 37–9.

Reekie, G. (1989) 'The shop assistants case of 1907 and labour relations in Sydney's retail industry' in S. Macintyre and R. Mitchell (eds) *Foundations of Arbitration: the Origins and Effects of State Compulsory Arbitration, 1890–1914*, Melbourne: Oxford University Press.

Reekie, G. (forthcoming) 'The sexual politics of selling and shopping', in S. Magarey, S. Rowley and S. Sheridan (eds) *Contesting the 1890s*, Sydney: Allen & Unwin.

Reekie, G. (forthcoming) *Temptations: Sex, Selling and the Department Store*, Sydney: Allen & Unwin.

Remm Property (Aust) Pty Ltd (1989a) 'Retailing Innovation', promotional brochure.

Remm Property (1989b) 'McWhirters Marketplace. What and Who? Your Questions Answered', promotional brochure.

Said, E. W. (1978) *Orientalism*, New York: Vintage.

Shergold, P. (1987) 'Prices and consumption', in W. Vamplew (ed.) *Australians. Historical Statistics*, Broadway, NSW: Fairfax, Syme & Weldon.

South Bank Corporation (1989) The Park Within the Building Within the Park': Your South Bank.

Sunday Mail, 9 April 1989.

Sunday Sun, 22 Jan., 16 March, 4 Dec. 1989.

Tatler. A Weekly Newspaper Published in the Interests of Fortitude Valley, 1 (1), 14 July 1905.

Walby, S. (1990) *Theorizing Patriarchy*, Oxford: Basil Blackwell.

Weekend Australian, 28–30 April 1989.

Zukin, S. (1988) 'The postmodern debate over urban form', *Theory, Culture and Society* 5 (2–3) (June): 431–46.

10

AESTHETICS OF THE SELF

Shopping and social being in contemporary urban Japan

John Clammer

INTRODUCTION: SHOPPING, SELF AND SOCIETY

Shopping is not merely the acquisition of things: it is the buying
of identity. This is true of all cultures where shopping takes place,
and the consumption even of 'necessities' in situations where there
is some choice, reflects decisions about self, taste, images of the
body and social distinctions. Japan, a society usually, and very
mistakenly, left out of discussions of the postmodern condition, is
well known as a place in which considerations of 'taste' have since
earliest historical times entered intimately into both consumption
and cultural production. The utensils for the tea ceremony, the
colour combinations of kimono and *obi* (the accompanying waist
sash), the severe economy of traditional domestic architecture, the
stress even today on the acquisition of skills in music and calligraphy, and innumerable other instances, all point to a culture in
which aesthetic values are considered to be not peripheral luxuries,
but central to the conduct of social life.[1] But yet central in an
interesting and perhaps even paradoxical way: first because this
aesthetic sensitivity is not necessarily expressed in any conven-
tionally 'artistic' form, but in the mundane activities of everyday
life (including, as we shall see, shopping), and this feature has led
at least one observer to characterize Japanese culture as a whole
as one of the everyday, with its lack of an indigenous monumental
architecture, its emphasis on the small-scale, the privileged role
that it gives to the practical and to feelings rather than to intellec-
tualization.[2] And second, because of the emphasis on social
cohesion in Japan, these 'artistic' activities are not thought of as
'individualistic' in any selfish sense, but on the contrary as creating
self-control. Group and individual are not polarized, but integrated

195

in the sense that the social nexus provides the greater context in which the aesthetic activities are carried out. And third, the visitor who arrives for the first time in Japan is often shocked by the apparently anarchic mess that seems to constitute most Japanese cities. But there is a logic here too: interior space, the private, can be managed. Exterior space does not belong to anybody in particular, so can be regarded as purely functional.

It is in relation to these themes that we will discuss Japanese shopping behaviour, especially as it manifests itself in Tokyo. Tokyo of course is not the whole of Japan, no more than London is England. It is a kind of heightened version of what goes on elsewhere in the country, faster-paced, bigger, and with an enormous concentration not only of population, but of businesses, the media, universities, fashion houses, department stores, publishers and booksellers, government bureaucracies, restaurants, theatres and the other paraphernalia of a major (and very affluent) capital city. It is also in Tokyo that one is constantly made aware of the contrasts of modern Japan – stores and temples, large boulevards of expensive shops and restaurants behind which still exist the narrow lanes of the old residential quarters with their little neighbourhood shops and itinerant vendors, the most bizarre of western youth-culture fashion next to ceremonial kimonos on the subway. If it is in Tokyo that the consumer culture of modern Japan has reached its apotheosis, it has done so in the context of a society in which both conformity and aestheticism have also reached high levels. It is the dialectic that this creates that makes the Japanese situation so challenging to analysis.

The construction of a sense of self in such a context is an interesting problem, since self is not defined so much in terms of an individual 'essence', but as relational. The presentation of the self as both internally integrated and socially acceptable requires a synthesis, one that when successfully achieved perhaps represents the true genius of Japanese culture. The self can be conceived by analogy with a work of art – as itself the product of a dialectical relationship between interior cultivation and external canons of acceptance. The mask and the reality are thus in a sense the same, or two aspects of the totality. Shopping – the material construction and adornment of this dialectical self – takes on an almost metaphysical significance as a result, since this self-identity must be constantly reaffirmed in ways that are socially visible as well as aesthetically pleasing. Shopping, however, is not just simple acquisition – it has symbolic, spatial, economic, class and gender aspects, and we need to turn to disentangling and clarifying these.

Shopping, although of course men also do it, is largely regarded as a female preserve, both shopping for daily necessities and for major consumer objects such as cars. There are several reasons for this: large numbers of Japanese women are housewives, expected after marriage, or certainly after the first baby, to devote themselves exclusively to the domestic well-being of their children and spouses, and possibly also of parents or elderly in-laws. Not only are women thus 'functionally' associated with shopping, but they are also thought, because of the small sizes of Japanese homes and the generally absent characteristics of their husbands, to have both the leisure and the interest. Given also the fact that many Japanese housewives largely control the family budgets, the 'femininity' of shopping comes to be established. And women do often shop for their husbands as well as for their children and themselves. But there are deeper reasons than these operative. Married women are seen as being primarily responsible for the education of their children and for the physical presentation of their families (in clean, up-to-date and neatly ironed clothes). Accusations of scruffiness – *darashi ga nai* – against one's children or husband involve a serious loss of face for the mother/wife. Japanese houses are frequently crowded and untidy within, but the family will leave the home invariably impeccably dressed (even when in casual clothes). With husbands usually absent for long working days, and children at school (including Saturdays), networks of friendships come into being amongst women of similar age in a neighbourhood (in addition to kin networks), and shopping together is one of the activities that cements and promotes these friendships. Interestingly it is out of these female networks that the albeit embryonic Japanese consumer movement has arisen. Concern about price, quality, safety and durability has quite naturally become a major concern of women, who are the primary purchasers of the things that their families consume.

The presentation of self in a very self-conscious culture – which Japan is, and meaning here both concern with the image of the country itself as it is perceived by outsiders, and concern amounting often to anxiety with the 'correct' appearance of one's individual self – requires the acquisition of the emblems appropriate to both self-image and objective status (as ranked that is by the rest of the society, since Japan, while relatively classless, is nevertheless very status-conscious). While education, career, travel and cultural accomplishments are also important aspects of this, so is the array of things with which one adorns oneself, family and home. What one *does* and what one *is* are to a great extent the same, and it is thought very desirable to present a rounded or 'total' and consistent image of oneself. A very visible aspect of this is the 'uniforms' that almost everyone in Japan wears (all the more obvious in a society in which 'real' uniforms are rarely seen, except on policemen). Students wear tartan shirts, jeans and clumpy boot-like footwear, and, if the weather is cold, bomber-jackets; businessmen and bureaucrats wear suits (blue is the favoured colour) with ties and white shirts. 'Intellectuals', which in Japan means writers, artists, poets, well-known journalists and classical musicians, and university teachers, wear either rather tweedy clothes, possibly with an open-necked shirt, or the same uniform as the businessmen, but with the vital addition of a beret, the sure sign of intellectual status. Youth-culture persons wear youth-culture uniforms, 'office ladies' (clerical workers) wear skirts with white blouses or business women's suits. The key is appropriate-ness: being not so much tidy as dressed for one's role. In Japan, all the world is indeed a stage.

THE ECOLOGY OF TASTE

This phenomenon creates an interesting mass market of great uniformity, which makes it relatively difficult to buy anything really unusual. Fashion magazines are full of the latest fads, but almost nobody wears them, except for fashion people themselves and a few media people and TV stars. Every Japanese man has a black suit, worn with a white tie to weddings and a black one to funerals. Shopping for originality would seem to be a frustrating experience in Japan unless one grasps the essential point that while generally acceptable fashion evolves very slowly and is con-servative, the secret of shopping is in the quality and the subtle not the gross differences. 'Taste' (within one's budget) becomes the vital quality to possess. One of the cognates for good taste (*shumi no ii*) is *johin de*, of which the root *kanji* (Chinese character) means literally 'above' and is also used in writing 'wisdom'. While high fashion is, as in other societies, the preserve of a few, neverthe-less high standards of taste usually prevail even in average or even 'low' fashion. Perhaps the word that best encapsulates this is *yoshiki* – 'style'. Another characteristic of this kind of relatively homogeneous mass market is fads. If a particular fashion variation is 'in' it will rapidly sweep the country, beginning in Tokyo or Osaka and spreading at least to the main urban centres, diffused through the, usually Tokyo-controlled, media, which is itself always alert for novelty.

The rule then is to make a clear statement of your gender, occupation and status, to be clean and neat (every Japanese neighbourhood has an amazing number of dry-cleaning stores and laundries), but not to be too different from others in your social category, even if that category is only temporary (when golfing wear golfing clothes, when hiking wear hiking clothes). The acquisition of these symbols can be structured in various ways in various contexts which involve the ecology of shopping and spatial practices.

Several of the same kinds of shopping sites can be found in Tokyo as in any big city in the industrialized world – large department stores concentrated especially in such central areas as the Ginza, Shibuya and Shinjuku, smaller but rather up-market boutiques in Aoyama, Azabu, Roppongi and Harajuku, large discount stores selling cut-price merchandise and usually situated in the suburbs, and local stores and small supermarkets scattered everywhere. Then there are the speciality areas – Kanda for books, Asakusabashi for toys, for instance; street markets selling cheap clothes, fruit, vegetables and Japanese foods; entertainment districts like Kabukicho full of bars, clubs, restaurants, theatres and 'adult shops'. Then there are individual shops known for specific wares, including shops selling kimonos and their accessories, specialized food shops, stationers, small craftsmen such as name-seal (*hanko*) carvers, who often also design and print the ubiquitous *meishi* or visiting cards. Mixed up with these are a huge number of coffee-houses, restaurants and snack places, often very small. A distinctive Japanese addition to the shopping scene is automatic vending machines that not only dispense soft-drinks and cigarettes, but also beer and liquor, socks, ties, women's stockings, coffee, hot noodles, magazines and practically everything else that can be packaged including, almost unbelievably, flowers and engagement rings. Such machines are everywhere, and it is reassuring to know that it is possible to buy a rose, a phonecard, a meal or a bottle of whisky in the middle of the night. An important ecological feature of many of these shopping areas is that they are concen-

199

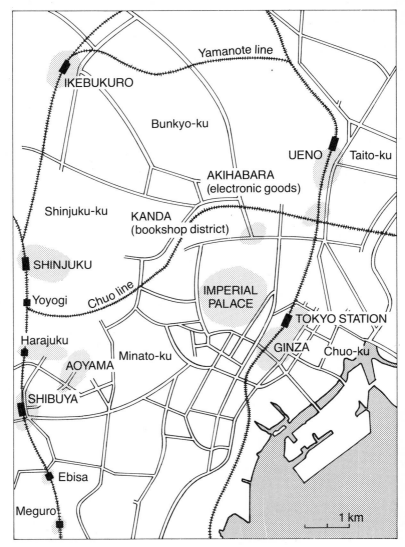

Figure 10.1 Sketch map of central Tokyo, showing
principal shopping districts

trated around the railway stations. The existence of a station, even
a quite minor one, is a sure sign of a concentration of shops,
coffee-houses, eateries and at least one bookstore. Some of the
large stores at railway stations actually own the railway, and the

200

station is literally in the basement (e.g. the Keio or Odakyu stores in Shinjuku or the Seibu store in Ikebukuro) and have branches of their stores at suburban stations along the line. In other cases stores have simply grown up around the stations to take advantage of the crowds that flow endlessly in and out. Some of these, that at first sight appear to be department stores, are actually large collections of independent shops and restaurants in the same building (e.g. the My Lord complex at Shinjuku station). In yet a further variation, huge underground shopping complexes have grown up underneath large stations. The biggest of these appears to be at Tokyo station, adjacent to the Ginza and a large business and government district, where hundreds of shops and restaurants provide all-weather, everyday shopping. This concept has spread to other cities too – Yokohama and Kyoto, for example. Many of these shops also operate for long hours, although the more 'down-market' the store, the longer it is likely to stay open, partly because large turnover is necessary to compensate for low profit margins, and partly because many of these small stores are family-owned and -run. Fast-food restaurants (both western and Japanese-style), 'convenience stores', i.e. small mini-markets, and neighbourhood bookstores, in particular, open for long hours.

The form of the latter appears to be a uniquely Japanese phenomenon. The number of bookstores is enormous, the smallest town or suburb having at least one and usually more. They open long hours, stock not only popular books but also the ubiquitous Japanese *manga* or comic books. Bookshops are always crowded with browsers, and there appears to be no limit to the time one can stand reading in such a store. The comic books themselves, some of which look like thick or book-length western comics and are printed on similar cheap newsprint, and others of which are properly bound books, cover a huge range of interests of both sexes and all age groups. There are *manga* for small children, for teens, adult females and especially for adult males; there is science fiction, romance, war, traditional Japanese tales, crime, pornography, information on economics and politics, humour, animal tales, mixtures of all of these and yet others besides. Due to the long commuting distances in Tokyo and other large cities, reading on the train is something of a national obsession – not only the *manga*, but books, magazines and newspapers are all consumed in this way at a prodigious rate, given the large population and universal literacy. Many bookshops also stock magazines, some sell little

201

else but *manga* and magazines, and kiosks at railway and subway stations supply a yet further range of titles. And the range is astonishing, with huge numbers of types or magazines to suit, again, every age and taste – fashion, travel, sport, news, cars, girls, wildlife, planes, ships, trains, health, children, interior decoration, art, music. More expensive specialized magazines not available at kiosks – such as on architecture or computing – can be bought in bookstores. Almost all are produced to high technical standards of design, printing and paper. Almost all are also discarded immediately on being read. There is only a very small second-hand book/magazine market in Japan, partly because of the Japanese distaste for used items, so most, once read, are either sold for nominal sums to waste-paper collectors or are simply thrown away. And indeed one's impression is that, whether in the bookstore or on the train, browsing is the way most are consumed. Books are read, and some comics too, but magazines and newspapers are scanned and discarded. Most magazines also carry a high volume of advertising, and it often seems to be this that attracts attention rather than the written content.

The bookshop and the big store share a common and desired characteristic – the ability to browse without any obligation to buy, and a great deal of shopping appears to be what used to be called 'window shopping', that culminates with a small purchase, or the purchase of something that one did not intend to buy, or simply ends in a coffee-house. The act of just going out, to see, be seen, to see what is new, is an important form of recreation and even exercise. But not all shopping is done in shops. Housewives have only recently but in increasing numbers begun to discover catalogue shopping, i.e. ordering by phone or mail from a glossy booklet provided sometimes by a store, sometimes by businesses that specialize in mail order, and sometimes by other housewives who have a small cottage industry going collecting orders and distributing a specific range of goods, for example imported wooden toys, vitamins or handicrafts. Two important varieties of this are door-to-door sales and membership of co-operatives. The first usually involves women who may sell products produced by the handicapped, cosmetics and, rather interestingly, condoms, which are the main means of birth control in Japan. These women, usually middle-aged married women, visit homes and apartment blocks during the day when young housewives are in and their husbands are out. Co-operatives have become an important part of Japanese retail trade, and it has been recently estimated that as much as thirty per cent of all sales are now via co-operatives. Again these vary: some, one joins as a member, and then orders from a catalogue at discount prices, or from the co-op truck which visits members' neighbourhoods at fixed intervals. Others are co-operatives of farmers, frequently those who only grow organic (chemical- and pesticide-free) foods, that sell their products, again, usually from trucks that tour neighbourhoods at specified days and times. Many of these one does not need to join, but although anyone can buy, they do in practice tend to develop their own regular clientele for their rather expensive but guaranteed-quality produce. A final recent innovation has been the appearance of 'do it yourself' stores where the materials needed for home construction, crafts, home arts such as knitting or oil painting, model making and the like are available. Furniture, bicycle kits, calligraphy equipment and almost anything imaginable that can be put together by oneself can be acquired in these stores, some of which (e.g. the Tokyu Hands chain) are large multi-storied buildings resembling department stores, and selling high-quality and by no means cheap products.

The symbolism and phenomenology of shopping that exists within these spatial, architectural and economic frameworks is intriguing, and, being in Japan, has its own cultural distinctiveness. To see and be seen, the shopper's 'gaze' directed both at the potential objects of consumption and at the other shoppers, is different in a small town where one is personally known, and in the vast metropolis. Tokyo contains twelve million people, and the total population of the city and the surrounding Kanto plain is over thirty million. The statistical possibility of meeting anyone you know, except in very well frequented places, is very small. This anonymity has its psychological advantages in a society where within the residential neighbourhood one's comings and goings, tastes and activities will be very well known. Shopping, while providing a legitimate and even necessary reason for going to town, is also liberating – one can spend,[3] acquire exciting new things and accordingly fine-tune one's image and be temporarily 'free'. Shopping is not necessarily mundane: it is adventure, safari, carnival, and contains unexpected 'risks' in what you may find and who you may meet. It is a kind of self-discovery. And by its very nature it possesses theatricality: one dresses up to go out and one shops to acquire the new persona, to modify the old one or to perfect the setting in which one is seen and known. *Where* one wants to be seen is consequently important. To 'be' amongst the boutiques of Aoyama or Azabu is phenomenologically different from being amongst the aisles of a suburban discount store. And since an important task in Japanese culture is to dissolve the distinction between having and being, shopping becomes an important existential project.

CHOICE AND BEING

This project has four key elements – eclecticism, wrapping, choosing and discarding. The modern Japanese house often contains the most amazing collection of artifacts – Japanese dolls, bits of western furniture, a piano standing on the *tatami* (rush matting), a kitchen containing the latest electrical conveniences and an ancient and primitive stove, pictures and souvenirs representing the spoils of foreign travels or of trips within Japan by family or friends. This wild eclecticism is not just, or even, bad taste: it represents a quality of the Japanese character – the ability not so much to synthesize as to juxtapose the inharmonious, and to live happily with the result because it works. Function is beauty. The excellence of Japanese industrial design is an example of this phenomenon working at another level: it is in the design of the practical and mundane that the merging of the function and aesthetics is most satisfactorily carried out. The first thing that must strike a shopper from a Second or Third World society, or even a neophyte shopper from a First World one, is the sheer profusion of things to be found, a cornucopia and an orgy of overchoice in which practically everything exists in multiple varieties. A visit to the extraordinary 'Electric City' district of Akihabara illustrates this very well. Dozens of stores, many of them multi-storied, contain literally millions of items of electrical equipment of all conceivable kinds. Actually choosing one, even a simple item like an electric fan or clock, becomes a feat of decision making. This range of choice gives a sense of power to the shopper – there is so much to choose or reject – but also a sense of confusion: the thing bought may well not in fact be the best or the latest. The role of the salesperson is important here, and most of them are men, in some cases on loan from the companies that actually make the stuff. They are supposed to *know*: they have a guru-like quality in this existential quandary, and their advice is taken very seriously and rarely rejected. They are not just sales-clerks, but priests: mediators between the innocent, ill-informed and choice-fatigued would-be consumer and the plethora of things themselves. Over-choice itself promotes eclecticism, especially in the absence of a central scale of values to structure that choice, and it is for this reason that Japan has been proposed as the pre-eminently post-modern society – as one having no central core of values (say in the Judeo-Christian sense) and as never historically having had one, except for an aestheticism joined to strong pressures of group conformity. According to this argument, Japan has not just become postmodern, it has always been that way ('transmodern'), and contemporary eclecticism is simply an expression of this. But the eclecticism is empirically apparent whatever its origins, and has different expressions: it is not just the random collection of unre-lated object, but differs with class, age, sex and self-image.[4] Seen from one angle a 'random' collection may be just that; seen from another it may be an indication of the cosmopolitan character of the individual collector. One may regard oneself as a *kokusaijin* – an international person – for instance, a person of varied cultural persona. Eclecticism would also seem to be a reflection of the Japanese characteristic of simultaneous self-confidence and inferi-ority complex. For every Japanese who is proud of his/her country's enormous economic success, there is another who is convinced of the inferiority of Japanese culture and character and the superiority of things foreign. Often the two attitudes are found in the same person. The use of things, especially objects that are semiotically ambiguous, to mediate this, is an understandable reaction. With careful planning one can be cosmopolitan and indigenous at the same time. Snoopy (of 'Peanuts' fame) is an example of this possibility, and (as a result?) is something of a cult figure in Japan. Little shops everywhere sell trinkets bearing his likeness, and young girls carry his image on bags, key-rings, umbrellas, and T-shirts. He is vaguely American and therefore modern, but he has also been assimilated in the same way that baseball has – indeed both are widely thought to be Japanese ideas borrowed by the North Americans. Above all, however, he is *kawaii* (cute), a concept used with incredible frequency in modern spoken Japanese (especially as used by women). Objects, then, are not neutral, but can be exploited in different and even contradictory ways to illustrate different facets of one's shifting or evolving identity.

The thing bought, however, is not just 'itself' and nor is it just the cluster of symbolic meanings attaching to it. It is indeed all of these too, but it is also transformed by one additional and quintessentially Japanese procedure: its wrapping. This may sound trivial, but in Japanese culture it is not. A serious literature exists in the art (literally the art, for it is so regarded) of wrapping things in paper, straw, cloth and in packing them in wooden boxes and other kinds of containers.[5] Shop assistants, assuming they have not already learnt the skill from their mothers, are taught how to wrap and tie expertly the merchandise that they are selling. The cheapest of the ubiquitous *obento* (lunch-boxes) bought at a railway station will be elegantly packaged and its contents laid out inside it an aesthetically pleasing fashion. And a small pair of disposable wooden chopsticks will be included with the purchase, also neatly packaged in a paper wrapping often decorated with elegant calligraphy. A Japanese is as likely to give as much atten-tion to the wrapping – the material, the way it is folded, the ribbons used to secure it – as to the contents of the package. To give a badly or inelegantly wrapped gift, or one not wrapped at all, is both rude and a negative reflection on one's own taste and sensibilities. Stationery stores have large sections for wrapping-paper, ribbons, labels, cards and the special kinds of decorative envelopes used for giving gifts of money. The humblest purchase is carefully wrapped and one is usually asked if it is a present. If it is, it will be wrapped and tied in an even more elaborate way, at no extra cost to the purchaser, the buying and the packaging being intimately linked and both part of the same philosophy of service.

This emphasis on packaging is an important facet of the fact that Japan is, on a very large scale, a gift economy of a kind that would be instantly recognized by any anthropologist.[6] Gift giving and receiving are ingredients of everyday culture. Gifts are given not only for birthdays and weddings, but also for funerals, when visiting someone's home, on the occasion of promotions or other similar events, and especially at mid-year and at New Year (*chugen* and *seibu*) when half-yearly bonuses are paid and when a nation-wide boom in gift giving occurs – to those who have done you favours, to those from whom you hope to receive favours, to bosses and to one's children's schoolteachers.[7] All the year round depart-ment stores stock appropriate gifts, but on these occasions they are full of them, advertising appears extolling certain products and parcel-delivery companies are inundated with work. Many families keep detailed record books of gifts sent and received, so that mistakes of reciprocity will not be made. The traditional gift-giving seasons are not the only occasions either. The Japanese (almost entirely non-Christian though they are) have discovered Christmas in a big way and even Easter to a degree, Mothers' Day, Fathers' day, Halloween and Valentine's Day (on which occasion women give gifts of chocolate to men – husbands, boyfriends, lovers, bosses). Life in Japan sometimes seems to be an endless round of gift giving, reflecting the networks of close social relationships that abound. On moving into a house or apartment one gives gifts to the neighbours on both sides and opposite; on returning from holiday one always brings gifts (*omiage*) for family, friends, secretary, office mates and neighbours, usually a regional speciality of wherever one has been, cakes, cookies and sweets being common choices. A great deal of shopping activity is not for oneself, but for gifts for others, and shops cater for this huge volume of gift giving, and every hotel in a resort area has a little shop selling souvenirs and local foods. Even railway stations reflect the gift economy, and in a popular tourist destinations like Kyoto there are gift shops not only around the station but within it and even on the platform, so that gifts for a suddenly remembered acquaintance can be bought at the very point of boarding the *Shinkansen* (bullet train) for the ride home. The actual shopping for gifts requires considerable cultural skill – for whom? How expensive? What kind of thing? And yet much of what is received is never consumed – it piles up or is given away again. This perpetual and enormous circulation of commodities – a gigantic kula-ring-like cycle of obligations and reciprocities, represents a key dimension of shopping behaviour in Japan, and a fascinating extension of the economics of the gift.

The art of choosing, as we have suggested, is a sophisticated one, whether for oneself or others. In buying a gift, for example, price is important, not only for one's own pocket book, but because to give a too expensive gift is to impose a heavy burden of reciprocity on the recipient, to give too cheap a one is an insult. In choosing for oneself, self-image comes into play. Here there are also some important contextual factors at work. Two groups are amongst the biggest consumers – youngish unmarried women who are between college and marriage, currently working and who are living at home and have few overheads; and youngish married or unmarried professionals who, because they cannot possibly ever afford a house in Tokyo, divert what would in other societies be mortgage savings into consumption. Both groups consider themselves sophisticated consumers, for whom consumption is indeed a way of life, and they are aided in this by the huge range of media, not only that carrying general advertising, but specialist consumer magazines and guides as well. The Japanese verb for shopping (*kaimono*) is written with the Chinese character for 'thing', and a leading consumer magazine, on sale at most news-kiosks, carries exactly this splendidly practical title – *Things*. It is, as a representative of its genre, a very interesting magazine – glossy, of nearly two hundred pages per issue, and containing nothing but advertisements and short articles on new products, including TVs and VCRs, cameras, watches, luggage, clothes, chairs, fashion accessories, toys, cars, pens, sunglasses, cigarettes, personal computers, lawnmowers, an endless succession of trivia – jigsaws, kits for making dinosaurs, tissue-holders, tiny first-aid kits, snuff, Wild Western-style embossed riding saddles, exotic clocks, art-nouveau decorations – new-product test reports on several items and a lead article on bourbon, with an illustrated guide to several dozen brands. Product guides of this kind (and there are many others, both rival general ones and ones specializing in cars, sporting goods, bridal wear, etc.) are themselves widely consumed – either for their aid in actually selecting an item or being alerted to the enormous range available, or because they are interesting in themselves, as attractive and fascinating guides to the inexhaustible range of possibilities – even if you do not actually want or need any of them. Such magazines are also an expression of the fine Japanese art of advertising. Adverts are everywhere – not only in magazines and newspapers and on six of the eight TV channels (two being state-run, non-commercial channels), but on walls, telephone poles, billboards, trains and subways, on every available surface, in neon all over commercial buildings and thrust in endless quantities into one's mail-box. As an incentive to consume, it is undoubtedly a powerful force, and like wrapping and the self, it is considered an art form.[8]

A thing once chosen, however, will not always be retained. It will, if bought as a gift, be given away. But it is just as likely to be rapidly discarded simply because it is no longer new. A certain day each month is 'heavy rubbish day' when unwanted large objects can be put out on the sidewalk for collection by the munici-

pal rubbish collectors or by private contractors. The most astonishing variety and volume of things are discarded – furniture, TVs,
bicycles, golf-clubs, all kinds of electrical appliances and just about
everything else that a modern household might possess. Students
and poorer people often furnish their dwellings with cast-offs of
this kind, which is not a bad idea since the objects are often in
almost mint condition. It is not uncommon for middle- and upper-
middle-class households to change their furniture, appliances, cur-
tains, even cutlery, every few years. New is good (and there may
be a deep-seated cultural attitude here originating in Shinto ideas
of purity). This high turnover means that constant shopping is
necessary, and constant awareness of what is on the market and
what is in fashion, which in turn requires a never-ceasing vigilance
on the part of the consumer. This mindset produces huge quantities of perfectly serviceable 'junk', and this logic applies even, or
especially, to cars. Very few old ones are to be seen on city roads,
and those that are are sometimes called *gaijin-kuruma*: 'foreigners'
cars' as only foreigners, who have little or no 'face', are willing to
drive around in them. Even the climate is roped in as a justification
here. Japan is markedly seasonal (Japanese sometimes refers to
themselves as 'ninety-day people' – fickle and rather changeable,
like the seasons which only last three months each) and certain
kinds of clothes are thought appropriate for each season, not only
in terms of warmth or coolness but also of colour and style. The
non-appropriate clothes are stored and/or discarded, and stores
exploit this seasonality by introducing even finer distinctions. In
1990, there were not only autumn clothes, but 'early autumn
clothes'. The logic of consumption expands here in culturally
interesting ways. Overnight, stores are transformed from late
summer to early autumn, and then instantly it is impossible to
buy late-summer clothes unless one knows the discount stores and
boutiques where out-of-season fashion is retailed at knock-down
prices. And this transformation is literally overnight. The Christmas season ends on Christmas Eve when the big stores simultaneously remove Christmas trees, decorations, seasonal music and
display themes and replace them by the following morning with
decorations and gifts for the much more culturally significant New
Year, which again, commercially speaking, ends as the shops close
on 31 December.

The situation that we are analysing here, while clearly a recognizable 'culture of consumption' by western capitalist standards,

is also one with its own distinctive characteristics. These include shopping to give away (the gift relationship), the predictability of the shopping cycle (its seasonality, constantly emphasized by the media, and especially on TV every night, where the characteristics of each season are dwelt on at length, and advice is given on where to go to view the best cherry blossoms, plum blossoms or maple leaves, as is appropriate), and in a sense its orderliness. The craziest object bought will still be wrapped in the most traditional manner and certain colours are still thought appropriate for each age group, season and even occupation. And there are yet other peculiarities. One of these is travelling abroad for the purpose, essentially, of shopping. Given the very high cost of living and inflated prices of Japanese commodities, it can be as cheap to vacation in Korea, South-East Asia, Taiwan or Hong Kong as it is to holiday in Japan, with the added incentive of being able to buy both international 'brand name' goods and Japanese-made products at far below their Tokyo prices (there being big price differentials between the cost of the same Japanese-made product at home and abroad). The desire for brand-name goods, especially French, Italian and British products – watches, luggage, shoes, leather products, perfumes and fashions – it is a well-known characteristic of Japanese shoppers, and one thoroughly exploited by shopkeepers in places like Singapore, Hawaii and Hong Kong. The motive is partly to buy quality goods, something that does, for once, last; and since one's foreign travels are likely to be less frequent after one's brief 'office lady' phase, it makes sense to buy while one can and has the ready cash.[9] But functionalism is not all: brand names possess a mystique, a cachet that creates the impression of sophistication, of internationalism, and of taste. The almost metaphysical levels that this can reach in Japan seem to transcend those found elsewhere, as revealed by the extraordinary success of the best-selling 'novel', *Nantonaku, kirisutaru* (*Somehow, crystal*), by Tanaka Yasuo, virtually plotless and consisting in large part of lists of brand-name goods and quasi-scholarly notes discussing these commodities, and which sold over three-quarters of a million copies and in doing so became something of a brand-name commodity itself.[10] The big stores in the major cities often have either special promotions of foreign brand-name goods or stock them permanently, Harrods of London and Laura Ashley being two currently popular examples in large stores in the Ginza area of Tokyo.

POSTMODERN JAPAN?

But if the ethnography of shopping in contemporary Japan is undoubtedly of considerable interest, does it help us to move beyond middle-range theory towards a comparative theory of post-modern societies? It would seem that it does, and this reopens the case for regarding, if not Japan as a whole, then at least its urban culture as an example of postmodernism incarnate. To assess this possibility we would have to begin with a subjectively and culturally constructed model for relating self and society – in this case the construction of self as social, that sociality being practiced and generated through participation in consumption. This participation both identifies and solidifies the sense of personal self, and confirms it as social through common membership of the shopping fraternity. The images of what one should be like – being fashionable, modern, while also being one's age and status, and continuing all the time to be Japanese (itself of course a social construct) – which are created through an enormous yet remarkably homogeneous media effort, can be fulfilled at a vast range of consumption sites. And here we also begin to see what makes the Japanese case so theoretically interesting. The aesthetics of the self in Japanese culture make that self vulnerable – it is liable to disintegration if it is not located in the social nexus and/or if the subjective means of its identity formation are disrupted. And this sets up what is perhaps the fundamental and persisting tension in Japanese society. The social order, certainly at least since Tokugawa times (the Shogunate of the period 1603–1868 which created and enforced a rigidly hierarchical and controlled social system) has been 'rational', but the basis of this rationality (or 'modernist' project), once one moves beyond mere crude social control, is and always has been, emotion. The modernist identification of self and task cannot be read in the same way as in the west – as primarily a function of goals and capitalist work relations – but rather on the analogy of the craftsman – a person so dedicated to a task that absorption *into* it becomes the end result. You do not so much *learn* a craft as *become* it. The role of intuition and subjectivity is very strong in Japanese culture (for example the emphasis, even if often overrated, on non-verbal communication, *haragei*, 'thinking with one's stomach').[11] Mood, atmosphere, feeling, are essential components of this, and this is a major reason why the Japanese are often accused by 'principled' westerners of being without ethics, or at best being situational ethicists. Feelings, especially consideration of *ninjo*, 'human feelings', are paramount over abstract principles. Shopping, then, is freedom, but freedom within the constraints so beloved by the Japanese, in which boundaries and limits confer rather than restrict freedom (the economy and restraint of *chanoyu*, the traditional tea ceremony, is a marvellous example of this). Excitement and tranquility are not, as for most westerners, opposites, but rather both aspects of an untranslatable 'spirit' in which grace and control are harmonized with pleasure and fun. Many middle-aged people remember the years of post-war privation before the current age of *akarui seikatsu*, the 'bright new life', came about. To be able to shop and choose and to create alternative identities within the bigger framework of a fundamentally conservative society is considered something really quite marvellous.[12]

This expanding range of possibilities, the fruit of affluence, offers new possibilities – the increasing public roles of women, the emergence of a distinctive youth culture, a rapidly burgeoning entrepreneurial sector, a flourishing arts and music scene – which while not necessarily challenging traditional Japanese sensibilities, are certainly extending and redefining them. If this interpretation is correct, Japan would represent a unique experience – the achievement of a form of postmodernity different from that so far described in the west, one without the fragmentary self and in which experiment in architecture, fashion and the arts co-exists with pragmatism and the continuous recreation of tradition (for example the now almost universal Shinto wedding ceremony, thought by many to be very ancient, was actually invented in 1900 for the marriage of the then crown prince). Certainly the Japanese intellectual community, very well versed as it is with trends of thinking elsewhere in the world, does not tend to theorize the situation so much as an attack on the modern as the creation of a distinctively Japanese form of modernity; not surprisingly, perhaps, in a society where media saturation and bullet trains paradoxically co-exist with a physical infrastructure that is often positively Third World in quality. If the true basis of postmodernity lies not in technology or particular styles of art or design, but in the collapse of metanarratives,[13] then Japan has, at least in this sense, been postmodern for a long time, since it is widely seen as a society in which such metanarratives have historically always been weak or absent. But the metanarrative argument is not all: the corresponding revaluation of self is an equally significant dimension. Although these things are very hard to measure, subjectively at least it appears that alienation is low in contemporary Japan, compared with other industrialized countries. The jarring changes of the last half century have not only been assimilated, but have been 'turned around' and presented back to the world as Japan's economic miracle – a success in creating a special brand of Asian capitalism based on a set of cultural and sociological behaviours so different from that experienced in the west that more than one observer has suggested that Japan is in fact the only really 'communist' state in the modern world.[14] Clearly there are critical dimensions to this too, such as whether or not commoditization of a capitalist kind is creating classes in a society that formerly did not have them (as indeed some have argued).[15] Nevertheless, what is interesting about Japan is that certainly the preconditions of post-modernity – the image of self, the central and accepted role of subjectivities, eclecticism, the centrality of feeling and atmosphere, the play element, the love of spectacle and the pose,[16] and the existence of a sensual rather than intellectual culture, as well as a materially advanced economy – all flourish. Japanese shopping is situated in this context: disturbingly familiar and yet disturbingly different, in a society semiotically charged, but in unfamiliar ways to the outsider. Here is a society which embodies a sensibility in which aesthetic values and social order continuously interact. Barthes rightly called Japan the 'Empire of Signs',[17] for it is surely a society in which the sign is central (and its ideographic script perhaps ensures this). A recently seen satchel, designed to look like a soap-flakes packet, has emblazoned on it, in English, the following cryptic message, a fitting epilogue to our exploration of Japanese shopping:

> Original Shopper's Bag; American Taste: We give you an answer to everything. You've always wanted to know about LOVE and HAPPINESS. Produced by Super Planning Company Limited. Made in Japan.

NOTES

NB: Japanese names are given in the usual order of surnames first unless a particular publication itself reverses this order.

1 A fact noted by Ezra Vogel in his historically fairly recent study of

what one might expect to be something of a cultural desert – a suburban Tokyo middle-class district: Vogel, E. (1973) *Japan's New Middle Class*, Berkeley: University of California Press.

2 Hasegawa, N. (1938) *Nihonteki Seikaku*; an English translation exists under the title *The Japanese Character: A Cultural Profile* (1982), Tokyo and New York: Kodansha. This is also reflected in many modern Japanese films, especially those of leading directors such as Ozu Yasujiro, which seem boring to many western viewers because of their slow pace and seeming lack of plot. This, however, is precisely the point – the dwelling in loving detail on the mundane, which for many Japanese reflects the essence of real life.

3 Certainly there are class limitations on expenditure, and on the kinds of things purchased, although most Japanese would today expect to possess 'necessities' like a TV and a washing machine. Although class consciousness is weak, differences in consumption patterns based on economic status are apparent, which suggests that the concept of 'consumption classes' is quite a useful way of looking at social stratification in Japan. For a useful exploration of class issues, see Steven, R. (1983) *Classes in Contemporary Japan*, Cambridge: Cambridge University Press; and for social divisions within the total political-economy, see Eccleston, B. (1989) *State and Society in Postwar Japan*, Cambridge: Polity Press.

4 Bourdieu, P. (1984) *Distinction: A Social Critique of the Judgement of Taste*, Cambridge, Mass.: Harvard University Press.

5 For example, Oka, H. (1967) *How To Wrap Five Eggs*, Tokyo: Bijutsu Shuppan-Sha.

6 Cf. Mauss, M. (1969) *The Gift*, London: Cohen & West.

7 There is a large literature on this. For example; Heibonsha Daihyakkajiten (1984) *Seibo/Chugen*, Tokyo: Heibonsha, and Befu Harumi (1974) 'Gift giving in a modernizing Japan', in Lebra, T. S. and Lebra, W. P. (eds) *Japanese Culture and Behaviour*, Honolulu: University of Hawaii Press.

8 Moeran, B. (1989) *Language and Popular Culture in Japan*, Manchester: Manchester University Press.

9 And indeed in a sense when one has to. Most Japanese take short holidays, often less than their official entitlement, and for the great majority in working life these are concentrated in the few days of 'Golden Week' in May when several public holidays fall together, in August during the school summer holidays, and at New Year, when many businesses close for up to four days. A major problem with this is that everyone is obliged to take their vacations at the same time, leading to massive congestion of roads, airports and long-distance train services.

10 Tanaka, Y. (1980) *Nantonaku, kirisutaru*, Tokyo: Bungei. There is a discussion of the book in English by Norma Field (1989) 'Somehow: the postmodern as atmosphere', in Miyoshi, M. And Harootunian, H. (eds) *Postmodernism and Japan*, Durham: Duke University Press.

11 E.g. Matsumoto, M. (1988) *The Unspoken Way: Haragei*, Tokyo and New York: Kodansha.

12 Cf. Vogel, op. cit.: 71–83, for a description of this in the late 1950s.
13 Lyotard, J.-F. (1984) *The Postmodern Condition*, Minneapolis: University of Minnesota Press.
14 Kenrick, D. M. (1990) *Where Communism Works: the Success of Competitive Communism in Japan*, Tokyo: Charles E. Tuttle.
15 As in the classical view of Nakane Chie that Japan is not a class but a ranked society: Nakane, C. (1970) *Japanese Society*, London: Weidenfeld & Nicholson. But see also the strong criticisms of this model in Mouer, S. and Sugimoto, Y. (1986) *Images of Japanese Society*, London: KPI.
16 Edwards, W. (1989) *Modern Japan through its Weddings: Gender, Person and Society in Ritual Portrayal*, Stanford: Stanford University Press.
17 Barthes, R. (1970) *L'empire des signes*, Paris: Flammarion.

11

NOTES FROM STORYVILLE NORTH[1]

Circling the mall

Janice Williamson

At work on a series of writings about West Edmonton Mall (WEM), I collect shopping stories. In one of my conversations, Ojibway performance artist Rebecca Belmore describes how she once acted in an artist's video tape shot at a Thunder Bay mall. Rebecca and her sister 'played Indian', circling round and round the mall in a car with a white driver while rapid-fire cash-register clatter sounded the attack. Mall as stockaded fort.

I laugh with complicity but wonder how my own circling around West Edmonton Mall relates to Rebecca's performance? I imagine myself on the seat beside her with a pocket full of credit cards and a memory of my cultural ancestors barricaded inside the stockade walls. I want to uncover our differences and commonalities. Is my circling of WEM motivated by a less acute sense of historical urgency? The Mall provides a world-within-a-world fantasy where cultural difference and class come into focus as tableau and entertainment. How do I make the Mall reveal the stories writ large in its design and architecture – stories which open up the historical present and past of Edmonton and the Western frontier? My motive is to read the Mall as symptom, signpost and map. In order to make this narrative possible, I rewrite the Mall as Storyville North, taking the name from one of WEM's theme streets. What is at stake in this response? In order to understand my own identity as a new Western settler, I flesh out the living history the Mall evokes.

Where does 'mall' come from? 'Mall' like *mal* (sick) or *male* (male) in French? I root through the dictionary to the mall in pall-mall, a seventeenth-century game in which wooden balls were driven down an alley through a raised ring, precursor to croquet. Later this gamesman's alley will name a London promenade. Or is it maul/moll in English -- 'maul', a wood-headed hammer word which when pushed transitive becomes 'to beat, bruise or mangle'. In WEM, what is object of this verb?

The Mall as fortress with dozens of obscure entrances provides protection from the disenfranchized: no homeless traffic here. As I approach WEM, a singular methodology eludes me so I work up the image of entrances, discontinuous passageways through the maze. 'Polymorphous orifices', says visiting American John Wynet on hearing about the fifty-eight entrances, 'opening preludes to the big fuck mall'. Is the Mall more orga(ni)sm, architecture as beehive, humming with life? Or is this animating metaphor nothing more than a romanticizing excision of the terms of mall production? How do I listen to the stories the Mall tells, the layered, multiple tracks of its voices, including those which ask 'who profits'? How do I reframe and retell the Mall's stories in relation to the politics of the local – the city of Edmonton and the Western prairie, the region the Mall and I call home?

To locate this home from the outside is to become subject to 'slumming' dismissals by those who refuse to see the extraordinary in the ordinary shopping mall. To analyse a shopping mall in Edmonton is to encounter 'why bother?' shrugs in a national context. Edmonton is home to the second largest university in Canada, assorted other post-secondary institutions and the provincial government, but to others elsewhere, it is often reduced to clichés of weather stories (inhabitants suffer nose-bleeds from lack of humidity) or tales of sexual and cultural backwardness. A typical *Globe & Mail* story in June 1991 about Edmonton tourism includes a comment by the designer of a local mechanical waterfall: 'I'm not putting people down . . . but not everybody has aesthetic taste. People in this city were still eating popcorn when people in other places were having coffee in street-front bistros.'

In a similarly dismissive way, several alienated academic colleagues ask, 'Why study the obvious, the banal, the alienated, when good books are published?' To write about the West Edmonton Mall, a critic has to avoid the highbrow posturing which negates this northern city and the pleasures inhabitants might find circulating in WEM. My own position responds to Iain Chambers' invitation to make the 'habitable' and '*our own*' an urban world 'in a perpetual tension between . . . presence and potential'. The twists and turns of my narrative follow my pleasures, anxieties and obsessions about this city.

217

West Edmonton Mall, a suburban centre, provokes me to an understanding that 'this world, this day-dream, is also our home'.[2]

In his analysis of an American suburb, John D. Dorst provides a possible strategy. He imagines his

> task as two-fold: first the formation of a collection – selecting and arranging; and then reading, or more specifically, reading critically as a rhetorician, looking for the 'motivations' of the texts . . . in other words . . . one . . . 'tells over again' and thereby 'relocates' the already inscribed citations by inserting them into a new context, in effect rewriting them.[3]

But how might a feminist revisionary reading differ from Dorst's? Ambivalence motivates my own writing about WEM, a tension between fascination and disassociation, a vacillation which reaches back into my own rural and then suburban childhood and through my academic training in literature, a discipline which traditionally ignores the popular.[4] My obsession with the Mall is both reconciliation and turning away, opening and exit.

One opening into the Mall recalls my own childhood. The shopping mall became performance space for this little girl growing up in Pickering, the rural outskirts of Toronto. Living out my mother's fantasies of escaping her small prairie hometown through the movies, at age 5 I began an 11-year training to become a Nordic Shirley Temple. At the Gladys Gayle School of Dance in the Ajax Shopping Centre, I danced tap, jazz, musical comedy, ballet, and for a few months, the highland fling. Even after my family moved deeper into the country, my mother drove me three times a week to my lessons. All day Saturday, I had classes or hung around the local restaurant sharing chips and gravy with my friends, gossiping about our tutus and turnout.

Outings with my mother included shopping expeditions for food, for ballet tulle and velvet, for polka-dot jumpers and hooped crinolines. I was the little girl who danced; fake marble corridors were my dressing room, rehearsal hall and stage. In the Pickering IGA or the local mall, I could not resist dancing and when no one was looking I would jeté my way past soup cans, propelled by piped-in stringed renditions of 'Chattanooga Choo Choo'. Muzak and music of the 1930s and 1940s helped me pursue my dancing starlet role, if only for the butcher, bagger or check-out 'girl'. Through the seemingly endless faux marble corridors of a Scarborough Mall, my fantasy matured into the fast-moving skirts of Ginger

Rogers; any staircase might yield the dapper Fred Astaire. I can still hear a precise tempo in elevators and airports, and remember the gestures well, the sweep of arms, tap of black patent feet, snap of head pirouetting through dry goods.

My mother was a 1950s head-turner; her platinum blonde hair, deep scarlet lips and precise mascara were achieved in extended experiments before a special back-lit mirror. My father liked her décolletage, so she scooped her neck for parties. Shopping with mother could produce unnerving identity crisis when clerks would comment, 'How could *you* be the mother of this girl?' In 1956, when my parents returned from Paris, I discovered the connection between shopping and mother. There on a postcard in front of the Eiffel Tower stood mother poised under her platinum bob in a fashionable Parisian coat. No longer shopper but commodity form, no longer tourist but emblem. Mother was now meta-mother, sign of an intimate elsewhere.

Father provided his own kind of shopping pleasures. An absent father like many of his generation, he sent me running from him in tears – 'making strange', mother later explained. But even in estrangement there were exceptional moments of pleasure. In the evening or on a Saturday, he would take me on his shoulders and parade through the local Hudson's Bay Store he managed. I would wear a smart new dress my mother had made. As we promenaded by the candy counters, women would coo about my good-little-girl looks, pressing gum balls and jelly babies into my sticky palms. My bangs were cut short and precise and in my lofty position under hot store lights, warmed by embarrassed pride, I could feel them wet against my forehead. This was my memory of father/daughter pleasure, an economy of gifts outside everyday exchange. On these shopping expeditions I could play the princess of gracious receiving.

This personal memory is of course specific to my experience. In shopping or shopping malls, in other women and men, class and cultural diversity produce different readings and meanings. A forty-year-old second-generation Canadian friend recounts how as a child she hated shopping with her mother, who was 'old' and did not speak English. Drifting three steps behind or in front of her mother, she would cringe as the grey-haired woman gesticulated and spoke Lithuanian. To make matters worse, the word for 'look here' sounded like 'shit.' Horrified, the daughter would cringe from the knowledge that her mother appeared not only ancient but foul-mouthed. At forty, my friend has the luxury of disappearing; her shopping is solitary and secretive, often a welcome but naughty diversion from something she ought to be doing.

I tell these stories to suggest the diversity of experience we have shopping and in malls. While the architecture and economic motivations of those who build the mall may remain fixed and dollar-specific, our experience of shopping malls is multiple. Philosophers and anthropologists tell us that the only communicable aspect of human experience is an interpretation. 'Knowledge of society is a king of text, a story about stories ... never final but always in process.'[5] This 'process' means that any interpretive work must be self-reflexive in order to account for the richness or impoverishment of each. Like any text, my reading of West Edmonton Mall is positioned and provisional.

In my initial visits to the Mall, its fantasies appeared as a theatre of the ridiculous. As I took on the persona of an Alice in Textland, a popular-culture detective lurking about the Mall, I abandoned ironic distance. Rather than a dismissive laugh, I became a critical collaborator in the performance, reading into and out of the historical simulations or artificial representations of Christopher Columbus's *Santa Maria*, the nineteenth-century Europa Boulevard or New Orleans' Bourbon Street. West Edmonton Mall's interior-design grab bag of submarines and palm trees, baby tigers and skating rinks, is constructed as cultural 'bricolage [or] an amalgam that incorporates all layers of history – past, present, and future; the real and imagined'.[6]

While this cultural eclecticism is a private enterprise marketing scheme, it can be understood like other cultures as 'constructions that take historical elements from different eras and sources ... [combining] images and words ... based on lived and imagined experience'.[7] The exotic in WEM's cultural imagery may be simply a manifestation of 'American cultural imperialism' or 'global economic imperatives'. But it can also be read in terms of Canada's frontier colonial attitudes. These Mall simulations are symptoms of Canada's heritage and habit of rummaging through the cultural baggage of Europe and the USA for signs of its own authenticity – for example, dredging up stories of New Orleans black jazz musicians and prostitutes playing turn-of-the-century Storyville tunes. Yet this explanation doesn't provide a sufficient reading of the phenomenon of West Edmonton Mall itself, the effects and meanings of its dizzying iconographic display in the middle of a northern prairie city, latitude 53°. I want to know not only what the elements in the Mall suggest, but why they mean what they seem to. A history and politics of location can be unearthed in what has been called the 'elsewhereness' of West Edmonton Mall.

While I don't pretend to unearth a 'truth' out of WEM's staged artifice, I want to sound the absent voices suppressed in the Mall, the indigenous and foreign tongues of 'Storyville North' which offer less status-quo points of view than the hegemonic 'official' stories. Representations of history in the Mall's visual narratives both reveal and obscure local history, writing over the real contradictions and conflicts which have determined the everyday life of Edmonton's generations. 'History' as coded in the mall is marked by signs of both excess and prohibition; desire, sexuality and the body are on the loose *and* on the run – simultaneously authorized *and* criminalized.

What do we read in the fact that women and visible minorities are both present and absent in WEM. Women fill many part-time, low-paid jobs, and people of colour are represented, as elsewhere in Edmonton, at the lower-paying levels. These groups are visually represented in decontextualized and deliberately alienated images. This blurring sends on vacation our critical understanding of the real relations of production and consumption within our community. White women and black men and women appear in dessicated simulations emptied of voice: the majority of the female sculptures show prostitutes; blacks are musicians; and the single representation of the native is the cigar-store Indian. Most notably underrepresented are native people who are invisible in the Mall even though there is a large Edmonton native population, much of it centred downtown. The Mall's displacement of the marketplace from the city centre meant those in its less affluent neighbourhoods would be less likely to travel to a distant suburban mall. Absent in the sculpted figures and human population of the Mall are the signs of difference within gender, class and race central to Edmonton's history.

BIG HOUSE

WEM once produced a transitory and modest glass display, 'A Glimpse of Jasper', a collection of stuffed sheep and tired landscape photographs. The circular case looked like a tourist landscaped globe I could pick up and shake to change the weather. Nature inside these curved glass panels was as 'real' as that speeding by me on the lookout for the quick fix of a sale. A year or so ago, even this 'glimpse' of the natural world outside WEM was replaced by a tourist T-shirt shop which included decals of the Rockies. Why not? In the world of wish-you-were-here, the after-image of the souvenir makes lived experience redundant.

But when we look outside the glass case of WEM, Edmonton's history provides antecedents for large-scale commercial structures. The beginnings of Edmonton have been traced to archeological digs of indigenous peoples dated between 3000 and 5000 BC near the site that would be established in 1795 as the fur-trade centre for the Hudson Bay Company. Edmonton House was founded in competition with nearby Fort Augustus, established the same year by the North West Company (the two companies would enact their rivalry through violent sabotage leading to death by starvation or murder until the companies eventually merged in 1821). Following one of many North Saskatchewan River floods, the chief trader decided to move Edmonton House up from the river to where the Alberta legislative buildings now stand. On this dry high ground, chief trader Rowand built his house and office, a three-storey wood structure, 30 by 80 feet. This edifice so impressed the natives that Edmonton House came to be known as 'Big House' in Cree and Blackfoot. Between 1870 and 1885 with the destruction of the buffalo herd and the military suppression of the Northwest Rebellion, 'the native majority on the Canadian Plains had become a dominated minority'.[8] By 1881, 263 were counted in Edmonton's census.[9] By the turn of the century, Alberta was advertising itself as part of the 'the last best west' in North America. Like other communities shopping for settlers, Edmonton was built on social-Darwinism's racist assumptions, typified by a remark in a 1906 *Edmonton Bulletin* story: 'The ideal of the West is not only greatness, but greatness achieved under the British Flag and stamped and moulded by the genius of race.'[10]

Between 'Big House' and 'World's Biggest Mall', 150 years of mainly white development and racism produced continued marginalization of indigenous peoples. The ongoing discouragement of non-white immigrants through a politics of 'Canadianization' for much of Alberta's history encouraged assimilation into the established values of early Anglo settlers by non-Anglo whites who could come to pass for Brits. The frontier primacy of the North Saskatchewan River as a canoe route for traders has been usurped in today's Edmonton by freeway rivers of cars built to serve the city's population of 780,000 inhabitants and a series of bridges which criss-cross North Saskatchewan and provide a route to WEM. Contemporary publicists erase this ethnocentric history in their white-washed celebratory prose trumpeting summer festivities of 'music, cultural exhibits and crafts and celebrations of our diverse ethnic heritage'.[11]

Like the original stockade, the Mall's exterior walls appear as a protective skin; fifty-eight entrances are marked without ceremony, suggesting that the world within the Mall is virtually autonomous. According to historians the original fortified stockade of Edmonton House had outside its walls 'a vegetable garden, a corral for livestock, and an area where the Indians pitched their tents when they arrived to trade'.[12] The traders in West Edmonton Mall are no longer natives bearing gifts and furs, but tourists or local residents. During the summer, one asphalt sea of cars expands into a special parking lot for RV homes pitched by travelling tourists.

The frontier represented in the Mall is that discovered by a full-sized replica of Christopher Columbus's *Santa Maria* beached inside its glass bubble. As though desperate in its attempt to locate its frontier life anywhere but Alberta, WEM shuffles history like trading cards and draws from the deck Bourbon Street, New Orleans, a comfortably distant cultural image.

OUR BOURBON STREET, LATITUDE 53°

WEM publicity characterizes the shopping centre's development as 'stages', implying an evolutionary growth. Our Bourbon Street opened in 1983 as a theme 'street' in the second of three stages of development. Included in these additions were the Ice Palace; an NHL-size rink; Fantasyland, 'the world's largest indoor amusement park'; 'dancing' water fountains (one plays classical music, the other modern music); and Our Bourbon Street, a corridor of restaurants and bars. Here the Mall becomes a more specific leisure environment, more 'city' than simply 'interior street'.

Transplanted north, Our Bourbon Street is named after the home of jazz, New Orleans' original Bourbon Street. Bourbon Street and Our Bourbon Street are each in themselves tourist reconstructions of (turn of the century) Storyville, through a contemporary reconstruction which encodes fantasies of the Mardi

223

Gras, the annual New Orleans carnival first held on Shrove Tuesday in 1857. WEM's interpretive reconstruction of Bourbon Street reflects this architectural history in wrought-iron balconies, arched doorways and shuttered windows. In one WEM tableau at the end of the street we are shown masqueraded signs of identities marked by gender, class, culture, and racial differences. A thick-hipped woman in gold stiletto heels is painted in a mermaid's wet suit. A serpent, sign of Medusa, mystery and castration, slithers across her forehead. Behind her a masked man in full Mardi Gras costume drawing on miscellaneous African elements signals a black man to the viewer. In the middle of this tableau, a black field hand in overalls bulging at the crotch plays the saxophone on a crate stencilled 'Dixie'; he's got rhythm and the plantation blues. In the Mall, history is recorded with advertising's inattentive grasp of particulars in a repertoire of stereotypes and 'cultural lessons half-learnt'.[13] What's missing in WEM's sculptural representations of southern blacks is their history as enslaved labourers. This absence is underscored in a New Orleans artifact which sits in regal splendour on Bourbon Street: the wrought-iron shoe-shine bench. The workers are absent; so are shoes and clients. This is a sign of class difference and of work, but there are no embodied subjects here, just an elegant, nostalgic trace of a lost past.

Carnivals explode with laughter, music and the destabilization of limits and boundaries. Theatre moves into the streets and the spectator becomes an active participant in the public drama. According to Mikhail Bakhtin's 'carnivalesque', this 'creates (through an authorized transgression of the usual norms) a second, inverted world, parallel to that of the official culture'.[14] But the carnival in Bourbon Street is a perverse simulation since the relation between spectator and actor is fixed. The actors are indeed dummies and the street only appears to be public; spectators rarely if ever participate in the street theatre.

STORYVILLE SOUTH

And what do we find when we visit the antecedent to WEM's New Orleans' theme street, the original Storyville? William Faulkner described New Orleans as 'a courtesan whose hold is strong upon the mature, to whose charm the young must respond'.[15] WEM's Our Bourbon Street translates Faulkner's New Orleans in spatial terms. The 'charm' of the courtesan is replaced by the seductions of the market-place.

New Orleans was a city founded on transgression. Established in the seventeenth century, this most important city in the French colony was populated with Parisian criminals transported by decree. Women among the settlers included exiles: 'in 1721, the Company of the West found it necessary to deliver to Louisiana a bevy of prostitutes from La Salpêtrière, a house of correction in Paris.'[16]

Fire in 1787 destroyed the French architectural history, and the French connection was entirely disrupted when the city was secretly sold to the Spaniards. New Orleans developed as one of the most filthy, disease-infested cities in North America due to corrupt government, a port's vagrant population, and the challenge of developing fetid swampland. The city became an urban hot potato, passing from owner to owner without its citizens' knowledge. It was secretly returned with the rest of Louisiana to France and then covertly sold by Napoleon Bonaparte to Thomas Jefferson. In 1802, it became an American frontier city.

Its history as a place of sexual corruption and lively vice continued for more than a hundred years. A visitor commented in the 1850s that 'sporting house' patrons included 'sailors, flatboatmen, dock workers, and warehousemen . . . wealthy upriver planters . . . gawking Hossiers and rube Texans . . . Southern planters and cracker farmers . . . Californians long on gold and short on experience, ard . . . mystified immigrants'.[17] By 1897, Storyville, a quarter of New Orleans devoted to the excesses of the body, was formally excluded from the following city ordnance:

> From and after the first of October, 1897, it shall be unlawful for any prostitute or woman notoriously abandoned to lewdness, to occupy, inhabit, live or sleep in any house, room or closet. . . . It shall be unlawful to open, operate or carry on any cabaret, concert-saloon or place where can can, clodoche or similar female dancing or sensational performances are shown.[18]

Storyville's community of black workers and unemployed created an eclectic musical brilliance in music halls and streets. This site became the birthplace of jazz, where according to one participant, 'music could begin sad with a spiritual, go to the blues and on to the work songs, the field holler learned in the cotton fields, on the river docks, [to] jail songs'.[19] To commemorate this musical history, near the entrance to WEM's Our Bourbon Street, a band of black minstrels beckons with a silent paralytic song. No city ordnances are necessary. In WEM, as in other shopping malls, private property masquerades as public space and all who enter are regulated. Researchers and photographers without permits can be charged with trespass. Marching bands and dance-hall girls need not apply.

New Orleans closed Storyville in 1917, forcing prostitutes to go underground. A series of haunting photographic images from this place remain to document some of these women. The Storyville portraits of the photographer Bellocq 'from the New Orleans red-light district, circa 1912,' were reprinted in the 1960s in a collection of prints from surviving glass-plate negatives.[20] In the photographs, women, mainly white women, stare out at the camera. Some are naked, others wear stockings, wild stripes or pastel sheers, or elaborate white-beaded dresses. Some recline on chaise-longues, others are seated formally on press-backed chairs. One sits jauntily beside a collection of doll chairs and a bottle of rum. Another caresses her pet dog while stretched out in a girlish pose. The photographic background is sometimes a white frame of photographer's paper which itself is edged by rooms of shabby whitewash or elaborate Victorian flock. The women dress themselves in pale cotton knickers or discreet pearl-studded high-necked dresses. A top-knotted woman leans back in her chair, arms boldly angled behind her head. On first glance, her long body stretched confidently towards the camera appears naked. A second look reveals a second skin, a monochromatic turtle-neck body stocking which shows no more than her silhouette. Masks disguise some of the nudes; some faces are scratched out, presumably to hide the subject's identity. Other women stand, ample-thighed or lithe, attentive eyes lit from within. Their bodies, inhabited with their being, are not simply put on display. Prostitutes in these photographs communicate something other than mere seduction of the viewer. There is desire and pleasure in their choice of costume or not, in their disclosures and veilings, in their gestures and wistful, strong or haughty, detached or ironic looks towards the camera. The Storyville they speak is their own.

GOOD GIRLS/BAD GIRLS

The Storyville North women of the night have no sympathetic photographer to represent them. On WEM's balcony above the Our Bourbon Street's minstrels, a woman of colour and a white woman beckon from above; 'A Steak Sandwich only $3.95', a sign announces. Woman *is* the city. Further down the street, a white woman in 1940s attire stands with hand on hip, smoking a cigarette behind a wrought-iron fence. A sign points the way up the stairs to the cleaners, the tailors, the rooms above. And what's hidden upstairs? When I first began my research I was shocked to discover at the end of the street that a woman's legs, one with a red garter tucked around her thigh, hung suspended just inside a window frame. When the Mall first opened, a recorded scream accompanied the mechanical thrust of the legs. Local feminists protested and the scream was silenced, but the legs remained, a sign of unreflective violence toward women. A few days after I presented my research in Edmonton, the windows were closed, obscuring the legs from view. In fact, the window-display legs are modelled on a New Orleans street where a woman on a swing arcs in and out of a window in seductive display. This referent is and was lost to most of those experiencing the Mall. What may have been intended as a parodic joke became a visual rhetoric of violence.

The figure of the prostitute is an important motif in WEM. On Europa Boulevard, WEM theatre casts a statuesque streetwalker in bronze. This fallen *femme de la rue* which the PR blurb euphemistically calls a 'Lady of the Street' is repeated in plaster figures of the prostitute on Our Bourbon Street. The Europa bronze sculpture of a woman stands beside a brass railing fingering an imaginary string of beads broken off by vandals. Her high-heeled pumps, short skirt and V-necked top reveal a full youthful body. Her face is lined with age. This woman is a sculpted representation of *la femme de la rue*, a street-smart female version of Walter Benjamin's *flâneur* in nineteenth-century Paris. While Benjamin's man of the street was a bohemian intellectual, a scholar 'on the road', the telling characteristic of WEM's mute woman as prostitute is the commodification of her body and her sexuality. In his essay, 'Paris, capital of the nineteenth century', Benjamin refers to the image of 'the prostitute, who is saleswoman and wares in one' as representa-

227

tive of 'the ambiguity attending the social relationships and products'.[21] Rachel Bowlby analyses and expands Benjamin's metaphor:

> It was above all to women that the new commerce made its appeal, urging and inviting them to procure its luxurious benefits and purchase sexually attractive images for themselves. They were to become in a sense like prostitutes in their active, commodified self-display, and also to take on the one role almost never theirs in actual prostitution: that of consumer.[22]

Woman-as-prostitute is the only representation of working women in WEM. At the entrance to Our Bourbon Street, life-sized mannequins depict the arrest of prostitutes. Two female prostitutes are accosted by a white male police officer. A Harlequin figure left over from another dismantled display looks on. One female figure's arm is tattooed with 'papa'; metal handcuffs dangle from her wrist. Another woman, eyes white with rage, shakes a clenched fist towards a white male law-enforcement officer whose power is expressed through his uniform and inscribed on the woman's body through his handcuffs.[23]

Bowlby notes that

> the commodity can be anything at all, since it is defined not by any substance or given utility, but simply by virtue of the fact that it 'goes to market,' in Marx's phrase, with a price, a social value: it can as easily take the form of a person or a person's time as that of a physical object.[24]

In WEM's representations of the prostitute, sexuality becomes property to be bought and sold, and the female body, a fetishized commodity form.

To characterize the prostitute this way is to deny her autonomy, her status as 'worker,' and fall into the trap of some who use the prostitute as a whipping girl, commodified body and victim. While Faulkner's New Orleans 'courtesan' is a clichéd romanticization, contemporary feminists call the victimized prostitute part of the 'good girl, bad girl' dichotomy where social-purity crusaders are whitewashed do-gooders. It is important to see these women as potentially active in order not to glorify the critic as heroine saving her 'fallen' sister.[25] Alternatively we can view these sculptures as a kind of contemporary Ovidian metamorphosis; just at the moment the bold goddess is about to be raped by any old god, the narrative conveniently arrests her in a holographic freeze-frame. What would happen if we made these statues come alive with the everyday stories of women who work as prostitutes? What would they reveal about WEM's market-place theatre?

In order to read this iconography, I look towards the hidden story of prostitution in Edmonton itself. The status of Edmonton's female prostitutes can be read in local newspaper stories of anonymous women found bludgeoned on the outskirts of the city, or in rumours about runaway girls working the 'second street' of West Edmonton Mall. Sex work figures as a significant though hidden contribution to the local economy – the Edmonton telephone book has sixteen pages of listings for escort services, erotic massages and prostitutes. Although the Mall won't tell and youth agencies remain silent in order to preserve the co-operation of the Mall, the West Edmonton Mall is a 'second street' and prostitution and drug rings pose a serious problem, particularly in the case of young runaways.[26] Ironically, the blurring of public and private property which appears to be signalled in the Mall's street-like simulations are erased by the Mall in response to problems with crime. There is in fact a four-man publicly funded police force which patrols the streets along with WEM's private security guards.

STORYVILLE NORTH

On hearing I was working on a 'cultural study' of the Mall, the father of one of my students invites me to give a slide show at the West Edmonton Rotary Club. He explains that while the club is now open to women, I and a few other guests will likely be the only women present. In a crowded hotel dining room, suited white men consume fruit salad or meat. Wicker baskets circulate, gathering money for charities. All men rise to shake hands with strangers and sing a sad song about loneliness and fellowship which makes me rethink any preconceptions I might have had about this gathering. The proceedings are timed to the minute and at one o'clock I stand to give my presentation. There has been a mix-up in their weekly newsletter. Part of the audience, under the impression I am a West Edmonton Mall publicist, prickles uncomfortably as my talk proceeds. In the darkened dining room, slides of dim corridors and twinkling lights along Bourbon Street's 'ceiling'

229

transform us into voyeurs of the Mall's simulated pleasures: full-skirted scarlet women, black jazz, hookers and revellers.

At the end of the evening, the master of ceremonies will reward me with a polaroid portrait in a presentation frame. In the photograph, my hands grip the oversized podium; my body and torso appear miniaturized and disappear behind the tilted surface. I'm in my father's house and all that is visible are my awkward grin and too-casual Reeboks. I would like to ask: if we were to hear the music of the Mall, would it be accompanied by a player piano of pedestrian noise hard-edge-amplified along corridors of marble and mirror? In circling the Mall, can we make Storyville North sing the uproarious sound we need to remember in Edmonton, a city that makes claims to the 'good life' pioneer jazz trombonist Kid Ory sought to escape – the city of 'white bread livin', tippin' your hat to the same wife all your life, sain' "yes sir" to the shitheads' (Longstreet, 1986: 4).[27]

The Rotarians become intense in response to my naming of WEM phenomena: 'the body as commodity', for instance, or 'racism'. Was I, among them, 'bad girl' or 'good'? In frustration, in the end, as though to provide a rationale beyond criticism, one man says, 'But West Edmonton Mall employs twenty thousand people.' His comment silences the room. My project of making 'this world, this dream-world, our home' sounds hollow to those who make of it a workplace.

NOTES AND REFERENCES

1 My thanks to engaged listeners and colleagues at the Universities of Alberta, Calgary, British Columbia, and York, and the Banff Centre for their insightful questions about variations of this work which included 'I-less and Gaga in Fantasyland Hotel'. This paper is work in progress towards a book, 'Of Arcades, Pleasure Domes and Plain Consuming: Pedestrian Feminist Readings of West Edmonton Mall'. I am grateful to Robert Wilson who initiated me into the unsolved mysteries of WEM. For several years I became the unofficial tour guide of the Mall for visiting cultural critics. My thanks to W. J. T. Mitchell, Dorothy Smith, Kathleen Martindale, Terry Goldie and Constance Penley for insightful talks, and to Cynthia Wright for sharing her expertise on counter-culture. The Banff Centre's Arts Journalism Programme offered skilled consultants and utopian space for writing this paper. Mark Czarnecki's gentle editorial insights moved me closer to finding my own voice in the Mall. Brian Rusted's expertise and conversations led to my eighteen-minute video, 'A pedestrian

feminist reading of West Edmonton Mall', which is available through Video Pool Inc., 300–100 Arthur Street, Winnipeg, Manitoba, R3B 1H3.

I am indebted to Meaghan Morris for introducing me to a 'pedestrian feminist' critique in her 'Things to do with shopping centres', in S. Sheridan (ed.) (1988) *Crafts: Feminist Cultural Criticism*, London: Verso. Two excellent studies of WEM are: J. S. P. Hopkins, 'West Edmonton Mall: landscape of myths and elsewhereness', *Canadian Geographer* 34 (1) (1990): 2–17; and R. Shields, 'Social spatialization and the built environment: the West Edmonton Mall', *Environment and Planning D: Society and Space* 7 (1989):147–64.

2 I. Chambers (1990) *Border Dialogues: Journeys in Postmodernism*, New York: Routledge: 62, 112.

3 J. D. Dorst (1991) *The Written Suburb: An American Site, An Ethnographic Dilemma*, Philadelphia: University of Pennsylvania Press: 206.

4 Meaghan Morris insists upon this strategy of ambivalence in her analysis of an Australian shopping centre:

> Ambivalence allows a thinking of relations between contradictory states: it is also a 'pose', no doubt, but one that is probably more appropriate to an everyday practice of using the same shopping centres often, for different reasons. . . . .Above all, it does not eliminate the moment of everyday discontent – of anger, frustration, sorrow, irritation, boredom, fatigue . . . Feminism is minimally a movement of discontent with 'the everyday' and with wide-eyed definitions of the everyday as 'the way things are'. . . . Like effective shopping, feminist criticism includes moments of sharpened focus, narrowed gaze – of sceptical, if not paranoid, assessment.
>
> (Morris: 197)

5 V. W. Turner and E. M. Bruner (1986) *The Anthropology of Experience*, Chicago: University of Illinois Press: 23.

6 Turner and Bruner, op. cit.: 25.

7 Turner and Bruner, op, cit.: 25.

8 H. Palmer with T. Palmer (1990) *Alberta: A New History*, Edmonton: Hurtig: 49.

9 Palmer, op. cit.: 62.

10 Palmer, op. cit.: 78.

11 Alberta Tourism (1991) *Touring Through Alberta*: 33.

12 Palmer, op. cit.: 18.

13 J. Berger (1972) *Ways of Seeing*, London: BBC: 140.

14 L. Hutcheon, (1988) 'Caveat lector: the early postmodernism of Leonard Cohen', *The Canadian Postmodern: A Study of Contemporary English-Canadian Fiction*, Toronto: Oxford University Press: 30.

15 W. Faulkner (1925) 'New Orleans', *The Double Dealer*, quoted in Frank Driggs and Harris Levine (eds) *Black Beauty, White Heat: Pictorial History of Classic Jazz 1920–1950*, New York: W. Morrow, 1982: 19.

16 L. Ostransky (1978) *Jazz City: The Impact of Our Cities on the Development of Jazz*, Englewood Cliffs: Prentice-Hall: 4.

17 Ostransky, op. cit.: 19.
18 S. Longstreet (1986) *Storyville to Harlem: Fifty Years in the Jazz Scene*, New Brunswick: Rutgers University Press: 40.
19 Longstreet, op. cit.: 30.
20 J. Szarkowski (ed.) (1970) *E. J. Bellocq: Storyville Portraits: Photographs from the New Orleans Red-Light District, Circa 1912*, New York: Museum of Modern Art.
21 Quoted in R. Bowlby (1985) *Just Looking: Consumer Culture in Dreiser, Gissing and Zola*, New York: Methuen: 10. The implications of the restriction of the 'flâneur' to the male gender in Benjamin and other modernist readers of public space are developed in Janet Wolff (1985) 'The Invisible Flâneuse: Women and the Literature of Modernity', *Theory, Culture and Society* 2(3): 37–46.
22 Bowlby, 11.
23 One day while passing this installation I encountered one of the few signs of shoppers' resistance to the representation of women in the Mall. Someone had stretched a woollen glove over this woman's enraged fist, taping the fingers into a defiant gesture against the officer of the law.
24 Bowlby, op. cit.: 26.
25 In England, nineteenth-century feminist reformers cried out for their 'fallen sisters', only to tumble into a dangerous alliance with evangelicals who campaigned for the end to prostitution. Most early feminists quickly disassociated themselves from this movement. The repression of prostitution between 1890 and 1914 had disastrous consequences: 'Prostitutes were uprooted from their neighbourhoods and forced to find lodgings in other areas of the city. Their activity became more covert and furtive. Cut off from any sustaining relationship, they were forced to rely increasingly on authorities', J. Walkowitz (1983). Male Vice and Female Virtue: Feminism and the Politics of Prostitution in Nineteenth-Century Britain', in Ann Snitow, Christine Stansell and Thompson (eds) *Powers of Desire: The Politics of Sexuality*, (New York: Monthly Review Press: 428). This moral outrage interrupted any attempts to regulate prostitutes and increase their health and safety; it confounded issues and disarmed the independent prostitute who became increasingly vulnerable to a pimp-driven economy – the entrepreneurial sex worker became male-dominated service worker.
26 For an exploratory analysis of the social issues in the Mall see an unpublished paper: P. McManus (1989). Social Issues Pertaining to the West Edmonton Mall', City of Edmonton – Community and Family Services Housing and Planning Branch, June. McManus claims that prostitution and drugs in the Malll require significant intervention by youth and social service organizations.
27 Kid Ory to Longstreet, in Longstreet, op. cit.: 4.

AUTHOR INDEX

233

SUBJECT INDEX